Big Data and Information Theory

Big Data and Information Theory are a binding force between various areas of knowledge that allow for societal advancement. Rapid development of data analytic and information theory allows companies to store vast amounts of information about production, inventory, service, and consumer activities. More powerful CPUs and cloud computing make it possible to do complex optimization instead of using heuristic algorithms, as well as instant rather than offline decision-making.

The era of "big data" challenges includes analysis, capture, curation, search, sharing, storage, transfer, visualization, and privacy violations. Big data calls for better integration of optimization, statistics, and data mining. In response to these challenges, this book brings together leading researchers and engineers to exchange and share their experiences and research results about big data and information theory applications in various areas. This book covers a broad range of topics including statistics, data mining, data warehouse implementation, engineering management in large-scale infrastructure systems, data-driven sustainable supply chain network, information technology service offshoring project issues, online rumors governance, preliminary cost estimation, and information system project selection.

The chapters in this book were originally published in the journal *International Journal of Management Science and Engineering Management*.

Jiuping Xu is Associate Vice President, Dean of Business School, and Director of Institute of Emergency Management and Reconstruction in Post-disaster of Sichuan University, Chengdu, China. He has published more than 700 peer-reviewed journal papers and over 40 books.

Syed Ejaz Ahmed is Dean of the Faculty of Mathematics and Science at Brock University, St Catharines, Canada. His research interests concentrate on big data, predictive modeling, data science, and statistical machine learning with applications.

Zongmin Li is Deputy Department Head of Management Science and System Science Department of Business School at Sichuan University, Chengdu, China. Her research interests focus on data-driven decision-making and big data analytics.

Big Data and Information Theory

Edited by
Jiuping Xu, Syed Ejaz Ahmed and Zongmin Li

Routledge
Taylor & Francis Group

LONDON AND NEW YORK

First published 2022
by Routledge
4 Park Square, Milton Park, Abingdon, Oxon, OX14 4RN

and by Routledge
605 Third Avenue, New York, NY 10158

Routledge is an imprint of the Taylor & Francis Group, an informa business

© 2022 International Society of Management Science and Engineering Management

British Library Cataloguing-in-Publication Data
A catalogue record for this book is available from the British Library

ISBN13: 978-1-032-26631-2 (hbk)
ISBN13: 978-1-032-26632-9 (pbk)
ISBN13: 978-1-003-28917-3 (ebk)

DOI: 10.4324/9781003289173

Typeset in Minion Pro
by codeMantra

Publisher's Note
The publisher accepts responsibility for any inconsistencies that may have arisen during the conversion of this book from journal articles to book chapters, namely the inclusion of journal terminology.

Disclaimer
Every effort has been made to contact copyright holders for their permission to reprint material in this book. The publishers would be grateful to hear from any copyright holder who is not here acknowledged and will undertake to rectify any errors or omissions in future editions of this book.

Contents

Citation Information

The following chapters were originally published in various issues of the *International Journal of Management Science and Engineering Management*. When citing this material, please use the original citations and page numbering for each article, as follows:

For any permission-related enquiries please visit:
http://www.tandfonline.com/page/help/permissions

Notes on Contributors

S. Ejaz Ahmed, Department of Mathematics and Statistics, Brock University, St Catharines, Canada.

Abdollah Babaeinesami, Department of Industrial Engineering, South Tehran Branch, Islamic Azad University, Tehran, Iran.

Alexander W. Blocker, Google, Inc., Mountain View, USA.

Fernando V. Bonassi, Google, Inc., Mountain View, USA.

Hugh A. Chipman, Acadia University, Nova Scotia, Canada.

Marina Dabic, Nottingham Trent University, UK.

Tugrul Daim, Department of Engineering and Technology Management, Portland State University, Engineering and Technology Management, USA.

Edward I. George, The Wharton School, University of Pennsylvania, Philadelphia, USA.

Anupam Haldar, Department of Mechanical Engineering, Netaji Subhash Engineering College, Kolkata, India.

Robert E. McCulloch, Booth School of Business, University of Chicago, USA.

Mounir Mesbah, Laboratoire de Statistique Théorique et Appliquée, Université Pierre et Marie Curie, Paris, France.

Samar Chandra Mondal, Department of Mechanical Engineering, Jadavpur University, Kolkata, India.

Sunday Olusanya Olatunji, Department of Computer Science, College of Computer Science and Information Technology, Imam Abdulrahman Bin Faisal University, Dammam, Kingdom of Saudi Arabia.

Dipika Pramanik, Department of Information Technology, Netaji Subhash Engineering College, Kolkata, India.

David Raffo, Portland State University, USA.

Nayem Rahman, Department of Engineering and Technology Management, Portland State University, USA.

Rosine Salman, Regence Group, Portland, USA.

Muizz O. Sanni-Anibire, Dammam Community College, King Fahd University of Petroleum and Minerals, Dhahran, Kingdom of Saudi Arabia.

Steven L. Scott, Google, Inc., Mountain View, USA.

Seyed Mohsen Seyedaliakbar, Department of Industrial Engineering, South Tehran Branch, Islamic Azad University, Tehran, Iran.

Nozer D. Singpurwalla, College of Science and Engineering, Department of Systems Engineering and Engineering Management, The City University of Hong Kong, Hong Kong.

Hamid Tohidi, Department of Industrial Engineering, South Tehran Branch, Islamic Azad University, Tehran, Iran.

Jiuping Xu, State Key Laboratory of Hydraulics and Mountain River Engineering and Uncertainty Decision-Making Laboratory, Sichuan University, Chengdu, China.

Jiali Yan, Business School, Sichuan University, Chengdu, China.

Bahadır Yüzbaşı, Department of Econometrics, Inonu University, Malatya, Turkey.

Rosli Mohamad Zin, School of Civil Engineering, Faculty of Engineering, Universiti Teknologi Malaysia (UTM), Iskandar Puteri, Malaysia.

Preface

In today's society, the application of big data has increasingly demonstrated its advantages, and it occupies more and more areas. Engineering management, supply chain, social media analysis, etc., various fields that use big data for development are helping companies/decision-makers continue to develop new businesses and innovate operating models. With the concept of big data and development of information theory, the methods of data mining, decision sciences, and business decisions have been comprehensively improved and optimized. In response to the background of big data era, *International Journal of Management Science and Engineering Management (IJMSEM)* published a special issue "Big Data and Information Theory" in 2016. This special issue was dedicated to celebrating the 95th birthday of Professor Lotfi A. Zadeh and was a great success with excellent collection of following papers:

1   Xu investigated engineering management in large-scale infrastructure systems, which were regarded as giant data-driven open complex systems with system complexities that encompass openness, human involvement, society, and the emergence of intelligence. Three open questions on the engineering management of infrastructure systems were proposed based on this precondition. (1) Is there an effective 3 M-based engineering management methodology for all large-scale infrastructure systems? (2) How can the morphism between problem groups and model fields in large-scale infrastructure systems be proven? (3) How can the morphism between model fields and algorithmic clusters in large-scale infrastructure systems be proven?
2   Scott et al. described a method of performing approximate Monte Carlo simulation from a Bayesian posterior distribution based on very large data sets. They have shown that there were models, some with non-Gaussian posteriors, for which the draws from workers can be combined using simple weighted averages.
3   Mesbah has presented the main modern statistical methods and models used in the validation and analysis of a quality-of-life measure in an epidemiological context. He presented three different applications to real data sets, including data from a large survey done in eight big European cities: the LARES study.
4   Ahmed and Yuzbasi presented efficient estimation and prediction strategies for the classical multiple regression model when the dimensions of the parameters are larger than the number of observations. These strategies were motivated by penalty estimation and Stein-type estimation procedures. The proposed strategy was applied to the analysis of several real high-dimensional data sets.
5   Singpurwalla tried to articulate the philosophical and mathematical underpinnings of the notion of dependence: what does it mean to assess it, how best to assess it, and how best to exploit it?

This book also contains following high-quality papers from more recent issues of *IJMSEM* related to big data and information theory:

1   Babaeinesami et al. proposed a new multi-objective model in the area of closed-loop supply chain problem integrated with lot sizing by considering lean, agility, and sustainability factors simultaneously. A new hybrid metaheuristic algorithm comprised a parallel Multi-Objective Particle Swarm Optimization algorithm, and a multi-objective social engineering optimizer was developed to deal with large size problems efficiency.
2   Salman et al. investigated Capability Maturity Models (CMMs)/ Capability Maturity Model Integration (CMMI) best practices and their effects on managing and mitigating critical issues associated with offshore development. Using a web-based survey, data were collected from 451 Information Technology (IT) and software development firms in the US. The results of the analysis showed that IT companies applying CMM/CMMI models have fewer issues associated with IT offshoring.

3   Yan used the Python crawler program to collect rumor-refuting microblogs. Statistical analysis methods ranging from correlation analysis to chi-square analysis and analytical methods like hot trend analysis, stage-based analyses of quantity, hot words, and subjects were used to study the dynamic evolution laws of online rumors from the perspective of quantity and content. Corresponding governance strategies were put forward.

4   Rahman discussed the findings of an empirical study of data warehouse implementation effectiveness. Eight variables were taken as predictive variables and four as response variables. The findings of the study showed that certain variables have a significant influence on the response variables for data warehousing success.

5   Sanni-Anibire et al. presented the application of Machine Learning techniques in the systematic development of a model to estimate the preliminary cost of tall building projects. The techniques considered include Multi-Linear Regression Analysis, k-Nearest Neighbors, Artificial Neural Networks, Support Vector Machines, and Multi-Classifier Systems. This research showed the potential of modern digital technologies such as machine learning to solve problems of the construction industry.

6   Pramanik et al. established a novel intelligent model by integrating fuzzy Shannon entropy and Fuzzy Technique for Order Preference by Similarity to Ideal Solution Method techniques as a decision tool for solving multiple-criteria decision-making (MCDM) problem using linguistic values, which smoothly aided decision-makers dealing with uncertain or incomplete information without losing existing quantitative information.

This book is suitable for big data analysis professionals, as well as researchers engaged in data mining and data-driven decision-making in universities and colleges. We welcome management science and engineering management professionals and researchers to contribute to *IJMSEM*. *IJMSEM* is a peer-reviewed quarterly journal that provides an international forum for researchers and practitioners of management science and engineering management. *IJMSEM* focuses on identifying management science problems in engineering and business, and using innovative management theories and methods to provide solutions. For more details about *IJMSEM*, please view: https://www.tandfonline.com/action/journalInformation?show=aimsScope&journalCode=tmse20

Jiuping Xu, Syed Ejaz Ahmed, Zongmin Li

2021.11.19

Engineering management: new advances and three open questions

Jiuping Xu

ABSTRACT

Big data has changed engineering management, which has consequently opened up many current and future scientific and technological challenges. This paper investigates engineering management in large scale infrastructure systems, which are regarded as giant data-driven open complex systems with system complexities that encompass openness, human involvement, society, and the emergence of intelligence. With the assistance of big data technologies and information theories, large scale infrastructure systems can be described as synergetic systems made up of 'Data Streams–Information Sets–Problem Groups–Model Fields–Algorithmic Clusters', so a 3 M-based engineering management based on meta-intelligence, meta-synthesis, and meta-technology is proposed as the methodological framework. Adjustability is explained as a precondition for the construction of large scale infrastructure systems, and three open questions on the engineering management of infrastructure systems are proposed based on this precondition. (1) Is there an effective 3 M-based engineering management methodology for all large scale infrastructure systems? (2) How can the morphism between problem groups and model fields in large scale infrastructure systems be proven? (3) How can the morphism between model fields and algorithmic clusters in large scale infrastructure systems be proven?

Introduction

Large scale infrastructure construction, such as oil and gas field development projects (Senouci, EI-Abbasy, & Zayed, 2014; Xu & Wu, 2015), water conservancy and hydropower engineering projects (Xu & Zeng, 2014, 2011; Zeng, Xu, Wu, & Shen, 2014) and urban transportation networks (Chang & Kendall, 2011), involves massive information, large investments, long construction periods, high risks, organizational complexity, and significant environmental impacts, all of which require complex systems engineering. The impact of human activities on natural systems has grown significantly, meaning that engineers now need consciously to employ engineering management systems. Realistically, engineering is at the heart of all infrastructure developments, so must be included when seeking to develop new theories and tools for complex engineering systems (Ottino, 2004). Improving construction efficiency and quality and reducing environmental impacts are the three core demands of current infrastructure development practice. With significant recent advances in information and engineering technologies, it is possible to move beyond traditional infrastructure construction engineering management practices. However, during this evolution, there are significant challenges, which this paper summarizes by focusing on three open questions that raise future research possibilities to determine effective solutions.

Opportunities within engineering development advances

Meta-intelligence through advances in big data analysis technology

Big data has become a current and future research frontier (Fung, Tse, & Fu, 2015; Lazer, Kennedy, King, & Vespignani, 2014; Lynch, 2008; Marx, 2013; Servick, 2015; Shneiderman, 2014; Wren, 2014) and has attracted significant research attention from the information sciences, governments and enterprise policy and decision makers, and technological development engineers (Chen & Zhang, 2014). It has also changed engineering management as it has opened up an ability to deal with current and future scientific and technological challenges. This is especially true in large scale infrastructure systems, which can be regarded as complex open data-driven giant systems with system complexities such as openness, human involvement, societal characteristics, and intelligence emergence.

Advances in information theory and computing technologies are reshaping the geographic scale of infrastructure developments from the local to the international, which can have both positive and negative impacts. For example, the merging of cyberspace with traditional infrastructure has created new functionalities and opportunities while simultaneously exposing the vulnerabilities of cyberspace. From an engineering perspective, understanding the interdependencies within infrastructure systems continues to be a major challenge both in terms of defining the appropriate theoretical constructs and in terms of defining and implementing the appropriate interventions given the fiscal realities. Infrastructure system engineering management under a big data environment emphasizes that meta-intelligence methodology should take an engineering management perspective with the support of advanced data acquisition, data storage, data management, and network intelligences. Meta-intelligence formation through the provision of more comprehensive focused information can support infrastructure construction and allow for intelligent construction.

Meta-synthesis through advances in complex system theory

Complex systems are a critical challenge as they can seriously affect future systems, human life, and cybernetics development (Aeppli & Chandra, 1997; Boumen, de Jong, Mestrom, van de Mortel-Fronczak, & Rooda, 2009; Foote, 2007; Leleur, 2008; May, 1972; Nadis, 2003). However, open complex giant systems are very challenging due to their inherent system complexities (Boumen et al., 2009; Cao, Dai, & Zhou, 2009). For open complex giant system problem solving, it is necessary to analyse the cooperative structures existing between people and systems and to study how people can better deal with and manage these open complex giant systems. In the 1990s, qualitative-to-quantitative meta-synthesis theory was proposed as an effective breakthrough methodology for the understanding and problem solving of open complex giant systems (Qian, 1991; Qian, Yu, & Dai, 1990, 1993). This method combined quantitative methods with qualitative knowledge through a synthesis of data-driven information and expert knowledge. Since that time, there has been a continuous endeavour to put these ideas into practice (Gu & Tang, 2005; Xu & Tao, 2012; Xu & Yao, 2011; Xu & Zhou, 2011). However, to date there has been little research focused on meta-synthesis-based engineering management for infrastructure systems, a technique which could provide significant improvements to construction quality and efficiency.

Meta-technology through advances in engineering management

The development of infrastructure engineering management has had a long history. From the beginning, engineering management has required theories or at least organized frameworks for engineering calculations (Ottino, 2004). Engineering management has been defined in many ways (Lannes, 2001). In 1916, Fayol (1949) first wrote *General and Industrial Management*, in which management was described as a process of planning, organization, coordination, directing, and controlling. Lock (1993) called Fayol the founding father of engineering management and modern management theory.

Bennett (1996) also cited Fayol's works as the origin of the management process that has formed the basis for most other work in this area. However, despite Fayol's pioneering work on management in the early 1900s, engineering management only emerged as a discipline in its own right in the latter part of the twentieth century (2014). Winston (2004)) stated that engineering leadership is the means to a more promising future for the engineering profession.

As one of the more important disciplines in engineering management, civil engineering management in the twenty-first century is expected to be dramatically different because of the growing and long-overdue realization that the traditional contract forms that have remained virtually unchanged since the 1860s have become obsolete (Barnes, 2000a, 2000b). During the past decade, against the background of the creation of independent business units within organizations, there have been major changes in the civil engineering management of safety, quality, and productivity (Hendrickson, 2012). Xu and Li (2012) concluded that engineering management should be based on ecological engineering, as this is an essential requirement for effective engineering management. At the same time, ecological engineering has been seen as the base and driver of comprehensive engineering management. With the above advances in engineering management, engineering management understanding has taken on a more focused system perspective, indicating that engineering technologies are becoming significantly more interdependent. Therefore, a meta-technology that establishes the technological basis for new advances in engineering management can be seen to be the most appropriate approach for the future.

Challenges in system engineering management

With the increasing demand for large scale infrastructure construction, many new challenges have emerged, some of which have remained unsolved and some of which have remained in the background. Based on the framework of a qualitative-to-quantitative meta-synthesis methodology, this paper describes large scale infrastructure systems as synergetic systems made up of 'Data Streams–Information Sets–Problem Groups–Model Fields–Algorithmic Clusters' as shown in Figure 1. To address this synergetic system, there are challenges

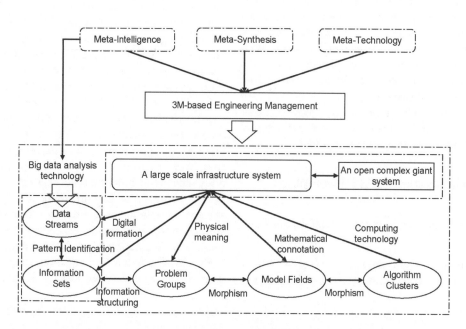

Figure 1. Synergetic system for 'Data Streams–Information Sets–Problem Groups–Model Fields–Algorithmic Clusters'.

that need to be overcome during the evolutionary process such as system efficiencies, accuracy, and effectiveness. The details are explained in the following.

In this paper, infrastructure systems are defined as networks of systems and processes that function cooperatively and synergistically to produce and distribute a continuous flow of essential goods and services. Such infrastructure systems can be found in dams, transportation systems, communications, manufacturing systems, and energy systems, amongst others. For example, an electrical power system depends on transportation services to deliver fuel to the power generating stations, but the production of that fuel depends in turn on the use of electrical power and the fuel needed for transportation services. An electrical power disruption can impact water provision, emergency services, finance, and government services, amongst others. All of these services are in turn dependent on the computing, networking, data, and control services provided by complex, multi-scale interdependent systems, and software, which cannot function without power. All systems and processes, however, are dependent on a human element. Taken all together, therefore, there is a complex set of interdependencies between the infrastructure services that are challenging to conceptualize, understand, model, and design across multiple scales. Our view of infrastructure, therefore, has evolved from just seeing a collection of discrete physical and human components, such as dams, roads, bridges and buildings, and engineering workers, to a tightly interconnected and interdependent ecosystem view made up of physical, cyber, and human components.

As shown in Figure 1, the 3 M-based engineering management of large scale infrastructure system construction can be regarded as an open complex giant system based on data streams integrated using big data analysis technology through a meta-intelligence methodology. Classified data streams using pattern identification form the information sets for the digital formation of the open complex giant system. The structured information is able to map to the problem groups that reflect the physical meaning of the system. To solve these problems, model fields are developed to describe the mathematical connotations, and algorithmic clusters are designed using computing technology. The question that needs to be solved immediately, however, is how to develop the model fields and design the algorithmic clusters so as to ensure the development of effective engineering management for large scale infrastructure system construction. To address this question, several challenges need to be overcome. The basic assumption is that effective engineering management does exist, yet proving its existence is complex. Furthermore, effective model fields and algorithmic clusters should reflect the characteristics of the problem groups accurately; therefore, there should be a morphism relationship between them. Yet, how can the morphism between the problem groups, the model fields, and the algorithmic clusters be defined and proved? As can be seen, significant further research is required. Problem groups, model fields, and algorithmic clusters are all regarded as domains in order to explain the morphism concept. A morphism definition is provided below.

Definition 1 – Morphism: A morphism from a source domain S and a target domain T is a map $f : S \to T$, such that the map f satisfies identity and associativity.

The definition for identity and associativity are provided as follows.

Definition 2 – Identity: For any domain X, a morphism $Id_X : X \to X$ is an identity morphism on X if and only if, for any morphism $f : S \to T$, we have $Id_X \circ f = f = f \circ Id_X$.

Definition 3 – Associativity: When the target domain for a morphism f is the source domain for a morphism g, and the target domain for a morphism g is the source domain for a morphism h, these morphisms satisfy associativity if and only if $h \circ (g \circ f) = (h \circ g) \circ f$.

The above definition for morphism refers to a structure-preserving mapping from a source domain to a target domain, within which the domains could be problem groups, model fields, or algorithmic clusters. To address these challenges, three open questions are raised in the following sections to stimulate future research. However, before moving to the discussion of the open questions, the essential precondition for the construction of large scale infrastructure systems is first explained.

Precondition for the construction of a large scale infrastructure system – adjustability

Before constructing a large scale infrastructure system, an important issue that needs to be considered is whether the infrastructure system will change the ecological environment and the geological structure of the neighbouring areas. The Three Gorges Dam is a typical example of several huge projects that are transforming China's environment (Stone, 2008). The Three Gorges Reservoir area plays a key role in economic development, national drinking water security, and ecosystem sustainability (Wei, Han, & Gao, 2016). However, while large scale hydropower projects may affect the ecological environment, whether they can change the geological structure is still in dispute.

A possible conjecture is that large scale infrastructure systems have an 'energy' that acts on the geological structure of the affected area as shown in Figure 2. In this conjecture, the stability of the geological structure of the affected area is determined by a singular point, which can be regarded as the threshold value for the 'energy'. Before the construction of large scale infrastructure systems, the 'energy' value is lower than the threshold, so the geological structure of the affected area is stable. After the construction of the large scale infrastructure system, if the 'energy' of the infrastructure system is sufficiently large, the total 'energy' at the affected area may increase and even exceed the threshold value, leading to instability in the geological structure at the affected area, which may result in an earthquake. However, proving the validity of this conjecture requires significant theoretical research. Yet if the conjecture is assumed to be true, we can define the adjustability of a large scale infrastructure construction system as outlined below.

Definition 4 – Adjustability: A large scale infrastructure construction system is adjustable if and only if the infrastructure system 'energy' is not large enough to increase the total 'energy' at the affected area and exceed the threshold value, thus leading to instability in the geological structure at the affected area. Otherwise, the large scale infrastructure construction system is not adjustable.

Based on the above definition, a large scale infrastructure system cannot be constructed when it is not adjustable. The adjustability of a large scale infrastructure system is, therefore, an essential precondition for its construction. The following three open questions are all based on this precondition so as

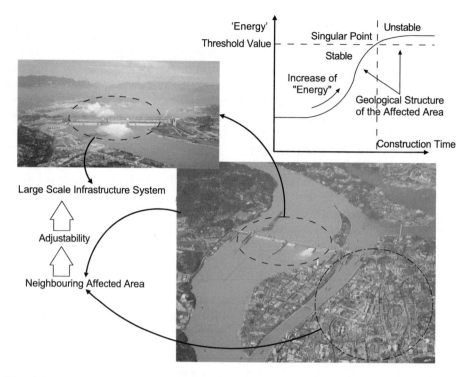

Figure 2. An example of the adjustability of a large scale infrastructure construction system.

to avoid human-caused disasters from the construction of non-adjustable infrastructure projects.

Question I: Is there an effective 3 M-based engineering management methodology for all large scale infrastructure systems?

It has been assumed that large scale infrastructure construction projects are open complex giant systems with complexities such as openness, human involvement, societal characteristics, and intelligence emergence. Complex systems have been recognized as one of the greatest challenges for current and future scientific and technological research. Large scale infrastructure construction project management is a challenge across multiple disciplines such as engineering management, system sciences, system engineering, cognitive sciences, information systems, artificial intelligence, and computer sciences. As a result, traditional problem solving engineering management methodologies are somewhat helpful but are far from a mature solution methodology. Large scale construction system problem solving is very challenging due to the inherent system complexities, many of which remain unrecognized or unperceived. For instance, it is not yet known if, and if so what kind of, collective intelligences can emerge from interactions between the wide range of system components. Furthermore, from a large scale infrastructure construction system problem solving philosophical perspective, the cooperation between people and systems needs to be studied to determine the roles people can play in better handling large scale construction systems. The qualitative-to-quantitative meta-synthesis theory has been proposed as a breakthrough and effective methodology for understanding the problem solving requirements of open complex giant systems. However, for most large scale construction projects, an effective 3 M-based engineering management methodology is still unexplored.

The meta-synthesis management system is the core methodology for infrastructure construction system 3 M-based

engineering management as it integrates meta-intelligence and meta-technology. In real world situations, some studies have found effective optimization methods for local problems. However, for large scale systems, the optimization methods for different local problems within the problem group may have conflicting objectives which eventually lead to ineffective global optimization across the whole system. To date, there has been no research that has sufficiently addressed this problem. Figure 3 shows an example of ineffective 3 M-based engineering management at large scale water conservancy and hydropower construction projects. Suppose that there are two optimization problems within the problem groups in the systems: a transportation network design problem and a construction site layout problem. To improve transportation network efficiency, an optimal strategy could be to increase the number and width of the roads. However, this would reduce the space for construction site layout and planning. The conflict between these two problem optimization objectives leads to an ineffective global optimization across the whole system.

Question II: How can the morphism between the problem groups and the model fields in large scale infrastructure systems be proven?

As discussed above, the establishment of effective 3 M-based engineering management for large scale infrastructure construction systems requires three types of system – problem groups, model fields, and algorithmic clusters – each of which reflects different aspects of the 3 M-based engineering management. The problem groups describe the physical meaning of the large scale infrastructure construction system, while the model fields express the mathematical connotations for the problem groups. The algorithmic clusters are problem solving technologies for the model fields, which are discussed further in Question III. For large scale infrastructure construction system 3 M-based engineering

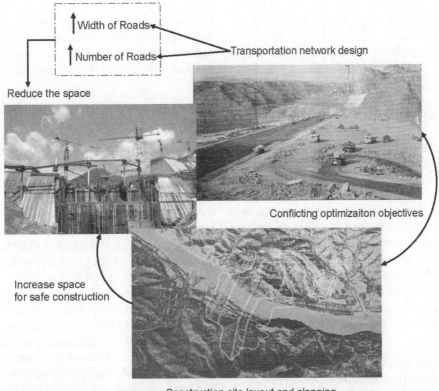

Figure 3. An example of ineffective 3 M-based engineering management in large scale water conservancy and hydropower construction projects.

management to be effective, there must be morphism between the problem groups and the model fields. The difficulties lie, however, in proving that morphism exists between the problem groups and the model fields.

However, as many studies have developed effective problem solving models, it is reasonable to believe that there is morphism between the problem groups and the model fields and that the effectiveness of a modelling approach is relevant to that morphism. However, defining the morphism requires more intensive theoretical research. As shown in Figure 4, to obtain the information sets to form the problem groups, real world problems are described using data streams classified by pattern identification. Therefore, several model fields with different constraints can be established for each problem group. Yet, as already mentioned, there is not yet any method to decide the type of morphism that exists between the problem groups and the model fields. In reality, there are two morphism types which may exist in these domains: homomorphism and isomorphism. Homomorphism can also be divided further into three types: monomorphism, epimorphism, and bimorphism, the definitions for which are as follows.

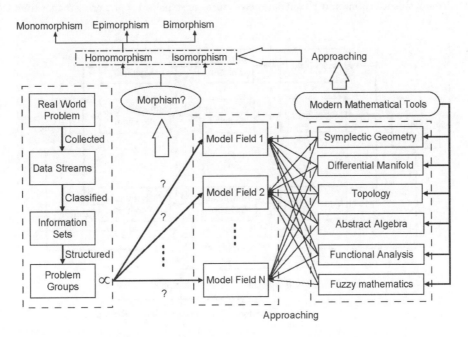

Figure 4. The challenging question of how to prove the morphism between the problem groups and the model fields.

Definition 5 – Monomorphism: A morphism $f : S \to T$ is a monomorphism if and only if $f \circ g_1 = f \circ g_2$ implies $g_1 = g_2$ for all morphisms $g_1, g_2 : Z \to S$.

Definition 6 – Epimorphism: A morphism $f : S \to T$ is an epimorphism if and only if $g_1 \circ f = g_2 \circ f$ implies $g_1 = g_2$ for all morphisms $g_1, g_2 : T \to Z$.

Definition 7 – Bimorphism: A morphism $f : S \to T$ is a bimorphism if and only if it is both a monomorphism and an epimorphism.

Definition 8 – Isomorphism: A morphism $f : S \to T$ is an isomorphism if and only if there exists a morphism $g : T \to S$ such that $f \circ g = Id_T$ and $g \circ f = Id_S$.

In fact, there is a limit to the model field which is either isomorphic or homomorphic to the problem groups. Modern mathematical tools such as symplectic geometry, differential manifolds, topology, abstract algebra, functional analysis, and fuzzy mathematics are useful in improving these model fields to approach the limit of the model field. The closer the problem group is to the limit of the model field, the more isomorphic or homomorphic it is. However, finding an appropriate way to measure the approach to this limit requires more research.

Question III: How can the morphism between the model fields and the algorithmic clusters of large scale infrastructure systems be proven?

Different from the morphism between the problem groups and the model fields ,which reflects description accuracy, the morphism between the model fields and the algorithmic clusters emphasizes computing consistency. The solution found using the algorithm clusters should be the desired solution for the optimized model fields. Yet again, proving that the morphism exists between the model fields and the algorithmic clusters in a large scale infrastructure construction project is also a challenge. In fact, when model fields have an analytical solution, it is possible to design exact algorithms. However, in large scale infrastructure construction systems, the model fields are usually NP-hard, so there is no analytical solution. Therefore, the algorithmic clusters may contain meta-heuristic algorithms to solve those models with no analytical solution. Meta-heuristic algorithms, however, can only approach the optimal solutions to the models, so the isomorphism or homomorphism between

the model fields and the algorithmic clusters is not absolute if some models have no analytical solution. As shown in Figure 5, defining the relativity of the isomorphism or homomorphism between the model fields and the algorithmic clusters is still a problem that requires focused research.

The significance of developing effective systems engineering management

Based on the above analysis, the following corollary is derived, which is critical to understanding the significance of developing effective systems engineering management for large scale infrastructure construction systems.

Corollary 1: The isomorphism or homomorphism between the problem spectrums, model fields, and algorithmic clusters in large scale infrastructure construction systems is a necessary condition for effective systems engineering management.

From the above corollary, an effective 3 M-based engineering management methodology could actually result in the digitized control of infrastructure system construction, which makes an intellectualized management of the system possible. One-to-one correspondence by mapping problem groups to model fields could significantly improve efficiency and quality, and isomorphism or homomorphism between the model fields and the algorithmic clusters could improve computing accuracy. These theoretical and technological improvements could change construction management and open up a new methodological world for infrastructure construction. 3 M-based engineering management will not only change infrastructure construction methods, but also improve our understanding of modern engineering essentials.

Conclusions

This paper examined engineering management at large scale infrastructure construction projects which have massive information, huge investments, long construction periods, high risks, organizational complexity, and widespread impact. With significant recent advances in information and engineering technologies, it is possible to change traditional infrastructure construction engineering management. The opportunities

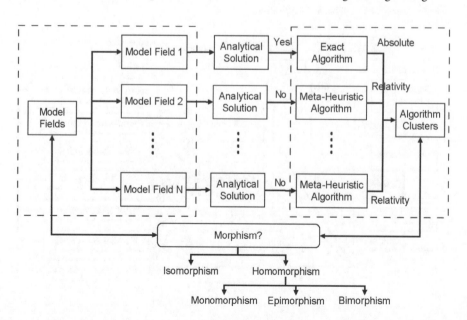

Figure 5. The challenging question of how to prove the morphism between the model fields and the algorithmic clusters.

within these engineering development advances were reviewed. With the assistance of big data technologies and information theories, large scale infrastructure systems were described as synergetic systems made up of 'Data Streams–Information Sets–Problem Groups–Model Fields–Algorithmic Clusters', and 3 M-based engineering management was proposed as the methodological framework to address this synergetic system. The challenges encountered during the evolutionary process were explained and summarized under three open questions to point to the solutions that are needed in future research. The understanding and insights raised under these three open questions can have both theoretical and practical significance for improvements in construction efficiency and quality, and reductions in environmental impacts – the three core demands of current engineering practice.

Acknowledgements

The author would like to thank the editors and anonymous referees for their helpful and constructive comments and suggestions, which have helped improve this paper.

Disclosure statement

No potential conflict of interest was reported by the author.

Funding

This work is supported by the Key Program of National Natural Science Foundation of China (grant number 70831005), and the Research Foundation of the Ministry of Education for the Doctoral Program of Higher Education of China [grant number 20130181110063].

References

Aeppli, G., & Chandra, P. (1997). Seeking a simple complex system. *Science, 275*, 177–178.

Barnes, M. (2000a). Civil engineering management in the new millennium. *Proceedings of The Institution of Civil Engineers-Civil Engineering, 138*, 73–78.

Barnes, M. (2000b). Civil engineering management in the Industrial Revolution. *Proceedings of The Institution of Civil Engineers-Civil Engineering, 138*, 135–144.

Bennett, F. L. (1996). *The management of engineering*. New York: John Wiley & Sons.

Boumen, R., de Jong, I. S. M., Mestrom, J. M. G., van de Mortel-Fronczak, J. M., & Rooda, J. E. (2009). Integration and test sequencing for complex systems. *IEEE Transactions on Systems, Man, and Cybernetics-Part A: Systems and Humans, 39*, 177–187.

Cao, L. B., Dai, R. W., & Zhou, M. C. (2009). Metasynthesis: M-Space, M-Interaction, and M-Computing for open complex giant systems. *IEEE Transactions on Systems, Man, and Cybernetics-Part A: Systems and Humans, 39*, 1007–1021.

Chang, B., & Kendall, A. (2011). Life cycle greenhouse gas assessment of infrastructure construction for California's high-speed rail system. *Transportation Research Part D: Transport and Environment, 16*, 429–434.

Chen, C. L. P., & Zhang, C. Y. (2014). Data-intensive applications, challenges, techniques and technologies: A survey on Big Data. *Information Sciences, 275*, 314–347.

Coates, G., Duffy, A. H. B., & Whitfield, I. (2004). Engineering management: operational design coordination. *Journal of Engineering Design, 15*, 433–446.

Fayol, H. (1949). *General and Industrial Management*. London, UK: Pitman.

Foote, R. (2007). Mathematics and complex systems. *Science, 318*, 410–412.

Fung, I. C., Tse, Z. T. H., & Fu, K. W. (2015). Converting big data into public health. *Science, 347*, 620–620.

Gu, J. F., & Tang, J. X. (2005). Meta-synthesis approach to complex system modeling. *European Journal of Operational Research, 166*, 597–614.

Hendrickson, C. (2012). Sustainable energy challenges for civil engineering management. *Journal of Management in Engineering, 28*, 2–4.

Lannes, W. J. (2001). What is engineering management? *IEEE Transactions on Engineering Management, 48*, 107–115.

Lazer, D., Kennedy, R., King, G., & Vespignani, A. (2014). The parable of google flu: traps in big data analysis. *Science, 343*, 1203–1205.

Leleur, S. (2008). Systems science and complexity: some proposals for future development. *Systems Research and Behavioral Science, 25*, 67–79.

Lock, D. (1993). *Handbook of engineering management*. Boston: Butterworth-Heinemann.

Lynch, C. (2008). Big data: How do your data grow? *Nature, 455*, 28–29.

May, R. M. (1972). Will a large complex system be stable. *Nature, 238*, 413–414.

Marx, V. (2013). The big challenges of big data. *Nature, 498*, 255–260.

Nadis, S. (2003). Complex system: All together now. *Nature, 421*, 780–782.

Ottino, J. M. (2004). Engineering complex systems. *Nature, 427*, 399–399.

Qian, X. S. (1991). Revisiting issues on open complex giant systems. *Pattern Recognit. Artif. Intell., 4*, 5–8.

Qian, X. S., Yu, J. Y., & Dai, R. W. (1990). A new scientific field-Open complex giant systems and the methodology. *Chin. J. Nature, 13*, 3–10.

Qian, X. S., Yu, J. Y., & Dai, R. W. (1993). A new discipline of science-The study of open complex giant system and its methodology. *Chin. J. Syst. Eng. Electron., 4*, 2–12.

Servick, K. (2015). Big data proposed study would closely track 10,000 New Yorkers. *Science, 350*, 493–494.

Senouci, A., EI-Abbasy, M. S., Zayed, T. (2014). Fuzzy-based model for predicting failure of oil pipelines. *Journal of Infrastructure Systems, 20*, 04014018.

Shneiderman, B. (2014). The big picture for big data: Visualization. *Science, 343*, 730–730.

Stone, R. (2008). Three Gorges Dam: into the unknown. *Science, 321*, 628–632.

Wei, X., Han, L., & Gao, B. (2016). Distribution, bioavailability, and potential risk assessment of the metals in tributary sediments of Three Gorges Reservoir: The impact of water impoundment. *Ecological Indicators, 61*, 667–675.

Winston, A. M. (2004). Engineering management - A personal perspective. *IEEE Transactions on Engineering Management, 51*, 412–413.

Wren, K. (2014). Big data, big questions. *Science, 344*, 982–983.

Xu, J. P., & Li, Z. M. (2012). A review on Ecological Engineering based Engineering Management. *Omega-International Journal of Management Science, 40*, 368–378.

Xu, J. P., & Tao, Z. M. (2012). *rough multiple objective decision making*. Boca Raton: Taylor & Francis Publishers.

Xu, J. P., & Yao, L. M. (2011). *Random-like multiple objective decision making*. Berlin: Springer-Verlag.

Xu, J. P., & Wu, Z. Z. (2015). *Tubular string characterization in HTHP oil and gas wells*. London: Taylor & Francis Publishers.

Xu, J. P., & Zeng, Z. Q. (2011). Applying optimal control model to dynamic equipment allocation problem: Case study of concrete-faced rockfill dam construction project. *Journal of Construction Engineering and Management, 137*, 536–550.

Xu, J. P., & Zeng, Z. Q. (2014). *Fuzzy-like multistage multiple objective decision making*. Heidelberg: Springer.

Xu, J. P., & Zhou, X. Y. (2011). *Fuzzy-like multiple objective decision making*. Berlin: Springer-Verlag.

Zeng, Z. Q., Xu, J. P., Wu, S. Y., & Shen, M. B. (2014). Antithetic method-based particle swarm optimization for a queuing network problem with fuzzy data in concrete transportation systems. *Computer-Aided Civil and Infrastructure Engineering, 29*, 771–800.

Bayes and big data: the consensus Monte Carlo algorithm

Steven L. Scott, Alexander W. Blocker, Fernando V. Bonassi, Hugh A. Chipman, Edward I. George and Robert E. McCulloch

A useful definition of 'big data' is data that is too big to process comfortably on a single machine, either because of processor, memory, or disk bottlenecks. Graphics processing units can alleviate the processor bottleneck, but memory or disk bottlenecks can only be eliminated by splitting data across multiple machines. Communication between large numbers of machines is expensive (regardless of the amount of data being communicated), so there is a need for algorithms that perform distributed approximate Bayesian analyses with minimal communication. Consensus Monte Carlo operates by running a separate Monte Carlo algorithm on each machine, and then averaging individual Monte Carlo draws across machines. Depending on the model, the resulting draws can be nearly indistinguishable from the draws that would have been obtained by running a single-machine algorithm for a very long time. Examples of consensus Monte Carlo are shown for simple models where single-machine solutions are available, for large single-layer hierarchical models, and for Bayesian additive regression trees (BART).

1. Introduction

This article describes a method of performing approximate Monte Carlo simulation from a Bayesian posterior distribution based on very large data sets. When the data are too large for a single processor, the obvious solution is to divide them among multiple processors. There are two basic methods of computing on the divided data. The first is to divide the work among multiple cores on the same chip, either on a multi-core central processing unit (CPU), or on a massively parallel graphics processing unit (GPU). The multi-core approach can be extremely effective (Suchard et al. , 2010; Lee, Yao, Giles, Doucet, & Holmes , 2010), but it has two limitations. The first is that multi-core computing cannot alleviate bottlenecks related to memory or disk. The second issue is programming. The multi-threaded code necessary for multi-core computing can be difficult to write, even for expert programmers, because it is subject to race conditions that are poorly understood and difficult to debug. GPU programming in particular requires very low level memory management that is difficult to abstract to higher level programming languages.

The alternative to multi-core computing is multi-machine computing, where data are divided among many different machines. Multi-machine computing provides scalable memory, disk, and processing power, so it can eliminate bottlenecks in all three traditional computing resources. However, multi-machine computing comes with a very high cost (in terms of efficiency) of communicating between machines. The multi-machine and multi-core approaches are complementary. If a multi-core solution is available it can be embedded in a multi-machine strategy, making each machine faster.

The primary difference between the multi-machine and multi-core computing models is communication, which is fast in multi-core systems and slow in multi-machine systems. Different communication costs imply that different algorithms are necessary for multi-core and multi-machine environments. On a multi-core system one can effectively parallelize a sequential algorithm by distributing the work required to implement an expensive step. For example, (Suchard et al. , 2010) achieve substantial speed increases by implementing a data augmentation algorithm on a GPU. Their algorithm is a standard data augmentation with the computationally intensive loop over the data done in parallel. Section 2 of this article presents a case study demonstrating the inefficiency of that algorithm in a multi-machine environment. It illustrates a fact which is well known to parallel computing experts, but often surprising to novices: passing messages among a large number of machines is expensive, regardless of the size of the messages being passed.

For Monte Carlo algorithms to succeed in a multi-machine environment, they must avoid regular communication between machines. Consensus Monte Carlo attacks the communication problem by dividing the data across multiple machines, with each machine independently sampling from the posterior distribution given its data. Posterior draws from each machine are then combined to form a consensus, system-wide belief about the model unknowns. The consensus Monte Carlo algorithm is embarrassingly parallel, as defined by the mapreduce framework (Dean & Ghemawat , 2008), so it can be run on virtually any system for parallel computing, including Hadoop (White , 2012), multi-core systems, or networks of workstations (Anderson, Culler, & Patterson , 1995).

Consensus Monte Carlo is one of several attempts to scale traditional statistical computation. Zhang, Duchi, and Wainwright (2012), and references therein, describe the literature on averaging frequentist point estimates for parameters

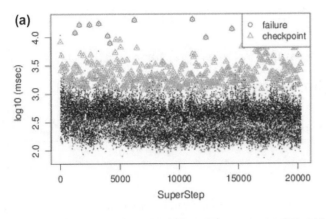 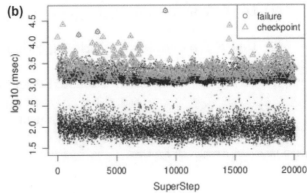

Figure 1. Step times for the naive MCMC algorithm in Section 2 with (a) 500 and (b) 50 machines.

of statistical models. Guha, Kidwell, Hafen, and Cleveland (2009) discuss distributed methods of visualizing large data sets. Kleiner, Talwalkar, Sarkar, and Jordan (2011) extend the bootstrap to distributed data with the 'bag of little bootstraps'. To the extent that bootstrap samples can be viewed as approximating posterior samples, this work can be considered an alternative to the work presented here. Returning to Bayesian inference, Huang and Gelman (2005) proposed a consensus Monte Carlo approach that is similar to ours, but with a different rule for combining posterior draws. For certain classes of models (and certain classes of model summaries), Bayesian inference can be conducted without Monte Carlo through clever approximations such as integrated nested Laplace approximation (INLA) (Rue, Martino, & Chopin , 2009), or variational Bayes (e.g. Hinton & Van Camp , 1993; Ghahramani & Beal , 2001; Jaakkola & Jordan , 2000). These approaches are effective, but there can be reasons to prefer Monte Carlo. For example, the computational cost of INLA is exponential in the dimension of the parameter space (or hyperparameter space in the case of hierarchical models), and the approximate posteriors delivered by variational Bayes give good approximations to individual marginal distributions, but not to the joint distribution as a whole. Posterior simulation by Monte Carlo is considerably more expensive than deterministic approximation algorithms, but it delivers the full posterior distribution. Although the approach presented here is limited to continuous parameter spaces, Monte Carlo methods can generally be applied to arbitrarily complex models.

The remainder of the article is structured as follows. Section 2 contains the case study, mentioned above, illustrating the high cost of communicating between processes in a multi-machine environment. Section 3 describes the consensus Monte Carlo algorithm, and then Section 4 provides a series of examples illustrating consensus Monte Carlo on a variety of simulated and real data sets. Section 5 is a concluding discussion.

2. Coordinating many machines is expensive

This section presents timings from a multi-machine Markov chain Monte Carlo (MCMC) algorithm, with the aim of illustrating just how expensive multi-machine communication can be. We focus on a single layer hierarchical logistic regression model

$$y_{ij} \sim \text{Binomial}(n_{ij}, p_{ij})$$
$$\text{logit}(p_{ij}) = \mathbf{x}_{ij}^{\mathrm{T}} \beta_i$$
$$\beta_i \sim \mathcal{N}(\mu, \Sigma) \tag{1}$$
$$\mu | \Sigma \sim \mathcal{N}(0, \Sigma/\kappa)$$
$$\Sigma^{-1} \sim W(I, \nu),$$

where $W(I, \nu)$ is the Wishart distribution with sum of squares matrix I and scale parameter ν. The precise numerical values of ν and κ used in the hyperprior are unimportant for this example. This model was applied to an internet advertising data set, where y_{ij} is the number of clicks on an advertisement with characteristics $\mathbf{x}_{ij}$ that was shown n_{ij} times. The hierarchy corresponds to different internet domains (e.g. espn.com versus nytimes.com). There are slightly more than 600,000 domains in our data set, each with its own β_i. The vector $\mathbf{x}_{ij}$ contains an intercept and seven dummy variables describing the color, font, and similar characteristics of the advertisement, so that the dimension of $\mathbf{x}_{ij}$ is eight. The number of distinct configurations of $\mathbf{x}_{ij}$ in each domain is small. It is bounded above by $2^7 = 128$, but it is rarely more than a few dozen, and often just a single observation.

The obvious parallel MCMC algorithm for this model partitions the complete data by domain across a set of worker machines, and assigns one worker to be the 'master node' responsible for the prior distribution. The algorithm then alternates between drawing each β_i given current values of μ and Σ, and then drawing μ and Σ given the set of β_i's. During the parallel data augmentation step, each machine simulates from $p(\beta_i | \mu, \Sigma, \mathbf{y})$ for its domains, and adds the draw to a set of low dimensional sufficient statistics $(\sum_i \beta_i, \sum_i \beta_i \beta_i^{\mathrm{T}})$. When a machine finishes drawing β_i for all of its domains, it sends its sufficient statistics to the master node, which accumulates sufficient statistics from different machines as they become available. Once all machines have reported, the master node draws μ and Σ, broadcasts them to the workers, and the cycle repeats. The algorithm was implemented in Pregel (Malewicz et al. , 2010), a system for distributed graph computing written by professional software engineers who are experts in parallel computation. The statistical computations were done in optimized C++ code.

There are potential issues with the adequacy of this model, the convergence rate of the MCMC algorithm, and the specific method used to sample the logistic regression coefficients. Set all these aside and focus on the amount of time required to perform an MCMC iteration. Figure 1 plots the time taken by each step in the algorithm from two separate runs with the same data on 500 and 50 machines. The draws of β_i and (μ, Σ) are separate 'SuperSteps' in Pregel, so each panel in Figure 1 represents 10,000 MCMC iterations, with two SuperSteps per MCMC iterate. The 500-machine run completed in 2.75 hours, which is very close to 1 iteration per second. The 50-machine run completed in around 5 hours. Notice that a ten-fold reduction in computing resources only produced a two-fold increase in compute time, so there is at least a factor of 5 inefficiency at play.

> (1) Divide **y** into shards $\mathbf{y}_1, \ldots, \mathbf{y}_S$.
>
> (2) Run S separate Monte Carlo algorithms to sample $\theta_{sg} \sim p(\theta|\mathbf{y}_s)$ for $g = 1, \ldots, G$, with each shard using the fractionated prior $p(\theta)^{1/S}$.
>
> (3) Combine the draws across shards using weighted averages: $\theta_g = \left(\sum_s W_s\right)^{-1}\left(\sum_s W_s \theta_{sg}\right)$.

Figure 2. The consensus Monte Carlo algorithm.

Job failures are a fact of life in multi-machine computing and are often discussed as a source of delay. Jobs can fail either because of faulty hardware or because of evictions in favor of higher priority jobs. To protect against job failures, Pregel periodically saves its state so that it can recover from a failure without completely restarting. The state-saving iterations are highlighted with triangles in Figure 1. Both runs lose about the same amount of time saving state. The iterations containing job failures are highlighted with circles. Each recovery from a failure takes a few tens of seconds. The 500-machine run experienced more failures, but not enough to factor materially into the efficiency difference between the two runs.

The source of the inefficiency can be seen in the lower of the two black bands in Figure 1. The bands represent even and odd numbered SuperSteps corresponding to the expensive β_i draws in the even steps and the cheap (μ, Σ) draws in the odd steps. As expected, increasing the number of machines leads to a decrease in the amount of time spent on the expensive step. The surprising thing is how much more expensive the 'cheap' steps become. In the 50-machine run, the (μ, Σ) draw takes a median of roughly $10^2 = 100$ milliseconds. In the 500-machine run it takes roughly $10^{2.4} \approx 250$ milliseconds. Logging in the C++ code shows that the actual time spent drawing μ and Σ is less than 1 millisecond, with the rest lost to communication overhead. The inefficiency is not coming from rare, catastrophic machine failures, but the consistently higher communication cost in iterations where no failures occurred. Ironically, CPU was the limiting resource in the single-machine version of this problem, but on a relative scale we wound up devoting almost no CPU time to our job!

We wish to emphasize that time is not being lost in what one might think are the obvious places: an imbalanced workload among the machines, inhomogeneous hardware, an inefficient broadcast of the parameters, reduction of the sufficient statistics, or a long transmission time on the network. All these possibilities were investigated and found to be performing efficiently. The problem is that we are communicating between machines at all. There is simply an overhead involved in getting a set of machines ready to send and receive messages, even if those machines are dedicated to your job. The cost is high enough that, in this case, a 500-machine job could achieve at most 4 iterations per second, on average, even if the machines had no data to process. The clear lesson is that if Bayesian posterior simulation is to be distributed across multiple machines, it must be done in a way that uses minimal communication.

3. Consensus Monte Carlo

The idea behind consensus Monte Carlo is to break the data into groups (called 'shards'), give each shard to a worker machine which does a full Monte Carlo simulation from a posterior distribution given its own data, and then combine the posterior simulations from each worker to produce a set of global draws representing the consensus belief among all the workers. Let **y** represent the full data, let $\mathbf{y}_s$ denote shard s, and let θ denote the model parameters. For models with the appropriate independence structure the system can be written

$$p(\theta|\mathbf{y}) \propto \prod_{s=1}^{S} p(\mathbf{y}_s|\theta)p(\theta)^{1/S}. \tag{2}$$

Notice that the prior distribution $p(\theta) = \prod_s p(\theta)^{1/S}$ is broken into S components to preserve the total amount of prior information in the system. Equation (2) assumes that batches of observations are conditionally independent across shards, given parameters, but it allows for arbitrary dependence within the elements of $\mathbf{y}_s$. Thus, for example, it can be used with hierarchical models with hyperparameters θ, as long as data in a single level of the hierarchy are not split across two different machines.

If each worker returned its posterior distribution as a mathematical function, then the worker-level distributions could be multiplied to form the overall 'consensus' posterior given the complete data. The difficulty is that the workers-level distributions are reported as Monte Carlo draws, so we need a way of combining the draws.

3.1. Combining draws by weighted averages

Suppose worker s generates draws $\theta_{s1}, \ldots, \theta_{sG}$ from $p(\theta|\mathbf{y}_s) \propto p(\mathbf{y}_s|\theta)p(\theta)^{1/S}$. One way to combine draws across workers is simply to average them. Suppose each worker is assigned a weight, representable as a matrix W_s. The consensus posterior for draw g is

$$\theta_g = \left(\sum_s W_s\right)^{-1} \sum_s W_s \theta_{sg}. \tag{3}$$

When each $p(\theta|\mathbf{y}_s)$ is Gaussian, the joint posterior $p(\theta|\mathbf{y})$ is also Gaussian, and Equation (3) can be made to yield exact draws from $p(\theta|\mathbf{y})$. To see this, suppose $S = 2$, and that $\theta|\mathbf{y}_1 \sim \mathcal{N}(\mu_1, \Sigma_1)$, and $\theta|\mathbf{y}_2 \sim \mathcal{N}(\mu_2, \Sigma_2)$. Then standard Bayesian calculations for the normal distribution give

$$\begin{aligned} p(\theta|\mathbf{y}) &\propto p(\theta|\mathbf{y}_1)p(\theta|\mathbf{y}_2) \\ &\propto \mathcal{N}(\theta|\tilde{\mu}, V), \end{aligned} \tag{4}$$

where $V^{-1} = \Sigma_1^{-1} + \Sigma_2^{-1}$ and $\tilde{\mu} = V(\Sigma_1^{-1}\mu_1 + \Sigma_2^{-1}\mu_2)$. Now let θ_1 be a draw from $\mathcal{N}(\mu_1, \Sigma_1)$ and let θ_2 be a draw from $\mathcal{N}(\mu_2, \Sigma_2)$. It is easily verified that

$$V\left(\Sigma_1^{-1}\theta_1 + \Sigma_2^{-1}\theta_2\right) \sim \mathcal{N}(\tilde{\mu}, V). \tag{5}$$

Taken together, Equations (4) and (6) suggest the algorithm in Figure 2. Although the algorithm is exact only for Gaussian posteriors, there are two reasons to believe that it is broadly useful. The first is that, under standard regularity conditions for asymptotic theory, posterior distributions tend towards a Gaussian limit in large samples (Le Cam & Yang , 2000). The second is that we will see examples in Section 4 where applying the method to non-Gaussian posteriors (without theoretical justification) works surprisingly well.

3.2. Choosing weights

The weight $W_s = \Sigma_s^{-1}$ is optimal (for Gaussian models), where $\Sigma_s = \text{Var}(\theta|\mathbf{y}_s)$. An obvious Monte Carlo estimate of Σ_s is the sample variance of $\theta_{s1}, \ldots, \theta_{sG}$. If the dimension of θ is very large, or if the model is very simple, one may prefer to weight sub-optimally in order to simplify the computation. If θ is high dimensional then it may be preferable to ignore the covariances in Σ_s, and simply weight each scalar element of θ by the reciprocal of its marginal posterior variance.

In many 'big data' problems the analyst is in control of the sharding process, so data can be sharded by randomly assigning each observation (or cluster of correlated observations) to a shard. One is tempted to argue that the posterior distributions in each shard will have roughly the same shape, and so the draws from different shards can be combined with equal weighting. However, large samples on each shard are necessary for the preceding argument to apply. In particular, each worker must have enough information to estimate all components of θ. Almost by definition, models that are complex enough to require very large data sets will have subsets of parameters that cannot be estimated on every shard. Section 4.3 provides an example where shard-level posterior distributions can be very different, even with IID data, because some observations are more informative than others. In practice, information-based weighting will usually be necessary.

3.3. Other potential consensus strategies

Strategies other than averaging could be used to form consensus posterior estimates. We focus on averages because they are simple and stable. For example, one could empirically estimate each worker-level posterior density using a kernel density estimate and then apply Equation (2) directly. This approach might work well in small models, but as the dimension of θ increases the kernel density estimates will become unreliable.

Huang and Gelman (2005) suggest four alternative methods for consensus posteriors, all of which are variants of either an explicit normal approximation or importance resampling. The consensus Monte Carlo method from Figure 2 is also rooted in normal theory, but it has the potential to capture non-normal features of the posterior such as fat tails or skewness that would be lost under an explicit normal approximation. We have not explored importance resampling methods because of the potential for importance resampling to collapse to a single point in high dimensions, and because of the potential difficulty in evaluating the likelihood $p(\mathbf{y}_s|\theta)$ in complex models, like hierarchical generalized linear models similar to Equation (1). On the other hand, consensus distributions based on averaging are obviously limited to continuous parameter spaces, while importance resampling methods could be applied more generally (e.g. to mixtures, or regression models with spike-and-slab priors).

Another alternative is to model (possibly non-parametrically) the draws of the posterior distribution, and then apply Equation (2) directly to the fitted models. This approach has been applied with some success by several authors, including Neiswanger, Wang, and Xing (2013), Wang and Dunson (2013), Wang, Fangjian, Heller, and Dunson (2015), and Srivastava, Li, and Dunson (2015). The primary differences among these articles are the methods used to model the posterior distribution. This is a promising approach for handling complex models with highly skewed or multimodal posteriors, but it can add a non-trivial amount of complexity, and the right way to model the posterior can depend on the model being fitted, the dimension and amount of data, and other factors. Given these challenges, the simplicity and robustness of forming consensus using weighted averages has considerable appeal.

3.4. More complex models

3.4.1. Nested hierarchical models

If the data have nested structure, where $y_{ij} \sim f(y|\phi_j)$ and $\phi_j \sim p(\phi|\theta)$, then consensus Monte Carlo can be applied to the hyperparameters in a straightforward way. If the data are partitioned so that no group is split across multiple shards, then the model satisfies Equation (2). One can run the consensus Monte Carlo algorithm, storing the draws of θ and discarding the draws of ϕ_j. Combining the draws of θ_{sg} based using empirical weights W_s estimated from the within-shard Monte Carlo variance produces a set of draws $\theta_1, \ldots, \theta_G$ approximating $p(\theta|\mathbf{y})$.

Conditional on the simulated draws of θ, sampling $\phi_j \sim p(\phi_j|\mathbf{y}, \theta) = p(\phi_j|\mathbf{y}_j, \theta)$ is an embarrassingly parallel problem. The simulated draws of θ can be broadcast back to the workers, which can simulate each ϕ_j in parallel. Each worker machine simulates ϕ_{jg} given the corresponding θ_g, with no need to communicate with other workers. Because $\theta \sim p(\theta|\mathbf{y})$, the second set of ϕ_j draws will have marginal distribution $p(\phi_j|\mathbf{y})$, whereas the first, discarded set follows $p(\phi_j|\mathbf{y}_s)$.

This procedure can be recursively applied as needed if the data are nested more than two levels deep.

3.4.2. Non-parametric regression

In a non-parametric regression model $y \sim \mathcal{N}\left(f(\mathbf{x}), \sigma^2\right)$ the goal is to compute $p(f(\mathbf{x})|\mathbf{y})$ where the form of f is unknown. Many non-parametric models either have no parameters to average or else the 'model parameters' are non-numerical constructs like decision trees (see Denison, Mallick, & Smith , 1998, and Chipman, George, & McCulloch , 2010). However, the predictive distributions from these models are often nearly Gaussian (possibly after conditioning on latent variables), so consensus Monte Carlo can be used to combine their predictive distributions at particular values of $\mathbf{x}$. Given training data $\mathbf{y}$ and a set of locations $\mathbf{x}_1, \ldots, \mathbf{x}_K$, where predictions are desired, one can run S separate Monte Carlo simulations to produce draws from $p(f(\mathbf{x}_k)|\mathbf{y}_s)$. At each $\mathbf{x}_k$, each worker's draws can be weighted by the inverse of the Monte Carlo estimate of the the within-worker posterior variance $s_{sk}^2 = \sum_{g=1}^{G}(f_{sg}(\mathbf{x}_k) - \bar{f}_s(\mathbf{x}_k))^2/(G-1)$, and averaged to form a consensus posterior distribution.

3.5. The potential for small-sample bias

Oddly enough, small sample bias can play a role when analyzing large data sets. When the data are divided among many machines, bias that vanishes in the full data may still be present in each shard. Zhang et al. (2012) discuss the issue of small sample bias in the context of frequentist point estimation. A similar effect can exist in Bayesian analysis, where the consensus posterior needs to be shifted because of an accumulation of small sample biases.

Figure 3 shows the effect of small sample bias in a toy simulation where $y_i \sim \mathcal{N}(\mu, 1)$, with $p(\mu) \propto 1$, where the parameter of interest is μ^2. The figure is based on a simulation of $n = 10{,}000$ observations from $y \sim \mathcal{N}(3, 1)$, with 10 equally weighted shards. The solid line in the figure is the posterior distribution based on all 10,000 observations, while the dashed line is the consensus Monte Carlo estimate.

Not all problems will exhibit meaningful small sample bias. In some cases the shard-level models will have sufficiently large sample sizes that small-sample bias is not an issue. In others, models can be unbiased even in small samples. When small sample bias is a concern, jackknife bias correction can be used to mitigate it through subsampling. The idea behind jackknife bias correction is to shift the draws from a distribution by a specified amount B determined by subsampling. Suppose $E(\theta|\mathbf{y}) = \theta + B/n$, so that the posterior mean is a biased estimate of θ. On each worker machine, take a subsample of size αn, where $0 < \alpha < 1$. Let $\mathbf{y}_{sub}$ denote the resulting distributed subsample, and construct consensus Monte Carlo draws from $p(\theta|\mathbf{y}_{sub})$. Then $E(\theta|\mathbf{y}_{sub}) = \theta + B/\alpha n$. Simple algebra gives an estimate of the bias term

$$\frac{B}{n} \approx \left(E(\theta|\mathbf{y}_{sub}) - E(\theta|\mathbf{y}) \right)\left(\frac{\alpha}{1 - \alpha} \right).$$

Subtracting the estimated value of B/n from each draw in the original consensus distribution gives a set of first order bias corrected draws. The dotted line in Figure 3 shows the effect of the bias correction in our example.

4. Examples

This section proceeds through a set of examples illustrating the consensus Monte Carlo algorithm. In each case, the goal is to see how the algorithm compares to a single-machine algorithm run on the same data. Thus the examples will have to be simple enough (or else the data small enough) for a single-machine run to be possible.

4.1. Binomial data with a beta prior

Figure 4(a) shows three Monte Carlo approximations to the posterior distribution of a binomial success probability. The data are 1000 Bernoulli outcomes with a single success, and the assumed prior is uniform. Two of the distributions in Figure 4 are made by directly drawing from the $Be(2, 1001)$ distribution. The distribution marked 'Consensus' was constructed by distributing the data across 100 independent Monte Carlo samplers, each with a $Be(.01, .01)$ prior distribution. One of the samplers is assigned the shard of data containing 9 failures and the single success. The remaining 99 samplers each observe 10 failures. The posterior draws were then combined using an unweighted average. This example is interesting because, even though the posterior is highly non-Gaussian, consensus Monte Carlo does an effective job capturing the distribution. Figure 4(b) highlights that the approximation is imperfect, in that it slightly under-weights the tails.

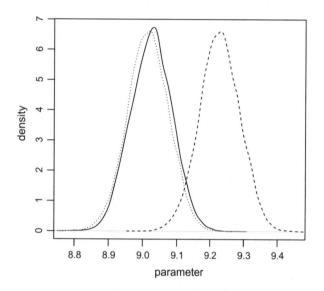

Figure 3. Example of small sample bias. The solid line is the posterior distribution of μ^2 as described in Section 3.5. The dashed line is the consensus Monte Carlo estimate. The dotted line is the consensus Monte Carlo estimate with a jackknife bias correction applied.

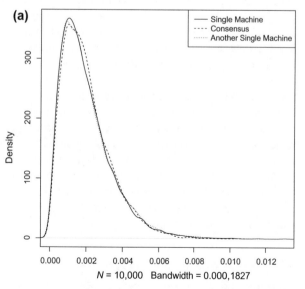

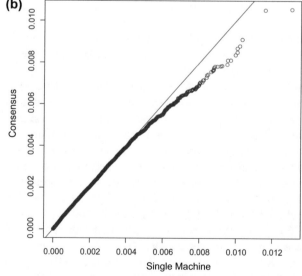

Figure 4. (a) Posterior draws from binomial data. (b) A qq plot showing that the tails of the consensus Monte Carlo distribution in panel (a) are slightly too light.

(a)
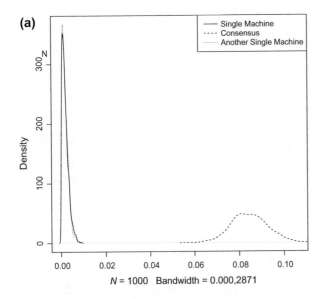

(b)
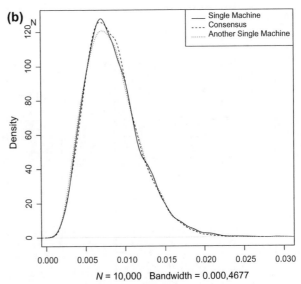

Figure 5. The consensus Monte Carlo distribution (a) performs badly when each worker receives a uniform prior, and (b)performs well with imbalanced shards, when properly weighted.

This example also illustrates that the procedure can be sensitive to the scale of the analysis. The shard-level prior $Be(.01, .01)$ is not the same as the full $Be(1, 1)$ prior raised to the .01 power. If the 100 workers had each been given the uniform prior then the estimated distribution would be seriously incorrect, as shown by Figure 5(a). The prior is very important because only a single success was observed. Giving each worker an additional 'prior success' corresponding to the uniform prior adds a substantial amount of prior information to the system. The influence of the prior, and thus the need for prior adjustment, becomes less dramatic when the data are more informative.

Figure 5(b) shows a different simulation where the workers are given different amounts of work to do. There were 5 workers each assigned 100, 20, 20, 70, and 500 binomial observations. The data were simulated from the binomial distribution with success probability .01. The workers were each given a $Be(1 / 5, 1 / 5)$ prior to match the $Be(1, 1)$ uniform prior used in the single machine analysis. This distribution is slightly less skewed than the one in Figure 4, because the simulation produced more than one success. The distribution is still noticeably non-Gaussian, and the consensus Monte Carlo estimate is very similar to the two single-machine analyses.

4.2. Gaussian data

The next test case is a multivariate normal model with unknown mean and variance. The test case has $\mu = (1, 2, 3, 4, 5)$ and

$$\Sigma = \begin{pmatrix} 1.00 & 0.99 & 0.98 & 0.00 & -0.70 \\ 0.99 & 1.00 & 0.97 & 0.00 & -0.75 \\ 0.98 & 0.97 & 1.00 & 0.00 & -0.60 \\ 0.00 & 0.00 & 0.00 & 1.00 & 0.00 \\ -0.70 & -0.75 & -0.60 & 0.00 & 1.00 \end{pmatrix}.$$

The model includes three deviates that are highly correlated with one another, one that is independent of everything else, and one that is anticorrelated with the first three. We consider a problem with 100 workers and examine how consensus Monte Carlo handles draws of Σ. We focus on Σ because the marginal

posterior of μ is multivariate T, which is sufficiently close to normal for the consensus draws to be nearly exact.

Figure 6 shows posterior draws of Σ based on simulated data with 50 observations per worker. The scale is different in each of the panels (which are arrayed as the elements of Σ) in order maximally to highlight differences in the consensus and single-machine draws. When viewed on the same scale, the differences between parameter values are far more important than the differences between methods. The consensus Monte Carlo estimates (shown as dashed lines) of the posterior appear to have a bias away from zero when compared to the single-machine algorithm (the solid lines).

The dotted lines are a jackknife bias corrected density estimate based on a 20% subsample. With 50 observations per worker, a 20% subsample is 10 observations. When paired with a corrected prior distribution (obtained by dividing both the prior sum of squares and prior sample size by S), a much smaller sub-sample would lead to an improper posterior. The bias correction generally seems to help in Figure 6(a), though for the variance term in element 4 it provides an adjustment were none is necessary.

Interestingly, when we double the sample size to 100 in Figure 6(b) the unadjusted consensus Monte Carlo estimates match the single-machine algorithm quite closely, while the jackknife bias adjustment winds up introducing a bias towards zero similar to the one it removed in Figure 6(a). We tried one more run with 1000 observations per worker, which we choose not to display because all the distributions match sufficiently closely that it is difficult to distinguish between them visually.

4.3. Logistic regression

Logistic regression is a widely used model for internet data because of the interest in whether a particular stimulus results in a user action such as a click, mouse-over, or similar observable event. Table (a) is a set of simulated data based on a hypothetical set of binary predictors that occur independently with the frequencies shown in Table (b). The first variable is an intercept, and the last is a rarely occurring variable that is highly predictive of an event when it occurs.

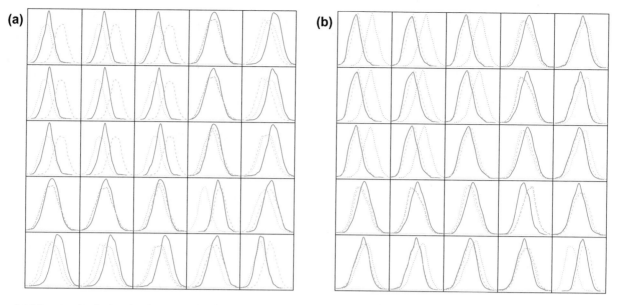

Figure 6. (a) Posterior distribution of Σ based on 100 workers, with 50 observations per worker. Red (solid) line is the single-machine algorithm. Green (dashed) line is the consensus Monte Carlo estimate. Blue (dotted) line is the bias corrected consensus estimate. (b) Same, but with 100 observations per worker. With 1000 observations per worker, all plots overlap essentially perfectly.

Table 1. (a) Data for the logistic regression in Figure 7. (b) The probability that each variable is active, and the true logistic regression coefficients used in the simulation.

y	n	x_1	x_2	x_3	x_4	x_5
266	2755	1	0	0	1	0
116	2753	1	0	0	0	0
34	1186	1	0	1	0	0
190	717	1	1	0	1	0
61	1173	1	0	1	1	0
37	305	1	1	1	0	0
68	301	1	1	1	1	0
119	706	1	1	0	0	0
18	32	1	0	0	0	1
13	17	1	0	1	1	1
18	24	1	0	0	1	1
8	10	1	1	0	1	1
2	2	1	1	1	0	1
7	13	1	0	1	0	1
2	2	1	1	1	1	1
3	4	1	1	0	0	1
			(b)			
Frequency	1	.2	.3	.5	.01	
Coefficient	-3	1.2	$-.5$	.8	3	

Figure 7(a) shows the posterior distribution of the coefficients in a logistic regression of y on x_1 through x_5. The single-machine 'overall' MCMC estimate is compared to consensus Monte Carlo estimates under three different weighting schemes. The 'matrix' scheme weights each worker's draws using the inverse of the sample variance matrix for β draws from that worker. The 'scalar' weighting scheme weights each individual component of β by the inverse of its scalar sample variance, ignoring covariances. The 'equal' scheme simply averages all draws with equal weights.

Despite the fact that all 100 workers faced identical sampling distributions, the equal weighting scheme fails badly because the workers are only 'equal' *a priori*. They don't see the same data. Out of 10,000 total observations, there are only 104 in which x_5 is active, and only 71 of those produce an event. Thus, many workers (roughly 1/3) have no information with which to measure the effect of x_5, and roughly another third have only a single observation, so a small subset of workers has all the information about this coefficient. The different subsets of workers can be seen in Figure 7(b). Those with no information about β_5 sample from the prior. Those that only get to

see a single observation sample from one of the the skewed distributions, depending on whether the single observation corresponded to a success or a failure. The subset of informed workers able to see multiple observations sample from the nearly normal distributions centered around 3. The empirical weighting schemes ('matrix' and 'scalar') are aware of the information asymmetry and can use it to place more weight on workers that have more information.

The information asymmetry is the main reason the equal weighting scheme misses so badly in Figure 7(a). The figure also shows substantial agreement between the single-machine overall MCMC algorithm and the 'matrix' and 'scalar' weighting schemes. Both schemes do a good job capturing not only the location and spread of the marginal distribution of the coefficients, but also the correlations between coefficients. The 'scalar' scheme tends to be over-dispersed relative to the 'matrix' scheme, but not terribly so.

Figure 8 shows how the various schemes perform as the sample size grows to 1,000 and 10,000 observations per worker. Both the matrix and scalar weighting methods do about equally well combining the worker draws. The equal weighting scheme is

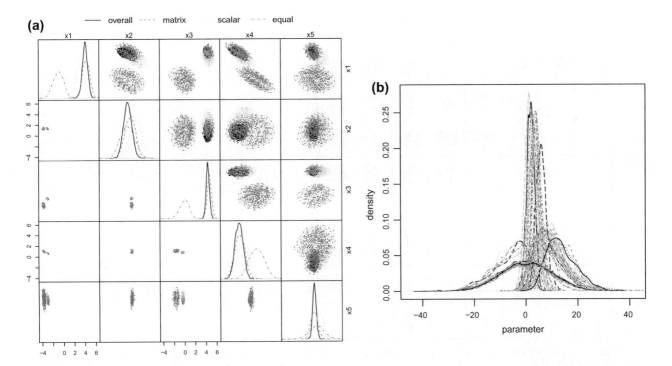

Figure 7. Logistic regression with 100 observations per worker. Panel (a) is a pairs plot comparing the single-machine MCMC estimate of the posterior distribution with the consensus Monte Carlo estimate under three different weighting schemes. Plots on and above the diagonal show the distributions on a scale just large enough to fit the plots in each dimension. Plots below the diagonal are on a common scale. The diagonal shows the marginal distribution of each coefficient. Panel (b) shows the worker-level marginal distributions for β_5.

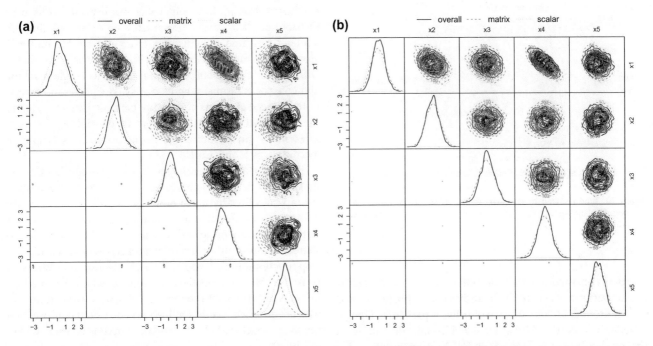

Figure 8. Logistic regression with (a) 1,000 and (b) 10,000 observations per worker. Compare to Figure 7(a). The equal weighting scheme is not shown here – in order better to focus on matrix and scalar schemes.

not shown in these plots. It still missed badly with 1,000 observations per worker, but it performs about as well as the other methods with 10,000 observations per worker. With so many observations, the differences between pairwise marginal distributions are vanishingly small when seen on a common scale.

4.4. Hierarchical models

We now consider fitting a hierarchical model to a large distributed data set of internet advertising data. The model is the hierarchical Poisson regression described in Equation (7), where y_{ij} is the number of times advertisement i from advertiser j was clicked, E_{ij} is the number of times it was shown, and $\mathbf{x}_{ij}$ is

a small set of predictor variables, including dummy variables describing the type of ad format the ad was shown in (e.g. part of a vertical versus a horizontal configuration, along the top versus along the side, etc.), and a continuous 'quality score' assigned by another model:

$$
\begin{aligned}
y_{ij} &\sim Po(E_{ij}\lambda_{ij}) \\
\log \lambda_{ij} &= \beta_j^{\mathrm{T}}\mathbf{x}_{ij} \\
\beta_j &\sim \mathcal{N}(\mu, \Sigma) \\
\mu &\sim \mathcal{N}(0, \Sigma/\kappa) \\
\Sigma^{-1} &\sim W(I, \nu).
\end{aligned}
\tag{6}
$$

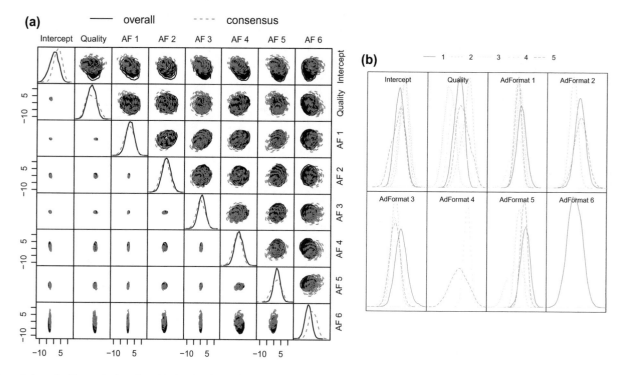

Figure 9. Posterior draws of μ based on the first five shards described in Section 4.4. (a) Posterior draws from the single-machine and consensus Monte Carlo algorithms. (b) Draws from the five worker machines.

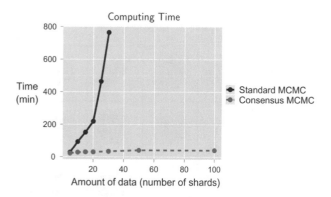

Figure 10. Time required to complete 10,000 MCMC draws with different numbers of shards under the single-machine and consensus Monte Carlo algorithm.

The data consisted of nearly 24 million observations regarding the performance of individual advertising creatives nested within around 11,000 advertisers using a particular Google advertising product. The data were divided into 867 shards, so that no shard contained more than 50,000 observations. A few shards contained between 10,000 and 20,000 observations, with a median shard size of about 27,000 observations. Most shards were close to the median. The model from Equation (7) was run on a single machine for 10,000 MCMC iterations using the MCMCglmm package from CRAN (Hadfield , 2010). Figure 9 shows the posterior draws of μ based on the first 5 shards of data under a single-machine run and the consensus Monte Carlo algorithm with 5 workers. We used only 5 of the 867 shards because of the long compute time for the single-machine run. The shards were combined by averaging draws based on the scalar precisions of each element of μ. There is general agreement between the single-machine and consensus algorithms. The largest disagreement is on *AdFormat 6*, about which only one of the five shards had any information. There was one shard that exhibited slow mixing on the *AdFormat 5*

coefficient, leading to a somewhat overdispersed consensus distribution. That could presumably be improved through a longer run time or by using a more efficient Monte Carlo algorithm on the worker machine. There were only two shards with information about *AdFormat 4*, but its single-machine and consensus estimates agree closely. The posterior correlations between elements of μ are not particularly strong, but to the extent that non-spherical errors are present (e.g. between *AdFormat 4* and the intercept), they appear to be well captured by consensus Monte Carlo.

Figure 10 shows what happens to the computing time as the number of shards increases. The single-machine algorithm scales linearly up to about 20 shards, at which point it encounters a resource limit and begins slowing down. We stopped experimenting with the single-machine run after 30 shards, because resource bottlenecks caused the machine to stop functioning, and we could not get the run to finish. With consensus Monte Carlo, the job completes within about 20–30 minutes, regardless of the number of shards. These times are with off-the-shelf R code. Optimized code would improve both the single-machine behavior and the run time on each worker machine.

The parameters of interest in this application are the advertiser-specific coefficients β_j. As mentioned in Section 3.4.1, these can be obtained with independent MCMC runs on each advertiser's data, given the draws of μ and Σ.

4.5. Non-parametric regression

We consider non-parametric regression models of the form

$$y_i \sim \mathcal{N}\left(f(\mathbf{x}_i), \sigma^2\right) \qquad (7)$$

independently across observations. Such models often lack interpretable sets of model parameters, so Bayesian inference focuses on the posterior distribution $p(f(\mathbf{x})|\mathbf{y})$ at a particular value of $\mathbf{x}$. As mentioned in Section 3.4.2, consensus Monte

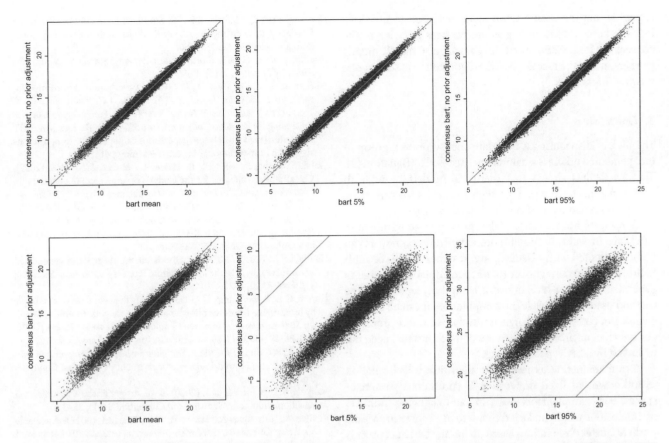

Figure 11. Comparing consensus BART with the single-machine algorithm. The three columns compare posterior means (left) and posterior 5% (center) and 95% (right) percentiles from the single-machine and consensus posterior distributions. In the top row the 30 workers were run with the same prior as the single machine. In the bottom row the prior was raised to the power 1/30.

Carlo can be applied to non-parametric regression models by fitting a separate model on each worker machine and averaging the draws from the worker-level predictive distributions.

As an example, consider the Bayesian additive regression tree (BART) (Chipman et al. , 2010), a tree-based algorithm for non-parametric regression, where

$$f(\mathbf{x}) = \sum_{t=1}^{T} f_t(\mathbf{x}) \qquad (8)$$

and each $f_t(\mathbf{x})$ is a decision tree. Each interior node j of tree t compares a specific element v_{tj} of $\mathbf{x}$ to a specific cutpoint χ_{tj}. Starting at the root of the tree, if node j has children and $x_{v_{tj}} \leq \chi_{tj}$ then $\mathbf{x}$ falls to the left child, otherwise it falls to the right. If node j is a leaf then it contains a mean parameter M_{tj} giving the contribution of tree t to $f_t(\mathbf{x})$. BART is an additive model that combines contributions from many trees.

The prior distribution for BART recommended by Chipman et al. (2010) consists of a prior over the topology of each tree, a prior over the parameters M_{jt}, and a prior on the residual variance σ^2. The prior probability that a node at depth d splits into children at depth $(d + 1)$ is $a/(1 + d)^b$. If there is a split, a variable v_{tj} is chosen uniformly from the set of available variables, and a cutpoint χ_{tj} uniformly from the set of available cutpoints. If there is no split, then the node is a leaf containing mean parameter M_{tj} with prior distribution $M_{tj} \sim \mathcal{N}(0, \tau^2)$, independently across t and j. A conditionally conjugate inverse gamma prior is assigned to σ^2.

We tested the consensus Monte Carlo algorithm with BART using simulated data from Friedman's test function: (Friedman , 1991)

$$f(\mathbf{x}) = 10 \sin(\pi x_1 x_2) + 20(x_3 - 0.5)^2 + 10x_4 + 5x_5 + \epsilon, \qquad (9)$$

where $\epsilon \sim \mathcal{N}(0, 3^2)$ is an independent error term. Our full data set contained 20,000 observations where each component of $\mathbf{x}_i$ was independently simulated from $\mathcal{U}(0, 1)$. We also simulated $x_6, \ldots, x_{10}$ as additional superfluous predictors. We chose 20,000 observations because that is close to the largest data set that the single-machine BART algorithm could handle in a reasonable time period. The consensus Monte Carlo algorithm was implemented using the *parallel* package from R on a 30-processor machine.

Figure 11 summarizes the results of two model runs on the same set of simulated data. In the top row, the single-machine algorithm and the worker machines in consensus Monte Carlo each used the recommended prior from Chipman et al. (2010). In the bottom row the prior was raised to the power 1/30 to account for the fact that there are 30 workers. With no prior adjustment, the single-machine and consensus algorithms essentially agree on both the posterior mean and the upper and lower posterior quantiles. When the prior is adjusted, the consensus Monte Carlo posterior becomes overdispersed. The prior distribution plays a significant role in determining the size of each tree in the BART algorithm. Much larger trees, and generally more diffuse posterior distributions, result from weakening the prior. Averaging over shards mitigates the overdispersion, but not enough to match the single-machine algorithm. Alternative strategies for prior adjustment, such as only modifying the prior on M_{tj} and σ^2, might still prove to be effective, and could potentially be necessary in other applications.

Interestingly, the consensus Monte Carlo algorithm actually fits the data slightly better than the single-machine algorithm. The correlation between the posterior means and the true function values for the single-machine run was .992. The same correlation for consensus Monte Carlo was .995. The reason is that the Monte Carlo algorithm used to fit BART tends to have trouble mixing as sample sizes grow large. The consensus Monte Carlo posterior is based on 30 rapidly mixing workers, while the single-machine algorithm is based on one slow mixing worker.

5. Discussion

The idea of distributing a Bayesian calculation to a group of independent workers is a natural one, justified by Equation (2). This article has shown that there are models, some with non-Gaussian posteriors, for which the draws from workers can be combined using simple weighted averages.

Consensus Monte Carlo scales to very large numbers of machines in ways that multi-core algorithms cannot. It can be implemented with existing code, whether single- or multi-threaded, and it is agnostic to the specific algorithm used to generate the worker-level draws. It is similarly agnostic to the method used to parallelize the computation. It can be used on a cluster of computers, a single multi-core or multi-processor computer, or an arbitrary collection of machines that need not be linked by a high speed network.

A fundamental weakness of the algorithm is its limitation to unknowns of fixed dimension in continuous parameter spaces. For example, label switching and changing numbers of dimensions would make it difficult to use consensus Monte Carlo to cluster observations based on infinite Dirichlet process mixtures. Similar issues make consensus Monte Carlo ill suited to model averaging using spike and slab priors.

There is a long list of open questions that needs to be addressed on consensus Monte Carlo. We need to understand better how the algorithm behaves as posterior distributions move away from Gaussianity. To the extent that averaging fails in non-Gaussian models, other methods of consensus should be explored. Improvements to the algorithm will probably involve a small number of between-machine communications, a handful of which would not fundamentally change the character of the method. Consensus Monte Carlo is likely to be useful with models that violate Equation (2), such as hierarchical models with crossed random effects, or Gaussian processes with non-trivial covariance functions, but these directions need to be explored.

Disclosure statement

No potential conflict of interest was reported by the authors.

References

Anderson, T.E., Culler, D.E., & Patterson, D. (1995). A case for NOW (Networks Of Workstations). *IEEE Micro, 15*(1), 54–64. Retrieved from http://dx.doi.org/10.1109/40.342018

Chipman, H.A., George, E.I., & McCulloch, R.E. (2010). BART: Bayesian Additive Regression Trees. *The Annals of Applied Statistics, 4*(1), 266–298.

Dean, J., & Ghemawat, S. (2008). MapReduce: simplified data processing on large clusters. *Communications of the ACM, 51*(1), 107–113.

Denison, D.G.T., Mallick, B.K., & Smith, A.F.M. (1998). Automatic Bayesian Curve Fitting. *Journal of the Royal Statistical Society, Series B, Methodological, 60*, 333–350.

Friedman, J. H. (1991). Multivariate adaptive regression splines. *The Annals of Statistics, 19*(1), 1–67.

Ghahramani, Z., & Beal, M.J. (2001). Propagation algorithms for variational Bayesian learning. T.K. Leen, T.G. Dietterich, & V. Tresp. (Eds.), *Advances in Neural Information Processing Systems 13, Proceedings of the 2000 Conference* (pp. 507–513). Boston, MA: MIT Press. Retrieved from http://papers.nips.cc/paper/1907-propagation-algorithms-for-variational-bayesian-learning.pdf

Guha, S., Guha, S., Kidwell, P., Hafen, R., & Cleveland, W.S. (2009). Visualization databases for the analysis of large complex datasets. In *Proceedings of the 12th International Conference on Artificial Intelligence and Statistic (AISTATS), 16–18 April 2009, Clearwater Beach, FL, Journal of Machine Learning Research: Workshop and Conference Proceedings.* 5, 193–200. Retrieved from http://ml.stat.purdue.edu/hafen/preprints/GuhaAISTATS2009.pdf

Hadfield, J.D. (2010). MCMC methods for multi-response generalized linear mixed models: the MCMCglmm R package. *Journal of Statistical Software, 33*(2), 1–22.

Hinton, G.E., & Van Camp, D. (1993). Keeping the neural networks simple by minimizing the description length of the weights. In *Proceedings of the Sixth Annual Conference on Computational Learning Theory (COLT '93), 26-28 July 1993, Santa Cruz, CA* (pp. 5–13). New York: ACM.

Huang, Z., & Gelman, A. (2005). *Sampling for Bayesian computation with large datasets (Technical Report).* Department of Statistics: Columbia University.

Jaakkola, T.S., & Jordan, M.I. (2000). Bayesian parameter estimation via variational methods. *Statistics and Computing, 10*(1), 25–37.

Kleiner, A., Talwalkar, A., Sarkar, P., & Jordan, M.I. (2011). A scalable bootstrap for massive data. *arXiv preprint arXiv:1112.5016.* Retrieved from http://arxiv.org/abs/1112.5016

Le Cam, L.M., & Yang,, G.L. (2000). *Asymptotics in Statistics: Some Basic Concepts.* New York: Springer-Verlag.

Lee, A., Yao, C., Giles, M. B., Doucet, A., & Holmes, C. C. (2010). On the utility of graphics cards to perform massively parallel simulation of advanced Monte Carlo methods. *Journal of Computational and Graphical Statistics, 19*(4), 769–789.

Malewicz, G., Austern, M.H., Bik, A.J.C., Dehnert, J.C., Horn,, I., Leiser, N., et al. (2010). Pregel: a system for large-scale graph processing. In *Proceedings of the 2010 ACM SIGMOD/PODS Conference (SIGMOD'10), 6-1 June 2010, Indianapolis, IN* (pp. 135–145). New York: ACM.

Neiswanger, W., Wang, C., & Xing, E. (2013). Asymptotically Exact, Embarrassingly Parallel MCMC. *arXiv preprint arXiv:1311.4780,*

Rue, H., Martino, S., & Chopin, N. (2009). Approximate Bayesian inference for latent Gaussian models by using integrated nested Laplace approximations. *Journal of the royal statistical society: Series b (statistical methodology), 71*(2), 319–392.

Srivastava, S., Li, C., & Dunson, D.B. (2015). Scalable Bayes via barycenter in Wasserstein space. *arXiv preprint arXiv:1508.05880.* Retrieved from http://arxiv.org/abs/1508.05880

Suchard, M. A., Wang, Q., Chan, C., Frelinger, J., Cron, A., & West, M. (2010). Understanding GPU programming for statistical computation: studies in massively parallel massive mixtures. *Journal of Computational and Graphical Statistics, 19*(2), 419–438.

Wang, X. & Dunson, D.B. (2013). Parallel MCMC via Weierstrass sampler. *arXiv preprint arXiv:1312.4605.* Retrieved from http://arxiv.org/abs/1312.4605

Wang, X., Fangjian, G., Heller, K.A., & Dunson, D.B. (2015). Parallelizing MCMC with random partition trees. Retrieved from http://dx.doi.org/10.13140/RG.2.1.2921.4883

White, T. (2012). *Hadoop: the Definitive Guide.* Sebastopol, CA: O'Reilly.

Zhang, Y., Duchi, J.C., & Wainwright, M.J. (2012). Communication-efficient algorithms for statistical optimization. *Proceedings of the 51st IEEE Annual Conference on Decision and Control (CDC 2012), 10-13 December 2012, Grand Wailea, Maui, HI* (pp. 6792–6792). IEEE.

Measurement and analysis of quality of life related to environmental hazards: the methodology illustrated by recent epidemiological studies

Mounir Mesbah

ABSTRACT

The measurement and analysis of health related quality of life for populations subject to environmental risks, and the measurement and analysis of the perception of these risks, require a rigorous scientific methodological approach. The proposed methodology is illustrated, based mainly on recent large epidemiological studies carried out in Europe. The first study was carried out during 2002 and 2003 in eight European cities, with the main goal of analysing the effect of the immediate environment on health status. At the end of the second study, conducted in 2005–2006 in several cities, a perception scale for air quality was developed and validated. The last study, conducted in 2012–2014 within the local population of an industrial platform, had as its main objective the characterization of the impact of this industrial site on environment and health. Health related quality of life (HrQoL) is one of the most important outcomes measured in clinical trials over the past 20 years. More recently, it has also become important in epidemiological surveys, where, unlike clinical trials, the number of end points involved is generally large. The measurement and statistical analysis of HrQoL and/or risk perception remain important scientific issues. It is generally done mainly by internal consistency methods, because external standards or experts are generally not available. These methods are based mainly on the statistical validation of measurement models using goodness-of-fit tests. We will show in this paper how such validation can be done using the empirical backward reliability curve (the α-curve).

1. Introduction

1.1. General

In epidemiological surveys, health related quality of life (HrQoL) is often considered as a global subjective health indicator. HrQoL is more and more recognized as an important specific end point, which is generally treated as a primary, or at least as a secondary, criterion in most epidemiological studies. For many reasons, as is easy to explain, the primary end point is generally the survival (duration of life) or another biological efficiency variable.

The World Health Organization (The WHOQoL Group, 1994) defines quality of life as: 'an individual's perception of his/her position in life in the context of the culture and value systems in which he/she lives, and in relation to his/her goals, expectations, standards and concerns. It is a broad-ranging concept, incorporating in a complex way the person's physical health, psychological state, level of independence, social relationships, and their relationship to salient features of their environment'.

Patient reported outcome (PRO) measurements are sometimes confused with quality-of-life measurements. Quality of life is a broad concept referring to all aspects of a person's well-being. Measurement of HrQoL is most of the time assessed through a patient questionnaire, where item (or question, or variable) responses are often categorical. In this paper, we present mathematical methods used in the statistical validation and analysis of HrQoL. These methods are based on the statistical validation of some essential properties induced by measurement models linking the observed responses and unobserved latent HrQoL variables.

In Section 2, some important measurement models used in HrQoL research are introduced. Within that section, we show how some important inequalities involving the Kullback–Leibler measure of association among conditionally independent variables can be very helpful in the process of validation. Then, the family of Rasch measurement models is introduced. The Rasch model can be considered as the standard of unidimensional measurement models. It must be used as a 'docking' target in building unidimensional scores. The statistical validation of health related quality-of-life measurement models is thoroughly considered in Section 3. First, we define the reliability of a measurement and we give its expression, and the expression for the reliability of the sum of item responses under a parallel model, which is estimated by Cronbach's α-coefficient. Then the backward reliability curve is presented, and its connection with the notion of unidimensionality is explained, and consequently how it can be used to check empirically the unidimensionality of a set of variables. Cronbach's α-coefficient is well known as a reliability or internal consistency coefficient, but is of little help in the process of validating questionnaires. On the other hand, the backward reliability curve can be very helpful in the assessment of unidimensionality, which is a crucial measurement property. We explain why, when such a curve is not increasing, the lack of unidimensionality of a set of questions is strongly suspected.

In Section 4, we say more about the construction of unidimensional HrQoL scores. This step generally follows the previous step of checking unidimensionality using the backward reliability curve. In a multidimensional context, the separability of measured concepts needs to be confirmed. Differential instrument functioning, or the invariance of measurements across groups, is an important property addressed within the same section.

The analysis of health related quality-of-life change between groups is tackled in Section 5. The direct statistical analysis of latent scores through a global latent regression model is briefly discussed.

Risk perception is a complex multidimensional phenomenon including the nature of the risk, personal characteristics, and also the subject's social and cultural background. It is a subjective judgment by which the individual understands and gives a meaning to a particular threat or hazard. The acceptability of a risk results partly from the balance between the perceived benefits and the negative effects of exposure. The risk, as defined by experts, does not always coincide with that perceived by laymen because different criteria are used to evaluate the risk; air pollution exposure is no exception. Some elements of the assessment are specific to the individual as a result of his/her life experiences and health status. Others are derived from the outside world via scientific knowledge or the media, beliefs, and ideas shared by the subject's group or social network.

Three real data examples are presented in Sections 7, 8, and 9.

1.2. Health related quality of life and housing in Europe

The possibility of a causal relationship between housing conditions and health is an interesting but difficult question. More than just one epidemiological study needs to be performed to count as strong evidence. Despite the difficulty and the cost of general population surveys, mainly when they are longitudinal and interventional, much progress has been made in gathering evidence of a causal relationship between housing conditions and human health. Using data from a large transversal epidemiological survey conducted in eight big European cities under the supervision of the WHO Environmental and Health program team based in Bonn, and called the 'Housing and Health' Large Analysis and Review of European Housing and Health Status (WHO LARES) survey, the associations between mental health and housing conditions have been analysed in depth (Bonnefoy, Braubach, Moissonnier, Monolbaev, and Röbbel, 2003; Bonnefoy et al., 2004; Fredouille, Laporte, and Mesbah, 2009; Mesbah, 2009). A total of 8519 questionnaires self-rated by all persons in selected dwellings were collected.

To this end, our statistical methodology involving psychometric methods to build and validate mental health measures and an adequate strategy to avoid errors and bias when researching risk factors among a large set of variables was applied. A large number of important new results in the field of housing and in the field of mental health came to light. More interestingly, these results seem to confirm: (1) the shelter theory of the dwelling, a psychological theory relating to the protective role of our own home; (2) the necessity for housing to constitute a bridge to the outside world; and (3) the recognition of the narcissistic function of the habitat as a true social representation of the self. The awakening to, and the respect for, these fundamental aspects of housing should allow actions of dwelling rehabilitation to be treated henceforth on a priority basis consistent with the effects of housing on the mental health of the inhabitants.

1.3. Risk perception research I: air pollution health effects

Despite improvements in air quality in developed countries, air pollution remains a major public health issue. To assess the health impact fully, we must consider that air pollution exposure has both physical and psychological effects; this latter dimension, less documented, is more difficult to measure and subjective indicators constitute an appropriate alternative. On the basis of the responses from 2522 subjects in 8 French cities, psychometric methods were used to construct a scale from 22 items that assess risk perception (anxiety about health and quality of life) and the extent to which air pollution is a nuisance (sensory perception and symptoms). Perception of air pollution by the general public is a key issue in the development of comprehensive risk assessment studies as well as in air pollution risk management and policy. This study offers a useful new tool for measuring such efforts and helping to set priorities for air quality improvements in combination with air quality measurements.

With regard to measuring the public's perception of air quality, several methods can be found in the literature. Some studies have considered the sensory aspects of air pollution: smell, dirt, or irritating effects, whereas others have allowed people to describe problems caused by air pollution. Whatever the approach, these simple indicators inevitably capture only one aspect of risk perception. In light of this, the present work has developed a new tool that includes many aspects of perception related to air pollution exposure. An air quality perception (AQP) scale has been drawn up and validated, using individual data collected during a French multi-city epidemiological study conducted in 2005–2006.

1.4. Risk perception research II: the environmental and health impact of an industrial site

The main goals of the study (Daniau, 2014; Daniau et al., 2015) were:

- to describe health events reported by the local population of the industrial site (Salindres, France), already identified in the literature as arising from exposure to a local source of pollution. These reported health events include perceived general health and anxiety;
- to compare the reported health in the local population of this industrial site to national references;
- to assess the association between the risk of occurrence of these reported health events and the exposure to health risk factors related to activities in the industrial site. In particular, the relationship between exposure to perceived pollution and psychological health is investigated; and
- to gain an exploratory perspective in understanding the role of attitudes towards the industrial site and the duration of residence in relationships between exposure to perceived pollution and psychological health.

2. Measurement models

2.1. Classical unidimensional models for measurement

Latent variable models involve a set of observable variables $A = \{\mathbf{X}_1, \mathbf{X}_2, \ldots, \mathbf{X}_k\}$ and a latent (unobservable) variable θ

which may be either unidimensional (i.e. scalar) or vector valued of dimension $d \leq k$. In such models, the dimensionality of A is defined by the number d of components of θ. When $d = 1$, the set A is unidimensional.

In an HrQoL study, measurements are taken with an instrument: the questionnaire. It is made up of questions (or items). The random response of a subject i to a question j is denoted as $\mathbf{X}_{ij}$. The random variable generating responses to a question j is denoted, without confusion, as $\mathbf{X}_j$.

The parallel model is a classical latent variable model describing the unidimensionality of a set $A = \{\mathbf{X}_1, \mathbf{X}_2, \ldots, \mathbf{X}_k\}$ of quantitative observable variables. Define $\mathbf{X}_{ij}$ as the measurement of subject i, $i = 1, \ldots, n$, given by a variable $\mathbf{X}_j$, where $j = 1, \ldots, k$, then

$$\mathbf{X}_{ij} = \tau_{ij} + \varepsilon_{ij}, \tag{1}$$

where τ_{ij} is the true measurement corresponding to the observed measurement $\mathbf{X}_{ij}$ and ε_{ij} is a measurement error. Specifying τ_{ij} as

$$\tau_{ij} = \beta_j + \theta_i$$

defines the parallel model. In this setting, β_j is an unknown fixed (non-random) parameter effect of variable j, and θ_i an unknown random parameter effect of subject i.

It is generally assumed to have zero mean and unknown standard error σ_θ. The zero-mean assumption is an arbitrary identifiability constraint with consequences for the interpretation of the parameter: its value must be interpreted as compared with the mean population value. *In our setting, θ_i is the true latent health related quality of life that a clinician or health scientist wants to measure and analyse.* It is a zero-mean individual random part of all observed subject responses X_{ij}, being the same whatever the variable X_j (in practice, a question j of an HrQoL questionnaire). The ε_{ij} are independent random effects with zero mean and standard error σ corresponding to the additional measurement error. Moreover, the true measure and the error are assumed uncorrelated: $\mathrm{cov}(\theta_i, \varepsilon_{ij}) = 0$. This model is known as the parallel model, because the regression lines relating any observed item X_j, $j = 1, \ldots, k$, to the true unique latent measure θ_i are parallel.

Another way to specify the model (1) is through conditional moments of the observed responses. So the conditional mean of a subject response is specified as

$$E[X_{ij}/\theta_i; \beta_j] = \beta_j + \theta_i. \tag{2}$$

Again, β_j, $j = 1, \ldots, k$, are fixed effects and θ_i, $i = 1, \ldots, n$, are independent random effects with zero mean and standard error σ_θ. The conditional variance of a subject response is specified as

$$\mathrm{Var}[X_{ij}/\theta_i; \beta_j] = \mathrm{Var}(\varepsilon_{ij}) = \sigma^2. \tag{3}$$

These assumptions are classical in experimental design. This model defines relationships between different kinds of variables: the observed score X_{ij}, the true score τ_{ij}, and the error ε_{ij}. It is interesting to make some remarks about the assumptions underlying this model: the random part of the true measure given by the response of individual i to a question j is the same whatever the variable j; θ_i does not depend on j; the model is unidimensional; and one can assume that in their random part all observed variables (questions X_j) are generated by a common unobservable (θ_i). More precisely,

let $X_{ij}^* = X_{ij} - \beta_j$ be the calibrated version of the response to item j of person i. Models (2) and (3) can be rewritten

$$E[X_{ij}^*/\theta_i; \beta_j] = \theta_i; \ \forall j, \tag{4}$$

with the same assumptions on β and θ and with the same conditional variance model.

Another important consequence of the previous assumptions, when the distribution is normal, is a conditional independence property: whatever j and j', two observed items X_j and $X_{j'}$ are independent conditional on the latent θ_i. So, even when normality cannot be assumed, it is essential to specify this property.

2.2. Classical multidimensional models for measurement

Classical multidimensional models for measurement generalize the previous simple parallel model:

$$X_j = \beta_j + \theta + \varepsilon_j$$

(the subject subscript i is forgotten without risk of confusion) from one true component θ to p true components θ_l, with $1 < l < p$.

First, remark that

$$X_j = \beta_j + \theta + \varepsilon_j \Leftrightarrow X_j - \beta_j = \theta + \varepsilon_j \Leftrightarrow X_j^* = \theta + \varepsilon_j. \tag{5}$$

In classical multidimensional models for measurement, also known as factorial analysis models, the observed item is a linear function of p latent variables:

$$X_j = a_{11}\theta_1 + a_{12}\theta_2 + \cdots + a_{1p}\theta_p + E_j. \tag{6}$$

This is usually written in matrix form:

$$X = AU + E, \tag{7}$$

where A is the factor loading matrix and U and E are independent.

Principal component analysis (PCA) is a particular factorial analysis model with $p = k$ and without error terms (E is not in the model). In PCA, components (θ_l) are chosen to be orthogonal ($\theta_l \perp \theta_m$) and with decreasing variance (amount of information). In practice, a varimax rotation is often performed after a PCA to allow better interpretation of the latent variable in terms of the original variables. It allows a clear clustering of the original variables into (unidimensional) subsets. In Section 3.2, we will show how this can be *checked* using a graphical tool, the backward reliability curve.

Parallel as well as factor analysis models are members of *classical* measurement models. They deal mainly with quantitative continuous responses, even if some direct adaptations of these models to more general responses are available today. In the next section, we present the *modern* approach, which includes the classical approach as a special case. Within this approach, qualitative and quantitative responses can be treated differently. Some useful general properties that are not well known but which are very important for the validation process of questionnaires are also presented. We introduce the Rasch model, and show how it can be interpreted as a nonlinear parallel model that is more appropriate when responses are categorical.

2.3. Latent variable models and graphical modeling

Modern ideas about measurement models are more general. Instead of arbitrarily defining the relationship between observed and the true latent as an additive function (of the true latent and the error), they just focus on the joint distribution of the observed and the true variables $f(X, \theta)$. We do not need to specify any kind of distance between X and θ. The error E and its relation to the observed X and the latent θ could be anything!

This leads us naturally to graphical modeling. Graphical modeling aims to represent the multidimensional joint distribution of a set of variables by a graph. We will focus on conditional independence graphs. The interpretation of an independence graph is easy. Each multivariate distribution is represented by a graphic, which is composed of nodes and edges between nodes. Nodes represent one-dimensional random variables (observed or latent, i.e. non-observed) while a missing edge between two variables means that those two variables are conditionally independent of the rest (all other variables in the multidimensional distribution). Since the pioneered work of (Lauritzen and Wermuth, 1989), many monographs on graphical modeling have become available (Edwards, 2000; Lauritzen, 1996; Whittaker, 1990).

One way to define *latent unidimensionality* in the context of a graphical model is straightforward: a set of variables X is unidimensional if there exists one and only one *scalar* latent variable θ such that each variable X is related to θ and only to θ. In Figure 1(a), the set of variables $X_1, X_2, \ldots, X_9$ is unidimensional. In Figure 1(b), the set of variables $X_1, X_2, \ldots, X_9$ is bidimensional. The unidimensionality is a consequence of the dimension of θ. The word *latent* means more than the fact that θ is not observed (or hidden). It means that θ is causal. The observed items X_j are caused by the true unobserved θ and not any other variable! This causal property is induced by the conditional independence property. If X_j is independent of $X_{j'}$ conditionally on θ, then knowledge of θ is enough. Such directed graphical models are also known as causal graphics or Bayesian networks.

2.3.1. Measure of association and graphical models

Let $K(f, g)$ be the Kullback–Leibler information between two distributions with respective density functions f and g:

$$K(f, g) = \int f(x) \log \left(\frac{f(x)}{g(x)} \right) \, \mathrm{d}x. \tag{8}$$

The *Kullback–Leibler measure of association* (KI) between two random variables X and Y with respective marginal distribu-

tions f_x and f_y and with joint distribution f_{xy} is given by

$$\mathrm{KI}(X, Y) = K(f_{xy}, f_y f_x). \tag{9}$$

In the same way, the measure of association between two variables X and Y *conditionally* on a third one Z is the *Kullback–Leibler measure of conditional association* ($\mathrm{KI}((X, Y)/Z)$) which, using similar straightforward notation, is given by

$$\begin{aligned} \mathrm{KI}((X, Y)/Z) &= K(f_{xyz}, f_{y/z} \times f_{x/z} \times f_z) \\ &= K(f_{xyz}, f_{yz} \times f_{xz}/f_z). \end{aligned} \tag{10}$$

Theorem 2.1: *Let X, Y, and Z be three random variables such that X is independent of Y conditionally on Z. Then, under mild general regularity conditions, we have*

(1) $\mathrm{KI}((X, Y)/Z) = 0$;
(2) $\mathrm{KI}((Y, Z)/X) = \mathrm{KI}(Y, Z) - \mathrm{KI}(X, Y)$;
(3) $\mathrm{KI}((X, Z)/Y) = \mathrm{KI}(X, Z) - \mathrm{KI}(X, Y)$;
(4) $\mathrm{KI}(X, Y) \leq \mathrm{KI}(X, Z)$ *and* $\mathrm{KI}(X, Y) \leq \mathrm{KI}(Y, Z)$.

Proof: (1), (2), and (3) can be easily derived. (4) is a direct consequence of (1), (2), (3) and the Cauchy–Schwartz inequality ($K(X, Y)$ is always positive). The interpretation of (2) and (3) is as follows: if we use KI as the measure of association, then the marginal association between two variables related by an edge in the graph G is stronger than the marginal association between two non-related variables.

Remark 1: If (X, Y) is normally distributed, then $\mathrm{KI}(X, Y)$ is a monotonic function of $\rho^2(X, Y)$, the square of the correlation coefficient. So $\mathrm{KI}(X, Y)$ can be considered as a generalization of $\rho^2(X, Y)$.

Remark 2: If (X, Y, Z) is normally distributed, then $\mathrm{KI}(X, Y/Z)$ is a monotonic function of $\rho^2(X, Y/Z)$, the square of the partial correlation coefficient. So, $\mathrm{KI}(X, Y/Z)$ can be considered as a generalization of $\rho^2(X, Y/Z)$.

Using result (4) of Theorem 2.1 and the collapsibility property of a graphical model (Frydenberg, 1990; Mesbah, Lellouch, and Huber, 1999), one can derive the following useful results.

Consequences

(1) In Figure 1(a), the marginal association between any observed item X and the latent variable θ is stronger than the association between two observed items.
(2) In Figure 1(b), the marginal association between any observed item X and its own latent variable θ is stronger

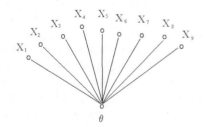

(a) One latent variable θ.

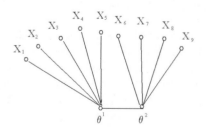

(b) Two latent variables θ^1 and θ^2.

Figure 1. Graphical unidimensional or bidimensional model.

than the association between that item X and another latent variable (other dimensions).

These two relationships between marginal measures of association are useful characterizations of the conditional independence property, which is a core property of latent variable models.

Remark 3: Under the parallel model presented in Section 2, whatever j and j', we have $\mathrm{Corr}(X_j, X_{j'}) = \rho$ and $\mathrm{Corr}(X_j, \theta) = \sqrt{\rho}$, so

$$\mathrm{Corr}^2(X_j, \theta) = \rho \geq \mathrm{Corr}^2(X_j, X_{j'}) = \rho^2.$$

This is a direct consequence of the fact that, under normality and the parallel model assumption, items are independent conditionally on the latent variable. Consequences (1) and (2) are very helpful in the process of questionnaire validation.

The graphical models framework is helpful for explaining the relationships between variables when some of these are observed and others are not. Historically, the Rasch model, which we are going to introduce in the next section, was established earlier – in the sixties of the last century – mainly as a measurement model more appropriate for binary responses, which frequently occur in HrQoL questionnaires. Nevertheless, its connection with graphical models through the conditional independence properties included within it, is recent.

2.3.2. The family of Rasch measurement models

The parallel model presented in Section 2 is a linear mixed model. When item responses are binary, ordinal, or categorical, the parallel model is inappropriate. For instance, when the item response is a Bernoulli variable X_{ij} taking values x_{ij} – coded for instance 0 (for 'failure' or 'false' or 'no') or 1 (for 'success' or 'correct' or 'yes') – theories of the exponential family and of generalized linear models (MacCullagh & Nelder, 1989) suggest to us an adapted generalized linear model alternative to model (2). Instead of the linear model

$$E[X_{ij}/\theta_i; \beta_j] = \beta_j + \theta_i, \tag{11}$$

define the generalized linear model, using the canonical link associated with the Bernoulli distribution,

$$\mathrm{Logit}(E[X_{ij}/\theta_i; \beta_j]) = \beta_j + \theta_i, \tag{12}$$

with, as previously, β_j a fixed effect and θ_i independent random effects with zero mean and standard error σ_θ. This model is known as the 'mixed Rasch model'. Its classical version, with θ_i assumed to be a fixed parameter, was introduced and popularized by the Danish mathematician George Rasch (1960) with the expression below. It is probably the most popular of modern measurement models in the psychometric context, where it is mainly used as a *measurement model*. Under the Rasch model framework, the probability of the response given by a subject i to a question j is

$$P(X_{ij} = x_{ij}/\theta_i; \beta_j) = \frac{\exp(x_{ij}(\theta_i - \beta_j))}{1 + \exp(\theta_i - \beta_j)}, \tag{13}$$

where θ_i is the person parameter: it measures the ability of an individual n, on the latent trait. It is the true latent variable on a continuous scale. It is the true score that we want to obtain,

using the *instrument* (questionnaire) including k items (questions) allowing us to estimate the true measurement (HrQoL) θ_i of person i. β_j is the item parameter. It characterizes the level of difficulty of the question. The Rasch model is member of the 'item response theory' (IRT) models (Fisher & Molenaar, 1995). When the number of modalities of item responses is more than two, the choice of a measurement model is more controversial. A large number of measurement models are possible. Item response theory is the field of psychometry devoted to that purpose. When the responses are ordinal, two reasonable choices could be the 'partial credit model' (PCM) or the 'graded response model' (GRM).

- Both are unidimensional models from the IRT family of measurement models.
- Both own the nice property of independence of observed variables conditional on the latent variable (Figure 1(a)).
- Both are logistic models.
- The raw score (sum of item responses) of an individual is a sufficient statistic for the latent parameter under the partial credit model.
- The raw score of an individual is not a sufficient statistic for the latent parameter under the graded response model.

See Dossar and Mesbah (2016), for more details.

2.3.3. The partial credit model

Let $X_j = x$ with $x = 0, \ldots, m$, the modalities of item j, and β_{jx} the parameter of modality x of item j. The partial credit model (Masters, 1982) is defined as:

$$\pi_{jx\theta} = \mathrm{Prob}(X_j = x \mid \theta) = \frac{\exp\left(\sum_{l=0}^{x}(\theta - \beta_{jl})\right)}{\sum_{k=0}^{m} \exp \sum_{l=0}^{k}(\theta - \beta_{jl})}$$

Constraints on the parameters are necessary to ensure the identifiability of parameters. This model is also known as model PCM at one parameter or polytomous Rasch model.

2.3.4. The graded response model

The graded response model (Samejima, 1969) is defined as

$$\mathrm{Prob}(X_j \geq x \mid \theta) = \frac{\exp\left[(\theta - \beta_{jx})\right]}{1 + \exp\left[(\theta - \beta_{jx})\right]},$$

with $\beta_{j1} \leq \beta_{j2} \leq \cdots \leq \beta_{jm}$. For $x = 0$ and $x = m$, by definition $\mathrm{Prob}(X_j \geq 0 \mid \theta) = 1$ and $\mathrm{Prob}(X_j \geq m+1 \mid \theta) = 0$, respectively. The probability of having an item score x is given by the difference

$$\begin{aligned}
\pi_{jx\theta} &= \mathrm{Prob}(X_j = x \mid \theta) \\
&= \mathrm{Prob}(X_j \geq x \mid \theta) - \mathrm{Prob}(X_j \geq x+1 \mid \theta) \\
&= \frac{\exp\left[(\theta - \beta_{ix})\right]}{1 + \exp\left[(\theta - \beta_{ix})\right]} - \frac{\exp\left[(\theta - \beta_{i(x+1)})\right]}{1 + \exp\left[(\theta - \beta_{i(x+1)})\right]}.
\end{aligned}$$

2.3.5. Rasch model properties

(1) *Monotonicity* of the response probability function.
(2) *Local sufficiency*: sufficiency of the total individual score for the latent parameter (considered as a fixed parameter).

(3) *Local independence* (items are independent conditional on the latent variable).
(4) *Non-differential item functioning* (conditional on the latent variable, items are independent of external variables).

The first property is an essential property for latent models. It is included in the Rasch model through the logistic link. The Mokken model (Molenaar & Sijstma, 2000) does not assume the logistic link, but rather a non-parametric monotone link function: this is appealing for the HrQoL field, but by relaxing the logistic link we lose the sufficiency property (2) of the total individual score, which is the most interesting characteristic property of the Rasch model in the HrQoL field. This property justifies the use of simple scores as surrogates for latent scores. Kreiner & Cristensen (2002) focus on this sufficiency property and define a new class of non-parametric models: the 'graphical Rasch models'. The last properties (3) and (4) are neither included in nor specific to the Rasch model, but are added general latent model properties.

Considering the latent parameter as a fixed parameter lead to a joint maximum likelihood method which, in this context, can be inconsistent (Fisher & Molenaar, 1995). A 'conditional maximum likelihood method' based on the sufficiency property gives consistent and asymptotically normal estimates for item parameters (Andersen, 1970).

When the latent parameter is clearly assumed to be random, estimation of (β, σ^2) can be obtained by the 'marginal maximum likelihood method'. In HrQoL practice, the distribution of the latent parameter is generally assumed to be Gaussian with zero population mean and unknown population variance σ^2. The likelihood function can be easily derived after marginalizing over the unobserved random parameter, the joint distribution of item responses, and the latent variable, and then using the local independence property one obtains

$$L(\beta, \sigma^2) = \frac{1}{(\sqrt{2\pi\sigma^2})^K} \prod_{i=1}^{K} \left\{ \int_{-\infty}^{+\infty} \prod_{j=1}^{J} \frac{\exp\left((\theta - \beta_j) x_{ij}\right)}{1 + \exp\left(\theta - \beta_j\right)} \right.$$

$$\left. \times \exp\left(\frac{-\theta^2}{2\sigma^2}\right) d\theta \right\}. \quad (14)$$

Estimation of β parameters can be obtained using Newton–Raphson and numerical integration techniques or an Expectation-Maximization (EM) algorithm followed by a Gauss–Hermite quadrature (Fisher & Molenaar, 1995; Hamon & Mesbah, 2002).

2.3.6. The remaining issue of estimation of latent parameters

Estimation of item parameters is generally the main interest in psychometrical area. Calibration of the HrQoL is the preliminary goal. When item parameters are known (or assumed as fixed and known) estimation of the latent parameter is straightforward. One easy method is just to maximize the classical joint likelihood method assuming that the latent parameter is a fixed parameter. Because item parameters are supposedly known, there is no problem of inconsistency estimation. Another popular estimator of latent parameters is the Bayes estimator, given by the posterior mean of the latent distribution (Fisher & Molenaar, 1995).

Other estimators can be obtained. Mislevy (1984) proposed a non-parametric Bayesian estimator for the latent distribution in the Rasch model. Martynov and Mesbah (2006) gave a non-parametric estimator of the latent distribution in a mixed Rasch model.

The posterior distribution of the latent parameter is defined as

$$P(\theta_i/x_i, \beta) = \frac{P(X_i = x_i/\theta_i, \beta) g(\theta_i)}{\int P(X_i = x_i/\theta_i, \beta) g(\theta_i) d\theta_i}. \quad (15)$$

The Bayesian modal estimator is $\widehat{\theta_i}$, the value of θ_i that maximizes the posterior distribution, while the Bayes estimator is given by

$$\widehat{\theta_i} = \int \theta_i P(\theta_i/x_i, \beta) g(\theta_i) d\theta_i. \quad (16)$$

The estimation of latent individual parameters in a frequentist point of view remains an issue. It is also done in a two step way. First, the item parameters are consistently estimated by a conditional or marginal maximum likelihood method, then their estimated values are plugged into a modified-likelihood function, assuming known values for item parameters. The argument of conditioning can be used to estimate directly the latent parameter, by the use of a likelihood function, conditional on the total item scores. The generally small number of items limits the use of this method in real practice.

In the next sections, we will show how the validation of questionnaires (Section 3) and the construction of scales (Section 4) can be performed.

3. Validation of measurement models

3.1. Reliability of an instrument: Cronbach's α-coefficient

A measurement instrument gives us values that we call observed measures. The reliability ρ of an instrument is defined as the ratio of the true over the observed measure. Under the parallel model, one can show that the reliability of any variable X_j (as an instrument to measure the true value) is given by

$$\rho = \frac{\sigma_\theta^2}{\sigma_\theta^2 + \sigma^2}, \quad (17)$$

which is also the constant correlation between any two variables. This coefficient is also known as the intra-class coefficient. The reliability coefficient, ρ, can be easily interpreted as a correlation coefficient between the true and the observed measure. When the parallel model is assumed, the reliability of the sum of k variables equals

$$\tilde{\rho}_k = \frac{k\rho}{k\rho + (1 - \rho)}. \quad (18)$$

This formula is known as the Spearman–Brown formula.

The Spearman–Brown formula indicates a simple relationship between $\tilde{\rho}_k$ and k, the number of variables. It is easy to show that $\tilde{\rho}_k$ is an increasing function of k. Figure 2 shows, as drawn on the same graph, these theoretical reliability curves corresponding to $\rho = 0.1; 0.2; \ldots; 0.9$.

The maximum likelihood estimator of $\tilde{\rho}_k$, under parallel model and normal distribution assumptions is known as the Cronbach's α-coefficient (CAC) (Cronbach, 1951; Kristof,

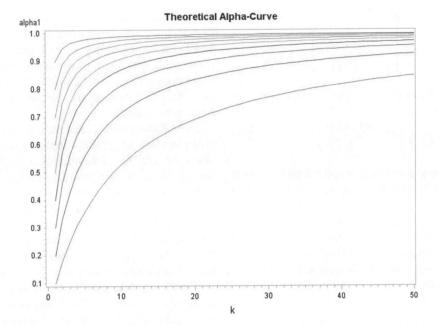

Figure 2. Theoretical relationship between α and the number of items.

1963). Its expression is

$$\alpha = \frac{k}{k-1}\left(1 - \frac{\sum_{j=1}^{k} S_j^2}{S_{\text{tot}}^2}\right), \tag{19}$$

where

$$S_j^2 = \frac{1}{n-1}\sum_{i=1}^{n}(X_{ij}-\overline{X}_j)^2$$

and

$$S_{\text{tot}}^2 = \frac{1}{nk-1}\sum_{i=1}^{n}\sum_{j=1}^{k}(X_{ij}-\overline{X})^2.$$

Under the parallel model, the *joint* covariance matrix of the observed items X_j and the latent trait θ is

$$V_{X,\theta} = \begin{pmatrix} \sigma_\theta^2 + \sigma^2 & \sigma_\theta^2 & \cdots & \sigma_\theta^2 & \sigma_\theta^2 \\ \sigma_\theta^2 & \sigma_\theta^2 + \sigma^2 & \sigma_\theta^2 & \sigma_\theta^2 & \sigma_\theta^2 \\ \vdots & \vdots & \vdots & \vdots & \vdots \\ \sigma_\theta^2 & \cdots & \sigma_\theta^2 & \sigma_\theta^2 + \sigma^2 & \sigma_\theta^2 \\ \sigma_\theta^2 & \cdots & \cdots & \sigma_\theta^2 & \sigma_\theta^2 \end{pmatrix},$$

and the *joint* correlation matrix of the observed items X_j and the latent trait θ is

$$R_{X,\theta} = \begin{pmatrix} 1 & \rho & \cdots & \rho & \sqrt{\rho} \\ \rho & 1 & \rho & \rho & \sqrt{\rho} \\ \vdots & \vdots & \vdots & \vdots & \vdots \\ \rho & \cdots & \rho & 1 & \sqrt{\rho} \\ \sqrt{\rho} & \cdots & \cdots & \sqrt{\rho} & 1 \end{pmatrix}.$$

The *marginal* covariance V_X and the correlation matrix R_X of the k observed variables X_j under the parallel model are

$$V_X = \begin{pmatrix} \sigma_\theta^2 + \sigma^2 & \sigma_\theta^2 & \cdots & \sigma_\theta^2 \\ \sigma_\theta^2 & \sigma_\theta^2 + \sigma^2 & \sigma_\theta^2 & \sigma_\theta^2 \\ \vdots & \vdots & \vdots & \vdots \\ \sigma_\theta^2 & \cdots & \sigma_\theta^2 & \sigma_\theta^2 + \sigma^2 \end{pmatrix}$$

and

$$R_X = \begin{pmatrix} 1 & \rho & \cdots & \rho \\ \rho & 1 & \rho & \rho \\ \vdots & \vdots & \vdots & \vdots \\ \rho & \cdots & \rho & 1 \end{pmatrix}.$$

This structure is known as being of *compound symmetry* type. It is easy to show that the reliability of the sum of k items given in (19) can be expressed as

$$\tilde{\rho}_k = \frac{k}{k-1}\left[1 - \frac{\text{trace}(V_X)}{J'V_X J}\right] \qquad (20)$$

with J a vector with all components equal to one, and

$$\alpha = \frac{k}{k-1}\left[1 - \frac{\text{trace}(S_X)}{J'S_X J}\right], \qquad (21)$$

where S_X is the observed variance, empirical estimation of V_X. There is, in recent literature, a comprehensible confusion between the Cronbach α as a population parameter (the theoretical reliability of the sum of items) and its sample estimate.

The exact distribution of α under the Gaussian parallel model and its asymptotic approximation are well known (van Zyl, Neudecker, and Nel, 2000). In the next sub-sections, we recall their main results.

3.1.1. Exact distribution of Cronbach's α-coefficient

Assuming the parallel model, and a Gaussian distribution of the latent and error components, we have

$$\frac{1}{1-\tilde{\rho}_k}(1-\alpha) \sim F_n^{n(k-1)}, \qquad (22)$$

where $F_n^{n(k-1)}$ is the Fisher distribution with n and $k-1$ degrees of freedom. A direct consequence is that, under the same assumptions, the exact population mean and variance of α are as follows:

$$E(\alpha) = \frac{n\tilde{\rho}_k - 2}{n - 2};$$

$$\text{Var}(\alpha) = \frac{2(1-\tilde{\rho}_k)^2 n(nk-2)}{(k-1)(n-2)^2(n-4)}\tilde{\rho}_k. \qquad (23)$$

3.1.2. Asymptotical distribution of Cronbach's α-coefficient

When the Gaussian distribution cannot be assumed but the parallel form remains, the following results are obtained:

(a) $E(\alpha) \to \tilde{\rho}_k$;

(b) $n\text{Var}(\alpha) \to \frac{2(1-\tilde{\rho}_k)^2 k}{(k-1)}\tilde{\rho}_k$; \qquad (24)

(c) $\alpha \to \tilde{\rho}_k$;

and

(d) $\frac{\sqrt{n}}{2}\ln(1-\alpha) \sim N\left(\frac{1}{2}\ln(1-\tilde{\rho}_k); \frac{k}{2(k-1)}\right)$ (25)

In addition, it is easy to show a direct connection between the CAC and the percentage variance of the first component in the PCA, which is often used to assess unidimensionality (Moret, Mesbah, Chwalow, & Lellouch, 1993). The PCA is mainly based on analysis of the latent roots of V_X or R_X (or, in practice, their sample estimate). The matrix R_X has only two different latent roots, the greater root is $\lambda_1 = (k-1)\rho+1$, and the other multiple roots are $\lambda_2 = \lambda_3 = \lambda_4 = \cdots = 1-\rho = (k-\lambda_1)/(k-1)$. So, using the Spearman–Brown formula, we can express the reliability of the sum of the k variables as

$$\tilde{\rho}_k = \frac{k}{k-1}\left(1 - \frac{1}{\lambda_1}\right).$$

This clearly indicates a monotonic relationship between $\tilde{\rho}_k$, which is consistently estimated by the CAC, and the first latent root λ_x, which in practice is naturally estimated by the corresponding value of the observed correlation matrix and thus the percentage variance of the first principal component in a PCA. So CAC can also be considered as a measure of unidimensionality.

Nevertheless, such a measure is not very useful because it is easy to show using the Spearman–Brown formula (19) that, under the parallel model assumption, the reliability of the total score is an increasing function of the number of variables.

So, *if the parallel model is true*, increasing the number of items will increase the reliability of a questionnaire. Moreover, this coefficient lies between zero and one. A value of zero indicates a totally unreliable scale, while a value of one means that the scale is perfectly reliable. Of course, in practice, these two scenarios never occur!

The Cronbach α-coefficient is an estimate of the reliability of the raw-score (sum of item responses) of a person *if the model generating those responses is a parallel model*.

It could be a valid criterion of the unidimensionality of such responses, if again those item responses are *generated by a parallel model*.

In the next section, we show how to build and to use a more operational and more valid criterion to measure the unidimensionality of a set of items: the backward reliability curve (the α-curve).

3.2. Unidimensionality of an instrument: backward reliability curve

Statistical validation of unidimensionality can be performed through a goodness-of-fit test of the parallel model or Rasch model. There is a large amount of literature on the subject, encompassing both classical and modern methods. These goodness-of-fit tests are generally very weak because their null hypotheses do not focus on unidimensionality: they include indirectly other additional assumptions (for instance normality for parallel models, local independence for Rasch models, etc.), so the departure from these null hypotheses is not specifically a departure from unidimensionality.

In the following, we present a graphical tool that is helpful in the step of checking the unidimensionality of a set of variables. It consists of a curve to be drawn in a stepwise manner, using estimates of reliability of sub-scores (the total of a subset included in the starting set).

The first step uses all variables and computes their CAC. Then, at every successive step, one variable is removed from the score. The removed variable is that one which leaves the score (the remaining set of variables) with a maximum CAC value among all other CACs of the remaining sets checked at this step. This procedure is repeated until only two variables remain. If the parallel model is true, increasing the number of variables increases the reliability of the total score, which is consistently estimated by Cronbach's α. Thus, a decrease of such a curve after adding a variable would cause us to suspect strongly that the added variable did not constitute a unidimensional set with variables already in the curve. This algorithm has been successfully used in the past in various medical applications (Curt, Mesbah, Lellouch, and Dellatolas, 1997; Moret et al., 1993; Nordmann, Mesbah, & Berdeaux, 2005).

Drawing the of backward reliability curve (BRC) of a set of *unidimensional* items is an essential tools in the validation process of an HrQoL questionnaire. Generally, when one develops an HrQoL questionnaire the main goal is to measure some unidimensional latent subjective traits (such as sociability, mobility, etc.). Use of the BRC in empirical data is very helpful for detecting non-unidimensional subsets of items. When the BRC is not an increasing curve, one can remove one or more items to get an increasing curve. So, if the reduced set gives an increasing curve, it is in some sense *more valid in terms of unidimensionality* than the previous one.

4. Construction of quality-of-life scores

4.1. From reliability to unidimensionality

Measuring individual quality of life is frequently done by computing one or various scores. This approach assumes that the set of items being considered represent a single dimension (one score) or multiple dimension (multiple scores). These scores can be considered as statistics, functions of individual measurements (for instance item responses). They must have good statistical properties.

Cronbach's α-coefficient, as an indicator of reliability of an instrument, is probably one of the most used in HrQoL fields or more generally in applied psychology. The big trouble with Cronbach's α as a reliability coefficient is the lack of a clear scientific rule to decide whether or not a score (based on a set of items) is reliable or not. We need to know a threshold to decide that the score is reliable or not. Following Nunnaly (1978), a scale is satisfactory when it has a minimal Cronbach's α value around 0.7. The 'Nunnally rule' is an empirical rule without any clear scientific justification. *So reliability is not a direct operational indicator.* The Spearman–Brown formula (18) is a direct consequence of parallel model assumptions. It implies that, when adding an item, or more generally increasing the number of items, the reliability of the sum of item responses must increase. This property is of course a *population property* characterizing the parallel model. Its sampling version is probably less regular. Cronbach's α-coefficient is the sampling estimate of the reliability of the sum of item responses. So, use of the backward reliability curve as an empirical rule to validate the parallel model graphically, and hence the *unidimensionality* of a set of items, is straightforward.

Use of the backward reliability curve *to find a unidimensional set of items* must be done in an *exploratory* way. It is a fast way to find *suspect* items, i.e. those items that must be removed to ensure an increasing curve and so a parallel model. It can also be used in a *confirmatory* way to assess a given set that has been supposed to be unidimensional. When a given set of items has a nice backward reliability curve (i.e. smoothly increasing in a close way to the one theoretical Spearman–Brown curve), one can perform additionally some statistical goodness-of-fit tests to check specific underlying properties. These consist mainly in validating the *compound symmetry structure* of the covariance matrix of the items, including the assumption of equality of item variances and item-latent variances. When the item responses are binary or ordinal one can test some underlying properties of the Rasch model (Hamon, Dupuy, and Mesbah, 2002). In practice, this is rarely done, because of the lack of implementation of such tests in most general statistical softwares. Under the Rasch model, a reliability coefficient close to Cronbach's α can be derived (Hamon & Mesbah, 2002). It can be interpreted in the same way as in parallel models. A backward reliability curve can be used at a first step followed by a goodness-of-fit test of the Rasch model.

Hardouin and Mesbah (2004) used a multidimensional Rasch model and Akaike information in a step-by-step procedure to obtain unidimensional clusters of binary variables in an exploratory way.

Mesbah (2015) used the BRC to identify a unidimensional subset of items from a set of questions coming from two different questionnaires.

Interpretation of multidimensional quality-of-life questionnaires may be difficult in real practice (Michel et al., 2015).

Most of the time in real HrQoL research, simpler validation techniques are often performed. More details are given in the next section.

4.2. Specificity and separability of scores

Measurement models considered here are very simple models based on unidimensionality principles. They can be defined as Rasch type models: parallel models for quantitative items and Rasch or partial credit models for ordinal items. Each '*unidimensional*' set of items is related to one and only one latent variable. There is no *confusion between 'concepts'*, so an item cannot be related directly to two latent variables. An item can be related to another latent variable only through its own latent variable. This is of course a strong property, which is hard to obtain in practice. HrQoL questionnaires are built using questions drawn with words, and often health concepts (psychological, sociological or even physical concepts) are not clearly separated. Be that as it may, measurement is generally considered as the beginning of '*science*', and science is hard to achieve.

So, correlations between each item and all unidimensional scores must be computed. This can be considered as part of the internal validation in a multidimensional setting, to ensure the *separability* of the subsets. The following attributes must be checked for each item:

(1) *specificity*: there is a strong correlation between that item and its own score, and
(2) *separability*: the item correlation between that item and its own score is higher than the correlation between the same item and scores built on other dimensions.

This is a direct consequence of Subsection 2.3. The first property is another view of the internal consistency condition of the *sub-scale*. Under the parallel model, that correlation is the same whatever the item, and it is also known as the intra-class coefficient. Cronbach's α is a monotone function of that value. It must be evaluated for each sub-scale. Item correlations between each item and all sub-scores must be tabulated (Nordmann et al., 2005; Wang, Liu, Chiu, & Tsai, 2016).

4.3. Graphical latent variable models for quality-of-life questionnaires

Graphical latent variable models for scales can be easily defined as graphical models (Lauritzen & Wermuth, 1989) built on multivariate distributions of variables with three kind of nodes:

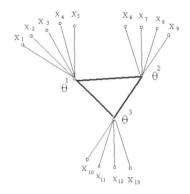
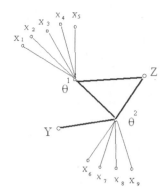

(a) Thirteen items and three latents.   (b) Nine items, two latents, and two covariates.

Figure 3. Graphical latent variable model.

- those corresponding to observed or manifest variables corresponding to items or questions;
- those corresponding to unobserved or hidden variables corresponding to latent variables; and
- those corresponding to other external variables.

Figure 3 shows two examples, the first (Figure 3(a)), with thirteen items related to three latent variables and without external variables, and the second (Figure 3(b)) with nine items related to two latent variables and two external variables Y and Z. The part of the graphic relating items and their corresponding latent variable is a graph, whereas previously, items were not, two-by-two, related by an edge. They were only related to the latent variable. One must also have the following properties:

(1) *monotonicity* – the marginal distribution of an item conditional on its latent variable must be a monotonous function of the latent variable;

(2) *non-differential item functioning* is a graphical property. There are no direct edges between nodes corresponding to any item and another latent variable or between any item and any external variable.

5. Analysis of quality-of-life change between groups

5.1. Use of HrQoL scores or global analysis

Development and validation of an HrQoL questionnaire is generally hard work requiring more than one survey and many real sets of data. When the structure of the questionnaire is stabilized, i.e. when the clustering of the items into subsets of unidimensional items is clearly defined, one needs simple rules for analysing data from studies including the HrQoL questionnaire simultaneously with other external variables. So, an HrQoL questionnaire, like any instrument, must include 'guidelines' for the statistical analysis step. Most of the time, for ease of use, only simple rules based on computing simple scores are included, such as the following.

(1) *Sum of item responses:* this score is a sufficient statistics for the latent parameter under the Rasch model. Under the parallel model, its reliability is estimated by Cronbach's α-coefficient. It is the simplest and easiest score to derive.

(2) *Weighted sum of item responses:* this is more complicated than the previous score. The weights are gen-

erally fixed and obtained with a principal component analysis previously performed in a 'large representative population'.

(3) *Percentage of item responses:* this score is similar to the first, with a different range of values. This range is between 0 and 100%. When a dimension includes k ordinal items with responses coded $0, 1, \ldots, m$ (all items with same maximum level m), this score is obtained by dividing the first score by km.

Unfortunately, the estimation of latent parameters is rarely suggested in guidebooks for HrQoL questionnaires because it requires the use of specific software, including a latent variable estimation section. Scores of type (2) need knowledge of 'good weights' given by the instrument developer, which is generally a marketing device to oblige any user of the questionnaire (for instance scientists, clinical investigators, pharmaceutical companies, etc.) to pay royalties. In practice, these weights are generally obtained in a specific population and are not valid for another one. Use of types (1) or (3) scores is, in our view, the best way to keep estimation simple, in particular when we do not have easy access to specific software for estimating Rasch type models.

5.2. Latent regression of HrQoL

It is usual to analyse HrQoL data with classical linear or generalized linear models, where the responses are scores of HrQoL built in a first step (measurement step). So, item responses are forgotten and replaced by surrogate summary scores. The analysis is of course easier and can be done using classical general software. Generally, one assumes that the distribution of scores is Gaussian, which is facilitated by the fact that most measurement models (parallel, Rasch, etc.) specify a Gaussian distribution for the latent variable. For instance, when the built score is a percentage, one can analyse its relation with other external variables by the mean of a logistic regression model which allows interesting interpretations in terms of odds ratios. Nevertheless, analysing surrogate scores as 'observations' instead of the actual observation, i.e. item responses, can give unsatisfactory results (Mesbah, 2004), mainly in terms of a lack of efficiency. So, when analysing the relationships between the latent HrQoL and any other external variables (for instance survival time, treatment, sex, age, etc.), it could be more efficient to consider a global model, even if one doesn't need to build new scores or to validate the measurement model once more. In fact, assuming some additional simple conditions that can be easily assumed in most real situations must lead to better statistical efficiency when considering such a global model. Building a global model taking into account the latent trait parameter, *without separation between the measurement and analysis steps*, is a promising latent regression approach (Christensen, Bjorner, Kreiner, and Petersen, 2004; Sébille & Mesbah, 2005) that is facilitated by today's increasing performance of computers. Nevertheless, this approach needs to be handled with care. Each practical case must be well analysed theoretically, with an in-depth investigation of which specific identifiability constraints we have to choose. We have to take care that this choice does not upset the interpretation of the final results.

Joint analysis of a longitudinal variable and event times is nowadays a very active field. Chi and Ibrahim (2006), Cowling, Hutton, and Shaw (2006), Dupuy, Grama, & Mesbah (2006), Dupuy and Mesbah (2002), Mesbah, Dupuy, Heutte, and Awad (2004), and Vonesh, Greene, and Schluchter (2006) are a few recent papers indicating that '[j]oint modeling of longitudinal and survival data is becoming increasingly essential in most cancer and AIDS clinical trials'.

Awad, Zuber, and Mesbah (2002) proposed analysing the degradation of HrQoL by considering the time of the first event when the degradation of HrQoL exceeds a prefixed threshold x, and a conservative log-rank test to compare treatment groups. Boisson, Mesbah, and Ying (2016) proposed a new test by combining the log-rank test along with a simulation based approach for p-value approximation.

Owing mainly to the complexity of the required computing programs, there is unfortunately no paper that considers the joint modeling of a longitudinal latent trait and an event time.

Another very popular method used in the 1990s of the last century was the quality adjusted time without symptoms of toxicity (Q-TWIST) approach (Gelber et al., 1996), in which the duration of life is simply divided into different categories corresponding to various states of health within given utilities. So it is a kind of weighted survival analysis (weighted by utility weights or HrQoL weights). It is a two-step approach, but the main criticisms are levelled at the fact that it uses utility values having in practice very poor measurement properties (Mesbah & Singpurwalla, 2008).

The approach of the present author can be considered as being in the framework of mixed models with a clear interpretation of the random factor as a latent trait, previously validated in a measurement step. Items are repeated measurements of such a true latent trait.

Computer programs are nowadays available even within general software (Hardouin and Mesbah, 2007) that allow building and estimating nonlinear models with random effects models.

6. Health related quality of life and housing in Europe

This example is based on a data set from the 'Housing and Health' WHO LARES survey. A total of 8519 questionnaires self-rated by each person in selected dwellings were collected, but only people older than eighteen were considered in the subsequent results. A total of 6920 valid questionnaires were retained.

An HrQoL score was derived after a preliminary exploratory phase based mainly on a PCA with varimax rotation, followed

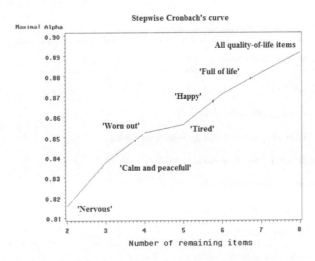

Figure 4. The empirical backward reliability curve for the quality-of-life scale.

by a confirmatory phase using the backward reliability curve method (see Figure 4, the curve for the finally built quality-of-life scale) and Rasch model methodology (the goodness-of-fit tests of Rasch models).

This score can be interpreted as the estimated probability of good HrQoL or as a proportion of the best HrQoL possible. This proportion is actually the ratio of two numbers: the numerator is the number of responses positively associated with good quality of life, the denominator is the maximum that the denominator can reach. So, *we can analyse this score by multiple logistic regression and present the odds ratio as the measure of association.* All computations were made with SAS® software.

The obtained odds ratios were estimated under multiple logistic regression models. The final model was chosen after parsimonious stepwise model selection. Table 1 shows the odds ratios between the quality of life of some selected significant housing condition factors for a few domains. Odds ratios greater than one mean that the factor is positively associated with the quality of life. On the other hand, when the odds ratio is smaller than one this means that the factor is negatively associated with the quality of life. The 95% confidence interval of this odds ratio is indicated in parentheses.

Nevertheless, we must be aware that the fact that the LARES survey was transversal (instead of longitudinal) and observational (instead of interventional) slightly limits the causal interpretation of housing factors revealed. Setting the evidence of a causal relationship is a more complex work.

7. Risk perception research I: air pollution health effects

7.1. Pilot study

7.1.1. Questionnaire and selection of sample populations

A pilot study was conducted to test the acceptability of an air quality perception (AQP) questionnaire and to improve the formulation of the question. In this pilot study, the questionnaire was designed with 54 ordinal questions dealing with the nuisances caused by air pollution in the fields of health, daily life, and local environment (all the questions are defined in Table 1). Two classical steps were followed to prepare the questionnaire: (i) a literature review from which questions relating to 'subjective' concepts were identified; and (ii) focus group meetings to draw up a list of questions relating to the perception of air quality, to formulate the wording, and to

Table 1. HrQoL and housing information.

Housing condition factor	Odds ratio (95% confidence interval)
Panel block	0.962 (0.932; 0.993)
Semi-detached housing unit	1.134 (1.077; 1.194)
Multifamily apartment block, up to six residential units	1.122 (1.084; 1.162)
In the urban centre close to a busy street	1.095 (1.057; 1.135)
Windows can be opened in flat	1.080 (1.037; 1.124)
Windows cannot be closed in flat	0.929 (0.910; 0.947)
Single-glazed windows	1.047 (1.020; 1.075)
Condensation signs at windows	0.937 (0.900; 0.975)
Wallpaper, paint, etc. peeling off walls	0.950 (0.924; 0.977)
Shared spaces are well maintained/taken care of	1.055 (1.027; 1.083)
One or two graffiti	0.891 (0.861; 0.923)
Vegetation/greenery visible on façades/windows/balconies	1.029 (1.006; 1.053)

structure the questionnaire. 'Nuisance' was ranked according to four levels classifying the perception intensity of the nuisance: never, occasionally, often, and always perceived. On the basis of a random selection of telephone numbers, 83 respondents were interviewed in three French towns with varying levels of air pollution: 26 interviews were carried out by telephone in Le Havre (northern France), 16 in Lyon (eastern France), and 41 in Rennes (western France).

7.1.2. Statistical analysis

Without clear a priori knowledge of the structure of the subjective concept we want to measure, principal component analysis (PCA) followed by a varimax rotation constitute an appropriate statistical method. This is an exploratory and preliminary analysis often used to identify clustering questions. However, statistical methods are needed to eliminate questions that do not guarantee the unidimensionality of the scale: in this case, it would mean that the scale measures more than one concept (the backward Cronbach curve). Statistical criteria were also used to assess the unidimensionality of the scale (the parallel model describing the unidimensionality of a set of variables and the reliability of the scale). Finally, the validity of the scale was verified.

7.1.3. Preliminary AQP scale

From the 54 initial questions, 22 were removed to ensure the unidimensionality of the scale after simultaneously applying the PCA and the step-by-step Cronbach curve previously described. The remaining 32 questions verified the standard statistical criteria required to validate a subjective scale. These 32 questions are split on three unidimensional groups (1, 2 and 3) with empirical backward reliability curves shown in Figure 5-7. The questions and more details about the results of the pilot study are given in Deguen, Segala, and Mesbah, (2007). These 32 questions have been included in the final questionnaire tested in the full study (Deguen, Segala, Pedrono, & Mesbah, 2012).

7.2. Epidemiological survey

7.2.1. Study areas, sample selection, and data collection

A typology of 52 French cities based on air pollution, demographic, and socioeconomic characteristics was realized. Averages of SO_2, NO_2, O_3, and PM10 concentrations in the year 2000 were used to estimate the air pollution level of each city; data were obtained from the local air quality monitoring association in each city. Demographic and socioeconomic data were obtained from the 1999 national census. The climate of each city was described by Météo France, the French weather national forecast service. A hierarchical classification was performed. The statistical units were aggregated with the wards method (Ward, 1963). Two statistical indicators (pseudo F and pseudo t2) were used to identify the best number of classes maximizing interclass variance and minimizing intraclass variance. Finally, the 52 French cities were distributed into 8 classes. These classes contrasted most and less polluted cities, and advantaged and deprived cities. Finally, other data, such as the housing market, for example, allowed discriminating the cities. Eight cities were selected at random (one from each class) to ensure characteristics diversity. A sample of 12,000 representative telephone numbers (1500 per city) was randomly selected from the France Telecom 'Pages Jaunes Marketing Services'. A total of 2522 answers (a participation rate of about 37%) were collected using an individual questionnaire administered by telephone between May 2006 and May 2007. The questionnaire included sociodemographic characteristics, occupation status, car and house ownership, smoking habits (passive smoking and smoker), and health status (chronic bronchitis, hay fever, depressed status, and asthma). The 32 questions selected in the pilot study were added to the questionnaire to collect data required to draw up the AQP scale. A general question about air quality, commonly used in literature studies dealing with AQP, was also included in the questionnaire as a validation question.

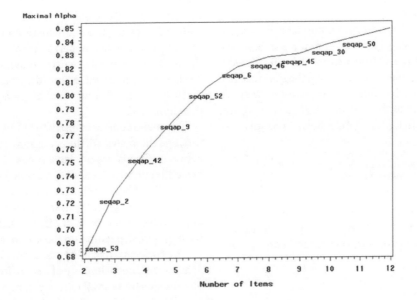

Figure 5. The empirical backward reliability curve for the perception scale: Group 1.

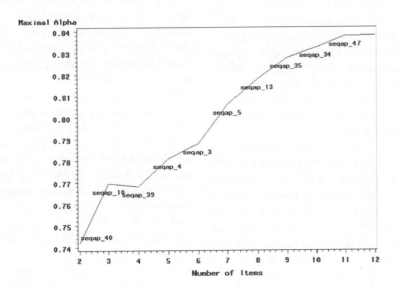

Figure 6. The empirical backward reliability curve for the perception scale: Group 2.

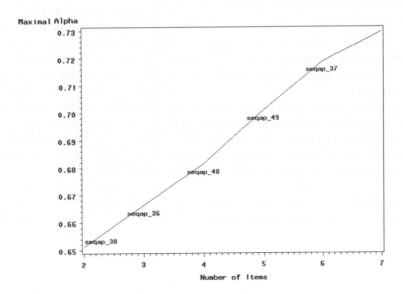

Figure 7. The empirical backward reliability curve for the perception scale: Group 3.

7.2.2. Scoring procedure

To quantify the degree of each reported nuisance more accurately, each question was assigned one of four possible values, 0 when the nuisance had never been perceived during the week preceding the interview, and 1, 2, or 3 when the nuisance had been perceived occasionally, often, or always, respectively. To obtain a global measure of the personal AQP, a score S_i was estimated for each subject, i, using the followed formula:

$$S_i = \frac{1}{3k - m_i} \sum_{j=1}^{n} X_{ij},$$

where k is the total number of questions in the AQP scale and m_i is the number of missing responses for subject i. The number 3 in the denominator is the maximum score for each question.

7.2.3. Final AQL scale

To test the robustness of this scale, the same methodological procedure as that used for the 83 respondents in the pilot study was conducted for another, larger, group of people. First, the backward Cronbach curve was used to eliminate some questions among the 32 questions composing the preliminary scale. Several questions seemed to be significantly correlated, giving redundant information; this high correlation had not been revealed in the pilot study because of low statistical power due to the small sample. Second, the validity of the AQP scale was assessed using the same indicators and statistical tests that had been applied in the pilot study.

Following this method, 10 questions were removed from the initial 32 questions. The 22 remaining questions covered different aspects of the perception of air pollution. Two principal aspects were clearly highlighted: (1) 'Nuisance' caused by air pollution, with sensory perception (odours, dust, etc.) and symptoms (irritation of the eyes, nose, or throat, headache, etc.), and (2) 'Risk perception', distinguishing subjects who were anxious about their health and their quality of life and those who took protection measures (staying indoors, thinking about moving home, etc.) against air pollution.

8. Risk perception research II: environmental and health impact of an industrial site

A cross-sectional survey was conducted in the year 2012 on a random sample of 1495 households selected from the population of the residents of 7 municipalities located in a 5km radius around the industrial site.

The reliability of standardized psychometric instruments in the study population was checked. Construction and validation of instruments to measure perceived pollution and attitudes towards the industrial site were developed, using the BRC method (Daniau, 2014; Daniau, Salvio, Wagner, Berat, Stempfelet, Kermarec, and Dab, 2015. Multiple linear regression analysis was used to examine the psychological health indicators (MCS, anxiety, insomnia) in relation to perception of the industrial pollution.

9. Conclusion

In this work, we have presented the main modern statistical methods and models used in the validation and analysis of a quality-of-life measure in an epidemiological context. The validation step is mainly internal and consists in analysing the unidimensionality of the set of items (questions) forming the scale. After giving the mathematical definition of unidimensionality (the parallel model) an empirical algorithm based on the backward reliability curve to assess the validity of such models was presented. Main ideas behind the extension to multi-dimensional scales and to categorical variables were then indicated.

The definition (or construction) of variables and indicators, and the analysis of the evolution of their joint distribution between various populations, times, and areas are generally two different, well-separated, steps in the work of a statistician in the field of health related quality of life.

The first step generally deals with the calibration and metrology of questionnaires. It is often called the measurement or scoring step, depending on the area of application.

The backward reliability curve can be used as a tool to confirm the unidimensionality of a set of items. When more than one dimension is available, the computation of scores, and correlations between items and scores, is useful for checking the separability of dimensions.

The second step is certainly more known by most statisticians. Linear, generalized linear, time series, and survival models are very useful models in this step, where the variables constructed in the first step are incorporated and their joint distribution with the other analysis variables (treatment group, time, duration of life, etc.) is investigated. HrQoL scores, validated during the first step, are then analysed, with complete omission of the real observations, i.e. item responses. The latent nature of the HrQoL concept is generally neglected.

Mesbah (2004) compared the simple strategy of separating the two steps with the global strategy of defining and analysing a global model including both the measurement and the analysis step. If, with a real data set, one finds a significant association between a built (from items) score and an external covariate, then the true association, i.e. the one between that external covariate and the true latent, is probably larger. So, if the scientific goal is to show an association between the true latent and the covariate, one does not need to use a global model: one may just use the model with the surrogate built score instead of the true latent. Conclusions drawn from the built score also stand for the true association.

But if one finds no significant association between the built score and the covariate, then the true association could be anything, and could perhaps be larger. So one has to consider a global model, even if one does not need to build new scores or to validate the measurement model.

Building a global model taking into account the latent trait parameter in a one-step method, i.e. without separation between measurement and analysis, is a promising latent regression approach (Christensen et al., 2004; Sébille & Mesbah, 2005) allowed by the increasing performance of computers. In the HrQoL field, most papers are devoted to a two-step approach in which the HrQoL scores are used instead of the original item responses data. Moreover, different scientific results are published in different kinds of scientific journal: those devoted to the validation of measurements and instruments, and more numerous others specializing in the analysis of previously validated measurements (Awad et al., 2002; Boisson et al., 2016).

Finally, we have presented three different applications to real data sets, including data from a large survey done in eight big European cities: the LARES study. We used data from this to derive quality-of-life related housing scores that can be easily interpreted in terms of odds ratios. Unlike quality-of-life measures obtained by themselves, and internally validated in a first step, quality-of-life related housing factors were obtained by using multiple logistic regression.

Disclosure statement

No potential conflict of interest was reported by the author.

References

Andersen, E. B. (1970). Asymptotic properties of conditional maximum likelihood estimators. *Journal of the Royal Statistical Society, Series B, 32,* 283–301.

Awad, L., Zuber, E., & Mesbah, M. (2002). Applying survival data methodology to analyze longitudinal quality of life data. In M. Mesbah, B. F. Cole & M. L. T. Lee (Eds.), *Statistical methods for quality of life studies: Design, measurement and analysis* (pp. 231–243). Boston, MA: Kluwer Academic.

Boisson, V., Mesbah, M., & Ying, Z. (2016). Log-rank-type test for evolution of health related quality of life. *Statistica Applicata - Italian Journal of Applied Statistics,* to be published

Bonnefoy, X., Annessi-Maesano, I., Moreno Aznar, L., Braubach, M., Croxford, B., Davidson, M., ...Rudnan, P. (2004). Habitat et Santé: État des connaissances. *Les echos du logement (Ministère de la Région Wallonne), 4,* 145–152.

Bonnefoy, X. R., Braubach, M., Moissonnier, B., Monolbaev, K., & Röbbel, N. (2003). Housing and health in Europe: Preliminary results of a pan-European Study. *American Journal of Public Health, 93,* 1559–1563.

Chi, Y. & Ibrahim, J. G. (2006). Joint models for multivariate longitudinal and multivariate survival data. *Applied Statistics, 62,* 432–445.

Christensen, K. B., Bjorner, J. B., Kreiner, S., & Petersen, J. H. (2004). Latent regression in loglinear Rasch models. *Communications in Statistics - Theory and Methods, 33,* 1295–1313. Retrieved from http://dx.doi.org/10.1081/STA-120030150

Cowling, B. J., Hutton, J. L., & Shaw, J. E. H. (2006). Joint modelling of event counts and survival times. *Applied Statistics, 55,* 31–39.

Cronbach, L. J. (1951). Coefficient alpha and the internal structure of tests. *Psychometrika, 16,* 297–334.

Curt, F., Mesbah, M., Lellouch, J., & Dellatolas, G. (1997). Handedness scale: How many and which items? *Laterality, 2,* 137–154.

Daniau, C. (2014). Surveillance épidémiologique fondée sur des indicateurs de santé déclarée: Pertinence et faisabilité d'un dispositif á l'échelle locale en santé environnement (Thèse de Doctorat de Sécurité Sanitaire -DOC39). Human Health and Pathology, Conservatoire National des Arts et Metiers (CNAM). Retrieved from https://tel.archives-ouvertes.fr/tel-01124371/file/2014CNAM0923.pdf

Daniau, C., Salvio, C., Wagner, V., Berat, B., Stempfelet, M., Kermarec, F., ..Dab, W., (2015). *Institut de veille sanitaire.* Health and quality of life of people living near a chemical industrial area. Retrieved from http://opac.invs.sante.fr/docnum.php?explnumid=9165

Deguen, S., Segala, C. & Mesbah, M. (2007). Measuring degradation of quality of life related to pollution in the SEQAP study. Chapter 25. F. Vonta, M. Nikulin, N. Limnios & C. Huber-Carol . (Eds.), *Statistical models and methods for biomedical and technical systems.* Boston, MA: Birkhäuser.

Deguen, S., Segala, C., Pedrono, G., & Mesbah, M. (2012). A new air quality perception scale for global assessment of air pollution health effects. *Risk Analysis, 32*(12), 2043–2054.

Dossar, P. & Mesbah, M. (2016). Cumulative or adjacent logits: Which choice for an ordinal logistic latent variable model?. *Communications in Statistics - Theory and Methods,* to be published

Dupuy, J.-F., Grama, I., & Mesbah, M. (2006). Asymptotic theory for the Cox model with missing time dependent covariate. *Annals of Statistics, 34*(2), 903–924.

Dupuy, J.-F. & Mesbah, M. (2002). Joint modeling of event time and nonignorable missing longitudinal data. *Lifetime Data Analysis, 8,* 99–115.

Edwards, D. (2000). *Introduction to graphical modelling* (2nd ed.). New York: Springer-Verlag.

Fisher, G. H. & Molenaar, I. W. (1995). *Rasch models, foundations, recent developments and applications.* New York: Springer-Verlag.

Fredouille, J. & Mesbah, M. (2009). Housing and mental health. Chapter 11 in: D. Ormandy. (Ed.), *Housing and health in Europe. The WHO LARES project.* Boston, MA: Routledge. Retrieved from https://www.routledge.com/products/9780415477352

Frydenberg, M. (1990). Marginalization and collapsibility in graphical interaction models. *Annals of Statistics, 18,* 790–805.

Gelber, R. D., Goldhirsch, A., Cole, B. F., Wieand, H. S., Schroeder, G., & Krook, G. E. (1996). A quality-adjusted time without symptoms or toxicity (Q-TWIST) analysis of adjuvant radiation therapy and chemotherapy for resectable rectal cancer. *Journal of the National Cancer Institute, 88,* 1039–1045.

Hamon, A., Dupuy, J. F., & Mesbah, M. (2002). Validation of model assumptions in quality of life measurements. In: C. Huber, N. Nikulin, N. Balakrishnan & M. Mesbah (Eds.), *Goodness of fit tests and model validity* (pp. 371–383). Boston, MA: Kluwer Academic.

Hamon, A., & Mesbah, M. (2002). Questionnaire reliability under the Rasch model. In M. Mesbah, B. F. Cole & M. L. T. Lee (Eds.), *Statistical methods for quality of life studies: Design, measurement and analysis* (pp. 155–168). Boston, MA: Kluwer Academic.

Hardouin, J. B., & Mesbah, M. (2004). Clustering binary variables in subscales using an extended Rasch model and Akaike information criterion. *Communications in Statistics - Theory and Methods, 33,* 1277–1294.

Hardouin, J. B., & Mesbah, M. (2007). The SAS macro-program %ANAQOL to estimate the parameters of item responses theory models. *Communications in Statistics - Theory and Methods, 36,* 437–453.

Kreiner, S., & Cristensen, K. B. (2002). Graphical Rasch models. In M. Mesbah, B. F. Cole & M. L. T. Lee (Eds.), *Statistical methods for quality of life studies: Design, measurement and analysis* (pp. 187–203). Boston, MA: Kluwer Academic.

Kristof, W. (1963). The statistical theory of stepped-up reliability coefficients when a test has been divided into several equivalent parts. *Psychometrika, 28,* 221–238.

Lauritzen, S. L. (1996). *Graphical models.* Oxford, UK: Oxford University Press.

Lauritzen, S. L. & Wermuth, N. (1989). Graphical models for association between variables, some of which are qualitative and some quantitative. *Annals of Statistics, 17*(1), 31–57.

MacCullagh, P., & Nelder, J. A. (1989). *Generalized linear models. Vol. 37 of Monographs on Statistics and Applied Probability.* London: Chapman & Hall/CRC. Retrieved from https://www.crcpress.com/Generalized-Linear-Models-Second-Edition/McCullagh-Nelder/9780412317606

Martynov, G. & Mesbah, M. (2006). Goodness of fit test and latent distribution estimation in the mixed Rasch model. *Communications in Statistics - Theory and Methods, 35,* 921–935. Retrieved from http://dx.doi.org/10.1080/03610920500501445

Masters, G. N. (1982). A Rasch model for partial credit scoring. *Psychometrika, 47,* 149–174.

Mesbah, M. (2004). Measurement and analysis of health related quality of life and environmental data. *Environmetrics, 15,* 471–481.

Mesbah, M. (2009). Building quality of life related housing scores using the LARES study - A methodical approach to avoid pitfalls and bias. Chapter 12. D. Ormandy. (Ed.), *Housing and Health in Europe. The WHO LARES Project.* Boston, MA: Routledge. https://www.routledge.com/products/9780415477352Retrieved from

Mesbah, M. (2015). Analysis of a complex longitudinal health related quality of life data by a mixed logistic model. Chapter 19in: Z. Chen , L. Aiyi, Y. Qu, L. Tang & Y. Tsong. (Eds.), *Applied statistics in biomedicine and clinical trials design - selected papers from the 2013 ICSA/ISBS joint statistical meetings.* New York: Springer-Verlag. (pp. 313–328). Retrieved from http://dx.doi.org/10.1007/978-3-319-12694-419

Mesbah, M., Dupuy, J. F., Heutte, N., & Awad, L. (2004). Joint analysis of longitudinal quality of life and survival processes. Chapter 38. N. Balakrishnan & C. R. Rao. (Eds.), *Handbook of statistics (23) - Advances in survival analysis.* Amsterdam: Elsevier North-Holland.

Mesbah, M., Lellouch, J., & Huber, C. (1999). The choice of loglinear models in contingency tables when the variables of interest are not jointly observed. *Biometrics, 48,* 259–266.

Mesbah, M., & Singpurwalla, N. (2008). A Bayesian ponders 'The Quality of Life'. Chapter 26. F. Vonta , M. Nikulin, N. Limnios & C. Huber-Carol. (Eds.), *Statistical models and methods for biomedical and technical systems.* Boston, MA: Birkhäuser.

Michel, P., Auquier, P., Baumstarck, K., Loundou, A., Ghattas, B., Lancon, C., & Boyer, L. (2015). How to interpret multidimensional quality of life questionnaires for patients with schizophrenia? *Quality of Life Research, 24*, 2483–2492.

Mislevy, R. J. (1984). Estimating latent distributions. *Psychometrika, 49*, 359–381. Retrieved from http://dx.doi.org/10.1007/BF02306026

Molenaar, I.W. & Sijstma, K. (2000). User's manual MSP5 for Windows: A program for Mokken scale analysis for polytomous items (Version 5.0), Groningen: ProGAMMA.

Moret, L., Mesbah, M., Chwalow, J., & Lellouch, J. (1993). Validation interne d'une échelle de mesure: Relation entre analyse en composantes principales, coefficient alpha de Cronbach et coefficient de corrélation intra-classe. *La Revue d'Epidémiologie et de Santé Publique, 41*(2), 179–186.

Nordmann, J. F., Mesbah, M., & Berdeaux, G. (2005). Scoring of visual field measured through Humphrey perimetry: Principal component, varimax rotation followed by validated cluster analysis. *Investigative Ophthalmology and Visual Science, 48*, 3168–3176. Retrieved from http://dx.doi.org/10.1167/iovs.04-1214

Nunnaly, J. (1978). *Psychometric theory* (2nd ed.). New York: McGraw-Hill.

Rasch, G. (1960). *Probabilistic models for some intelligence and attainment tests.* Copenhagen: Danmarks Paedagogiske Institut.

Samejima, F. (1969). *Estimation of ability using a response pattern of graded scores.* Psychometrika Monograph, No. 17.

Sébille, V. & Mesbah, M. (2005). Sequential analysis of quality of life Rasch measurements. M. Nikouline, D. Commenges & C. Huber. (Eds.), *Probability statistics and modeling in public health. In honor of Marvin Zelen* (pp. 421–439). New York: Kluwer Academic.

The WHOQoL Group (1994). The development of the World Health Organization quality of life assessment instrument (the WHOQoL). In J. Orley & W. Kuyken (Eds.), *Quality of life assessment: International perspectives.* Heidelberg: Springer-Verlag.

van Zyl, J. M., Neudecker, H., & Nel, D. G. (2000). On the distribution of the maximum likelihood estimator of Cronbach's alpha. *Psychometrika, 65*, 271–280.

Vonesh, E. F., Greene, T., & Schluchter, M. D. (2006). Shared parameter models for the joint analysis of longitudinal data and event times. *Statistics in Medicine, 25*, 143–163.

Wang, M. Y., Liu, I. C., Chiu, C.-H., & Tsai, P. S. (2016). Cultural adaptation and validation of the Chinese version of the fatigue severity scale in patients with major depressive disorder and nondepressive people. *Quality of Life Research, 26*, 89–99.

Ward, J.H. (1963). Hierarchical grouping to optimize an objective function. *Journal of the American Statistical Association, 58*, 234–244.

Whittaker, J. (1990). *Graphical models in applied multivariate statistics* (1st ed.). New York: Wiley.

Big data analytics: integrating penalty strategies

S. Ejaz Ahmed and Bahadır Yüzbaşı

ABSTRACT

We present efficient estimation and prediction strategies for the classical multiple regression model when the dimensions of the parameters are larger than the number of observations. These strategies are motivated by penalty estimation and Stein-type estimation procedures. More specifically, we consider the estimation of regression parameters in sparse linear models when some of the predictors may have a very weak influence on the response of interest. In a high-dimensional situation, a number of existing variable selection techniques exists. However, they yield different subset models and may have different numbers of predictors. Generally speaking, the least absolute shrinkage and selection operator (Lasso) approach produces an over-fitted model compared with its competitors, namely the smoothly clipped absolute deviation (SCAD) method and adaptive Lasso (aLasso). Thus, prediction based only on a submodel selected by such methods will be subject to selection bias. In order to minimize the inherited bias, we suggest combining two models to improve the estimation and prediction performance. In the context of two competing models where one model includes more predictors than the other based on relatively aggressive variable selection strategies, we plan to investigate the relative performance of Stein-type shrinkage and penalty estimators. The shrinkage estimator improves the prediction performance of submodels significantly selected from existing Lasso-type variable selection methods. A Monte Carlo simulation study is carried out using the relative mean squared error (RMSE) criterion to appraise the performance of the listed estimators. The proposed strategy is applied to the analysis of several real high-dimensional data sets.

1. Introduction

The representation and modeling of high-dimensional data, where the sample size (n) is smaller than the size of data elements (d) associated with each observation, is an important feature in a host of social sciences, bio-informatics, medical, environmental, engineering, and financial studies, among others. The rapid growth in the size and scope of data sets in a host of disciplines has created a need for innovative statistical strategies in data analysis. Classical methods are based on the assumption that $d < n$ to obtain a meaningful statistical output. The existing classical strategies do not provide solutions related to so-called 'big data'. The term big data is not well defined, but its problems are real and statisticians need to play a more important role in this arena. Big data, or 'data science', is an emerging field. There are many challenging questions. For example, how to acquire, manage, process, analyse, and make sense of big data? Clearly, big data is the future of research in a host disciplines, and trans-disciplinary programs are required to develop the skills for data scientists, so-called. For example, many security agencies are using sophisticated number-crunching, data mining, or big data analytics to reveal patterns in information provided by air carriers about passengers. There is an increasing demand for efficient prediction strategies for such analysis of high-dimensional data, i.e. data sets where the number of observed data elements (sample size) substantially smaller than the number of subjects or number of predictors in a regression context; for example, data arising from gene expression arrays and social network modeling, and clinical, genetics and phenotypic data. Existing techniques that deal with high-dimensional data mostly rely on various

ℓ_1 penalty regularizers. Due to the trade-off between model complexity and model prediction, the statistical inference of model selection becomes an extremely important and challenging problem in high-dimensional data analysis. Over the past two decades, many penalized regularization approaches have been developed to do variable selection and estimation simultaneously. Among them, the least absolute shrinkage and selection operator (Lasso) is one of the recent approaches (Tibshirani, 1996). It is a useful technique due to its convexity and computation efficiency. The Lasso approach is based on squared error and a penalty proportional to regression parameters. Schelldorfer, Bühlmann, and van de Geer (2011) have provided a comprehensive summary of the consistency properties of the Lasso approach. Efron, Hastie, Johnstone, and Tibshirani (2004) introduced the least angle regression algorithm, which is a very fast way to draw the entire regularization path for a Lasso estimate of the regression parameters. Penalized likelihood methods have been extensively studied in the literature, see for example Tran (2011), Huang and Zhang (2008), Kim, Choi, and Oh (2008), Wang and Leng (2007), Yuan and Lin (2006), Leng, Lin, and Wahba (2006), and Tibshirani, Saunders, Rosset, Zhu, and Knight (2005). The penalized likelihood methods have a close connection to Bayesian procedures. Thus the Lasso estimate corresponds to a Bayes method that puts a Laplacian (double exponential) prior on the regression coefficients. Recent results (Armagan, Dunson and Lee, 2013; Bhattacharya, Pati, Pillai, and Dunson, 2012; Carvalho, Polson, and Scott, 2010) have demonstrated that better desirable results can be obtained by using priors with heavier tails than the double exponential prior, in particular, priors with polynomial tails. Our study has concentrated on the widely recognized penalty estimators Lasso, adaptive Lasso (aLasso), and the smoothly clipped absolute deviation method (SCAD).

We consider the estimation problem of regression parameters when there are many potential predictors in the initial/working model and

(1) most of them may not have any influence (sparse signals) on the response of interest;
(2) some of the predictors may have strong influence (strong signals) on the response of interest;
(3) some of them may have a weak-to-moderate influence (weak–moderate signals) on the response of interest.

It is possible that there may be extraneous predictors in the model. Consider a situation in which the main concern is the effect of treatment or the effect of biomarkers; extraneous nuisance variables may be laboratory effects if several laboratories are involved, or the age and sex of patients. The analysis will be more precise if 'nuisance variables' can be left out of the model. This leads to the consideration of two models: the full model that includes all predictors and possible extraneous variables, and a candidate submodel that includes the predictors of main concern while leaving out extraneous variables. Further, it is important that we do not automatically remove all the predictors with weak signals from the model. This may result in selecting a biased submodel. A logical way to deal with this framework is to use pretest model selection and estimation strategies that test whether the coefficients of the extraneous variables are zero and then estimate parameters in the model that include coefficients that are rejected by the test. Another strategy is to use Stein-type shrinkage estimators where the estimated regression coefficient vector is shrunk in the direction of the candidate subspace. This 'soft threshold' modification of the pretest method has been shown to be efficient in various frameworks. Ahmed, Hossain, and Doksum (2012) among others have investigated the properties of shrinkage and pretest methodologies for host models.

The model and some estimators are introduced in Section 2. In Section 3 we showcase our suggested estimation strategy. The results of a simulation study that includes comparison of the suggested estimator with penalty estimators are reported in Section 4. Application to real data sets is given in Section 5. Finally, we offer concluding remarks in Section 6.

2. Estimation strategies

In this communication, we consider a high-dimensional linear regression sparse model:

$$y_i = \sum_{j=1}^{d} x_{ij}\beta_j + \varepsilon_i, \quad 1 \le i \le n << d, \qquad (1)$$

where y_i are the observed response variables with predictors x_i, and β_j are the regression parameters. Further, ε_i are independent and identically distributed random errors with center zero and variance σ^2.

Regularization techniques are helpful in dealing with the problem when the number of features, d, is much larger than the number of data points, n. The solution is based upon a stringent assumption that the true underlying model is sparse in terms of the ℓ_0 norm of the regression parameters. How-

ever, in an effort to achieve meaningful estimation and selection properties, most Lasso-type penalties make some important assumptions about both the true model and the designed covariates. For example, the true model is often assumed to be sparse such that

- most of the regression coefficients are zero except for a few;
- all non-zero β_j are larger than the noise level, $c\sigma\sqrt{(2/n)\log(d)}$ with $c \ge 1/2$.

Further, additional assumptions made regarding the designed covariates include the adaptive irrepresentable condition and the restricted eigenvalue conditions. We refer to Zhao and Yu (2006), Huang and Zhang (2008), and Bickel, Ritov, and Tsybakov (2009) for some insights. In general, the Lasso penalty tends to select an over-fitted model since it penalizes all coefficients equally Leng et al. (2006). In the reviewed literature, several modifications and methodologies have been suggested to improve the prediction accuracy of the Lasso strategy. For example, SCAD Fan & Li (2001), adaptive Lasso (Zou, 2006), MCP (Zhang, 2010), and several others. These methods select a submodel by shrinking some regression coefficients to zero and providing shrinkage estimators for the remaining coefficients. However, these methods may force the relatively weaker coefficients towards zero as compared with Lasso, resulting in under-fitted models subject to a much larger selection bias in the presence of a significant number of weak signals.

In this paper we consider the estimation and prediction problem for sparse regression models when there are many potential predictors that have a weak influence on the response of interest. The analysis will be relatively more precise if 'weak effect' variables can be weighted for the ultimate model prediction. This leads to the consideration of two models: on one hand, an over-fitted model that includes predictors with strong signals and possibly some predictors with weak signals selected by Lasso; on the other hand, an under-fitted model that possibly includes predictors with strong signals while leaving out weak-effect predictors by using SCAD or aLasso. One way to deal with this framework is to use Stein-type shrinkage estimators where the estimated regression coefficient vector is shrunk in the direction of the under-fitted model. This 'soft threshold' modification of the pretest method has been shown to be efficient in various frameworks. Ahmed et al. (2012) among others have examined the properties of Stein-type shrinkage estimation strategies for a host of models.

Consider the following regression model:

$$Y = X\beta + \varepsilon, \qquad (2)$$

where $Y = (y_1, y_2, \ldots, y_n)'$ is a vector of responses, X is an $n \times d$ fixed design matrix, $\beta = (\beta_1, \ldots, \beta_d)'$ is an unknown vector of parameters, $\varepsilon = (\varepsilon_1, \varepsilon_2, \ldots, \varepsilon_n)'$ is the vector of unobservable random errors, and the superscript $(')$ denotes the transpose of a vector or matrix. We do not make any distributional assumption about the errors except that ε has a cumulative distribution function $F(\varepsilon)$ with $E(\varepsilon) = 0$, and $E(\varepsilon\varepsilon') = \sigma^2 I$, where σ^2 is finite.

For $n > d$, the classical estimator of β minimizes the least squares function and is given by

$$\widehat{\beta}^{\text{LSE}} = (X'X)^{-1}X'Y.$$

However, we are dealing with a high-dimensional situation, i.e. $n < d$, so $(\mathbf{X}'\mathbf{X})^{-1}$ will not exist and thus there will be no solution. However, one can employ the generalized inverse to revert the problem. In the current set-up we are assuming that the model is sparse so it is desirable to use the penalized likelihood method to obtain a meaningful solution, as discussed briefly in our introduction. Penalty estimators are a class of estimators in the least penalized squares family of estimators, see Ahmed (2014). This method involves penalizing the regression coefficients, and shrinking a subset of them to zero. In other words, the penalizing procedure produces a submodel and subsequently estimates the submodel parameters. Several penalty estimators have been proposed in the literature for linear and generalized linear models. In this section, we consider Lasso, SCAD, adaptive Lasso, and minimax concave penalty (MCP) (Zhang, 2010). By shrinking some regression coefficients to zero, these methods select parameters and perform estimation simultaneously. Frank and Friedman (1993) introduced bridge regression, a generalized version of penalty (or absolute penalty type) estimators. For a given penalty function $\pi(\cdot)$ and regularization parameter λ, the general form can be written as

$$S(\varepsilon) = (\mathbf{y} - \mathbf{X}\varepsilon)'(\mathbf{y} - \mathbf{X}\varepsilon) + \lambda\pi(\beta),$$

where the penalty function is of the form

$$\pi(\beta) = \sum_{j=1}^{d} |\beta_j|^{\gamma}, \quad \gamma > 0. \tag{3}$$

The penalty function in (3) bounds the L_γ norm of the parameters in the given model as $\sum_{j=1}^{d} |\beta_j|^{\gamma} \leq t$, where t is the tuning parameter that controls the amount of shrinkage. We see that for $\gamma = 2$ we obtain ridge estimates that are obtained by minimizing the penalized residual sum of squares

$$\widehat{\beta}^{\text{ridge}} = \arg\min_{\beta} \left\{ \sum_{i=1}^{n} \left(y_i - \beta_0 - \sum_{j=1}^{d} x_{ij}\beta_j \right)^2 + \lambda \sum_{j=1}^{d} \beta_j^2 \right\}, \tag{4}$$

where λ is the tuning parameter that controls the amount of shrinkage. Frank and Friedman (1993) did not solve for the bridge regression estimators for any $\gamma > 0$. Interestingly, for $\gamma < 2$, it shrinks the coefficient towards zero, and depending on the value of λ, it sets some of them to be exactly zero. Thus, the procedure combines variable selection and shrinking of the coefficients of penalized regression.

An important member of the penalized least squares family is the L_1 penalized least squares estimator, which is obtained when $\gamma = 1$, and is called Lasso.

2.1. The least absolute shrinkage and selection operator (Lasso)

Lasso, which was proposed by Tibshirani (1996), performs variable selection and parameter estimation simultaneously. Lasso is closely related to ridge regression. Lasso solutions are similarly defined by replacing the squared penalty $\sum_{j=1}^{d} \beta_j^2$ in the ridge solution (4) with the absolute penalty $\sum_{j=1}^{d} |\beta_j|$ in

the Lasso,

$$\widehat{\beta}^{\text{Lasso}} = \arg\min_{\beta} \left\{ \sum_{i=1}^{n} \left(y_i - \beta_0 - \sum_{j=1}^{d} x_{ij}\beta_j \right)^2 + \lambda \sum_{j=1}^{d} |\beta_j| \right\}. \tag{5}$$

Although the change apparently looks subtle, the absolute penalty term made it impossible to have an analytic solution for the Lasso. Originally, Lasso solutions were obtained via quadratic programming. Later, Efron, Hastie, Johnstone, and Tibshirani (2004) proposed least angle regression (LAR), a type of stepwise regression with which the Lasso estimates can be obtained at the same computational cost as that of an ordinary least squares estimation. Further, the Lasso estimator remains numerically feasible for dimensions of d that are much higher than the sample size n.

Ahmed, Doksum, Hossain, and You (2007) proposed a penalty estimator for partially linear models. Further, they reappraised the properties of shrinkage estimators based on the Stein-rule estimation for the same model.

2.2. Smoothly clipped absolute deviation (SCAD)

Although the Lasso method does both shrinkage and variable selection due to the nature of the constraint region, which often results in several coefficients becoming identically zero, it does not possess oracle properties, as discussed in Fan and Li (2001). To overcome the inefficiency of traditional variable selection procedures, they proposed SCAD to select variables and estimate the coefficients of variables automatically and simultaneously. This method not only retains the good features of both subset selection and ridge regression, but also produces sparse solutions, ensures continuity of the selected models (for the stability of model selection), and has unbiased estimates for large coefficients. The estimates are obtained as

$$\widehat{\beta}^{\text{SCAD}} = \arg\min_{\beta} \left\{ \sum_{i=1}^{n} \left(y_i - \beta_0 - \sum_{j=1}^{d} x_{ij}\beta_j \right)^2 + \lambda \sum_{j=1}^{d} p_{\alpha,\lambda} |\beta_j| \right\}.$$

Here $p_{\alpha,\lambda}(\cdot)$ is the smoothly clipped absolute deviation penalty. The SCAD penalty is a symmetric and quadratic spline on $[0, \infty)$ with knots at λ and $\alpha\lambda$, whose first order derivative is given by

$$p_{\alpha,\lambda}(x) = \lambda \left\{ I(|x| \leq \lambda) + \frac{(\alpha\lambda - |x|)_+}{(\alpha - 1)\lambda} I(|x| > \lambda) \right\}, \quad x \geq 0. \tag{6}$$

Here $\lambda > 0$ and $\alpha > 2$ are the tuning parameters. For $\alpha = \infty$, the expression (6) is equivalent to the L_1 penalty.

2.3. Adaptive Lasso

Zou (2006) modified the Lasso penalty by using adaptive weights on L_1 penalties on the regression coefficients. Such a modified method was referred to as adaptive Lasso. It has been shown theoretically that the adaptive aLasso estimator is able to identify the true model consistently, and the resulting estimator is as efficient as the oracle.

The aLasso $\widehat{\beta}^{\text{aLasso}}$ are obtained by

$$
\widehat{\boldsymbol{\beta}}^{\text{aLasso}} = \arg\min_{\beta} \left\{ \sum_{i=1}^{n} \left(y_i - \beta_0 - \sum_{j=1}^{d} x_{ij}\beta_j \right)^2 \right.
$$
$$
\left. + \lambda \sum_{j=1}^{d} \widehat{w}_j |\beta_j| \right\}, \tag{7}
$$

where the weight function is

$$
\widehat{w}_j = \frac{1}{|\widehat{\beta}_j^*|^\gamma}; \quad \gamma > 0
$$

and $\widehat{\beta}_j^*$ is a root-n consistent estimator of β. Equation (7) is a 'convex optimization problem and its global minimizer can be efficiently solved' (Zou, 2006).

2.4. Minimax concave penalty (MCP)

Zhang (2010) suggested an MCP estimator given by

$$
\widehat{\boldsymbol{\beta}}_n^{\text{MCP}} = \arg\min \left\{ \sum_{i=1}^{n} \left(y_i - \sum_{j=1}^{d} x_{ij}\beta_j \right)^2 + \sum_{j=1}^{d} \rho_\lambda(|\beta_j|, \gamma) \right\},
$$

where $\rho_\lambda(\gamma)$ is the MCP penalty given by

$$
\rho_\lambda(\gamma) = \int_0^t (\lambda - x/\gamma)_+ \, dx,
$$

where $\gamma > 0$ is a regularization parameter.

The above methods have been extensively studied in the literature. A large amount of research is ongoing, and it is hard to keep track of all the interesting work in this area. It has been pointed out in the review literature that penalty estimators are not efficient when the dimension d becomes extremely large compared with the sample size n. There are still challenging problems when d grows at a non-polynomial rate with n. Furthermore, non-polynomial dimensionality poses substantial computational challenges.

However, the main objective of this communication is to improve the estimation accuracy of the active set of the regression parameter by combining an over-fitted model estimator with an under-fitted one. As stated earlier, Lasso produces an over-fitted model as compared with SCAD, aLasso, and other variable selection methods. The Lasso strategy retains some regression coefficients with weak effects as well as some with weak effects in the resulting model. On the other hand, aggressive variable selection strategies may force moderate and effects coefficients towards zero, resulting in under-fitted models with fewer variables having strong effect. The idea here is to combine estimators from an under-fitted model with an over-fitted model using a nonlinear shrinkage technique.

3. Integrating submodels

In this section we show how to combine two submodels produced by two distinct variable selection techniques. The idea is to work with a sparse model that will have all the predictors included, and then to apply two variable selection methods with high and low penalties, respectively. Finally, we combine the estimates from the two models to improve post estimation and prediction performance, respectively.

3.1. Working model

Consider the following high-dimensional sparse regression model with strong and weak-to-moderate signals:

$$
Y = X\beta + \varepsilon, \quad d > n. \tag{8}
$$

Suppose we can divide the index set $\{1, \ldots, d\}$ into three disjoint subsets: S_1, S_2, and S_3. In particular, S_1 includes indexes of non-zero β_i's that are large and comfortably detectable. The set S_2, being the intermediate, includes indexes of those non-zero β_j with weak-to-moderate but non-zero effects. By the assumption of sparsity, S_3 includes indexes with only zero coefficients and can be easily discarded by existing variable selection methods. Thus, S_1 and S_3 are able to be retained and discarded by using existing variable selection techniques, respectively. However, it is possible that S_2 may be covertly included either in S_2 or S_3 depending on existing Lasso-type methods. For the case when S_2 may not be separated from S_3, some work has been done in this area (see Zhang and Zhang [2014] and others). Hansen (2013) has shown using simulation studies that such a Lasso estimate often performs worse than the post selection least squares estimate. To improve the prediction error of a Lasso-type variable selection approach, some (modified) post least squares estimators are studied in Belloni and Chernozhukov (2009) and Liu and Yu (2013).

However, we are interested in cases when covariates in S_1 are kept in the model, and some or all covariates in S_2 are also included in S_1, which may or may not be useful for prediction purposes. It is possible that a particular variable selection strategy may produce an over-fitted model, i.e. retain predictors from S_1 and S_2. On the other hand, other methods may produce an under-fitted model keeping only predictors from S_1. Thus, the predictors in S_2 should be subject to further scrutiny to improve the prediction error.

We partition the design matrix such that $\mathbf{X} = (\mathbf{X}_{S_1}|\mathbf{X}_{S_2}|\mathbf{X}_{S_3})$, Further, $\mathbf{X}_1$ is an $n \times d_1$, $\mathbf{X}_2$ is an $n \times d_2$, and $\mathbf{X}_3$ is an $n \times d_3$ submatrix of predictors, respectively; and $d = d_1 + d_2 + d_3$. Here we make the usual assumptions that $d_1 \leq d_2 < n$ and $d_3 > n$.

Thus, our working model is rewritten as

$$
Y = X_1\beta_1 + X_2\beta_2 + X_3\beta_3 + \varepsilon, \quad d > n, \ d_1 + d_2 < n. \tag{9}
$$

3.2. Over-fitted model

We apply a variable selection method which keeps both strong and weak–moderate signals as follows:

$$
Y = X_1\beta_1 + X_2\beta_2 + \varepsilon, \quad d_1 \leq d_2 < n. \tag{10}
$$

Recall that the Lasso strategy, which usually eliminates the sparse signals and retains weak–moderate and strong signals in the resulting model, may be considered to be an over-fitted model.

3.3. Under-fitted model

Now we apply a variable selection method that keeps only strong signals and eliminates all other signals in the resulting model. Thus we have

$$Y = X_1 \boldsymbol{\beta}_1 + \varepsilon, \quad d_1 < n. \qquad (11)$$

One can use a SCAD or aLasso strategy, which usually retain the strong signals and may produce lower-dimensional models as compared with Lasso. Such a model may be called an under-fitted model.

We are interested in estimating $\boldsymbol{\beta}_1$ when $\boldsymbol{\beta}_2$ may be a null vector, but we are not sure. We suggest a Stein-type shrinkage strategy for estimating $\boldsymbol{\beta}_1$ under this real situation. In essence, we would like to combine the estimates of the over-fitted model with the estimates of an under-fitted model to improve the efficiency of an under-fitted model.

3.4. Integrated estimation strategy

In the sprit of Ahmed (2014), the shrinkage estimator of $\boldsymbol{\beta}_1$ is defined by combining the over-fitted model estimate $\widehat{\boldsymbol{\beta}}_1^{OF}$ with the under-fitted $\widehat{\boldsymbol{\beta}}_1^{UF}$ as follows:

$$\widehat{\boldsymbol{\beta}}_1^S = \widehat{\boldsymbol{\beta}}_1^{UF} + \left(\widehat{\boldsymbol{\beta}}_1^{OF} - \widehat{\boldsymbol{\beta}}_1^{UF}\right)\left[1 - (d_2 - 2)W_n^{-1}\right], \quad d_2 \geq 3,$$

where the weight function W_n is defined by

$$W_n = \frac{n}{\widehat{\sigma}^2}\left(\widehat{\boldsymbol{\beta}}_2^{LSE}\right)'(X'_{S_2}M_1X_{S_2})\widehat{\boldsymbol{\beta}}_2^{LSE},$$

$$M_1 = I_n - X_{S_1}\left(X'_{S_1}X_{S_1}\right)^{-1}X'_{S_1},$$

$$\widehat{\boldsymbol{\beta}}_2^{LSE} = \left(X'_{S_2}M_1X_{S_2}\right)^{-1}X'_{S_2}M_1y,$$

and

$$\widehat{\sigma}^2 = \frac{1}{n-1}\left(y - X_{S_1}\widehat{\boldsymbol{\beta}}_1^{UF}\right)'\left(y - X_{S_1}\widehat{\boldsymbol{\beta}}_1^{UF}\right).$$

The $\widehat{\boldsymbol{\beta}}_1^{UF}$ may be a SCAD or an aLasso estimator, and $\widehat{\boldsymbol{\beta}}_1^{OF}$ is a Lasso estimator.

In an effort to avoid the over-shrinking problem inherited by $\widehat{\boldsymbol{\beta}}_1^S$ we suggest using the positive part of the shrinkage estimator of $\boldsymbol{\beta}_1$ defined by

$$\widehat{\boldsymbol{\beta}}_1^{PS} = \widehat{\boldsymbol{\beta}}_1^{UF} + \left(\widehat{\boldsymbol{\beta}}_1^{OF} - \widehat{\boldsymbol{\beta}}_1^{UF}\right)\left[1 - (d_2 - 2)W_n^{-1}\right]^+.$$

In the following section, we conduct a Monte Carlo simulation study to appraise the performance of the listed estimators.

4. Simulation study

We consider a Monte Carlo simulation, and simulate the response from the following model:

$$y_i = x_{1i}\beta_1 + x_{2i}\beta_2 + \cdots + x_{pi}\beta_d + \varepsilon_i, \quad i = 1, 2, \ldots, n, \quad (12)$$

where ε_i are i.i.d. $N(0,1)$ and $x_{ij} = (\xi^1_{(ij)})^2 + \xi^2_{(ij)}$ with $\xi^1_{(ij)} \sim N(0,1)$ and $\xi^2_{(ij)} \sim N(0,1)$ for all $i = 1, 2, \ldots, n, j = 1, 2, \ldots, d$. We consider the following two situations for simulating the data.

(a) We let

$$\boldsymbol{\beta}_1 = \Big(\underbrace{1, 1, \ldots, 1}_{d_1=5}\Big)', \quad \boldsymbol{\beta}_2 = \Big(\underbrace{\kappa, \kappa, \ldots, \kappa}_{d_2}\Big)'$$

and $\boldsymbol{\beta}_3 = \mathbf{0}'_{d_3}$.

We choose $n = 75, 150, 200$, $d_2 = 45, 95, 145$ and $d_3 = 100, 300, 600$ suitably so that $d_1 + d_2 < n$.

(b) We keep all values the same as in (a) except

$$\boldsymbol{\beta}_1 = \Big(\underbrace{3, 3, \ldots, 3}_{d_1=5}\Big)'.$$

4.1. Model selection

In this subsection, we investigate the performance of Lasso, SCAD, and aLass as variable selection criteria, respectively. For purposes of visualization, we plot these methods with different values of signals in Figures 1, 2, and 3. We use $(n, d_1, d_2, d_3) = (75, 5, 45, 100)$ in the case of $\boldsymbol{\beta}_1 = (1, 1, 1, 1, 1)'$ for the sake of brevity.

The figures show the percentage of predictors selected for each method, respectively. For example, if the percentage of any one predictor is 100, then this predictor is always selected for all simulation steps. Similarly, if the percentage of any one predictor is zero, then this predictor is never selected in the simulation steps. The findings are summarized in Table 1 and Figures 1, 2, and 3.

According to Table 1, if $\kappa = 0.05$, then all three methods always select strong predictors, while Lasso selects more weak variables than SCAD and aLasso; see also Figure 1. On the other hand, for $\kappa = 0.50$, Lasso is more powerful than both SCAD and aLasso with regard to selecting predictors with strong signals, although SCAD and aLasso are also competitive. It can safely be concluded that Lasso selects more predictors than SCAD and aLasso in the presence of weak–moderate signals; see also Figure 2. When $\kappa = 0.90$, Lasso's performance is the best with regard to selecting influential predictors, whereas the performance of SCAD and aLasso is rather poor; we refer the reader to Figure 3.

Based on this limited simulation study, we are inclined to conclude that, in general, Lasso may produce an over-fitted model while SCAD and aLasso may result in an under-fitted model.

In the following subsection we appraise the performance of the proposed estimators based on simulated data.

4.2. Estimated performance

The performance of an estimator is evaluated by using the relative mean squared error (RMSE) criterion. The RMSE of an estimator $\boldsymbol{\beta}_1^*$ with respect to $\widehat{\boldsymbol{\beta}}_1^{OF}$ is defined as follows:

$$\text{RMSE}\left(\boldsymbol{\beta}_1^*\right) = \frac{\text{MSE}\left(\widehat{\boldsymbol{\beta}}_1^{OF}\right)}{\text{MSE}\left(\boldsymbol{\beta}_1^*\right)}, \qquad (13)$$

where $\boldsymbol{\beta}_1^*$ is one of the listed estimators. The results for the simulated RMSEs of the listed estimators are reported in Tables 2 and 3.

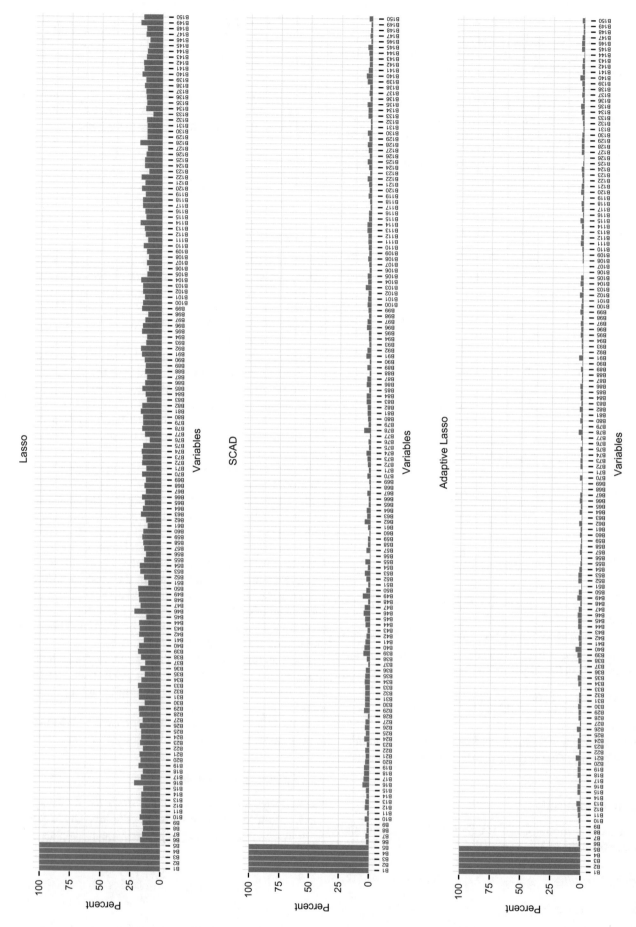

Figure 1. The percentage of times each predictor was selected. $\kappa = 0.05$.

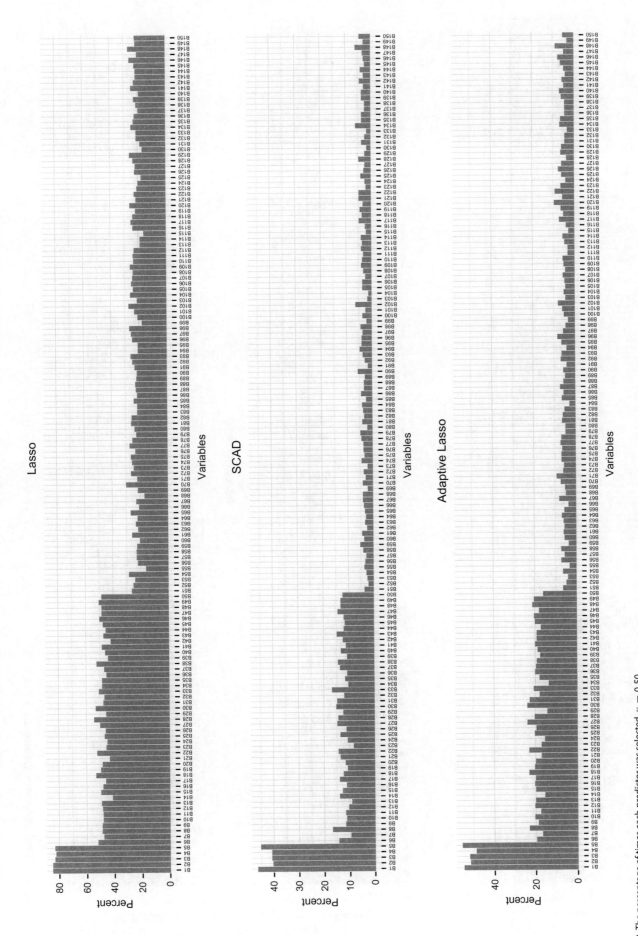

Figure 2. The percentage of times each predictor was selected. $\kappa = 0.50$.

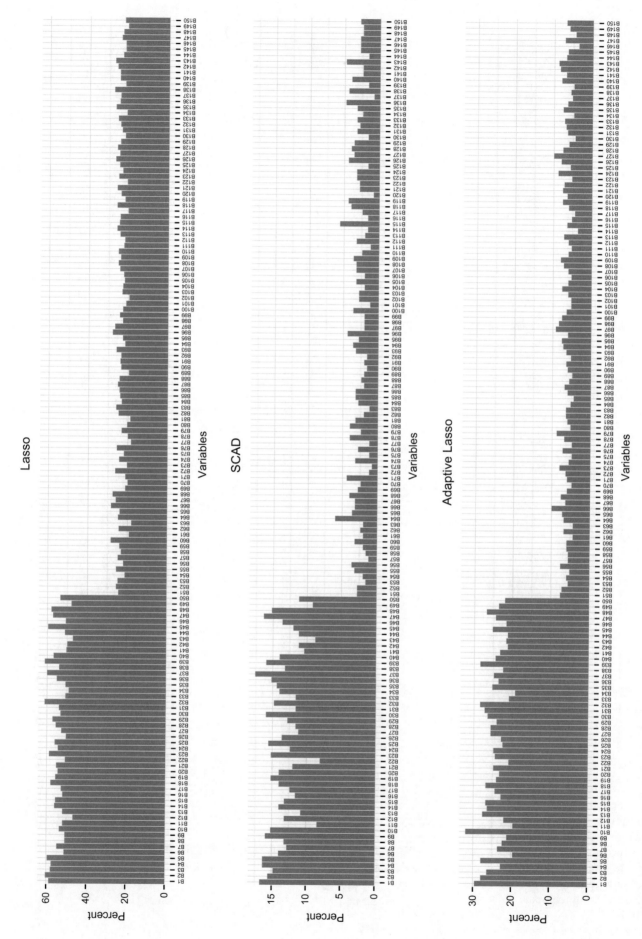

Figure 3. The percentage of times each predictor was selected. $\kappa = 0.90$.

Table 1. The percentage of times each predictor was selected.

	Strong signals			Weak–Moderate and no signal		
κ	Lasso	SCAD	aLasso	Lasso	SCAD	aLasso
0.05	100.00	100.00	100.00	14.84	2.77	1.72
0.50	83.68	42.72	52.56	30.72	6.25	9.88
0.90	58.88	16.00	26.96	33.02	5.94	11.84

Table 2. RMSE of the estimators for case (a).

			Model 1		Model 2	
n	(d_2, d_3)	κ	$\widehat{\beta}_1^{SCAD}$	$\widehat{\beta}_1^{PS}$	$\widehat{\beta}_1^{aLasso}$	$\widehat{\beta}_1^{PS}$
75	(45,100)	0.00	3.516	1.788	3.317	1.613
		0.05	3.035	1.722	3.166	1.610
		0.90	0.643	1.326	0.662	1.266
		0.95	0.584	1.343	0.620	1.273
150	(95,300)	0.00	4.470	1.612	4.839	1.561
		0.05	4.071	1.602	4.171	1.533
		0.90	0.364	1.276	0.374	1.245
		0.95	0.331	1.225	0.346	1.199
200	(145,600)	0.00	4.976	1.513	5.352	1.482
		0.05	4.770	1.477	5.237	1.453
		0.90	0.329	1.212	0.331	1.191
		0.95	0.287	1.181	0.293	1.160

Table 3. RMSE of the estimators for case (b).

			Model 1		Model 2	
n	(d_2, d_3)	κ	$\widehat{\beta}_1^{SCAD}$	$\widehat{\beta}_1^{PS}$	$\widehat{\beta}_1^{aLasso}$	$\widehat{\beta}_1^{PS}$
75	(45,100)	0.00	3.541	1.773	5.833	1.907
		0.05	3.200	1.740	5.456	1.892
		0.90	0.826	1.398	0.790	1.366
		0.95	0.715	1.365	0.695	1.337
150	(95,300)	0.00	1.926	1.391	7.207	1.637
		0.05	1.690	1.336	7.154	1.614
		0.90	0.397	1.240	0.405	1.263
		0.95	0.374	1.231	0.379	1.256
200	(145,600)	0.00	1.711	1.376	7.499	1.573
		0.05	1.612	1.236	7.208	1.552
		0.90	0.324	1.251	0.326	1.244
		0.95	0.300	1.214	0.300	1.207

Table 4. Variable selection and relative prediction error.

		Number of selected predictors			RPE		RPE	
Data	(n, d)	Lasso	SCAD	aLasso	SCAD	Shrinkage	aLasso	Shrinkage
Eye data	(120,200)	25	9	11	0.929	1.009	1.308	1.384
Expression data	(30,403)	30	9	10	0.963	1.009	0.971	1.062

It is important to keep in mind that, for smaller values of κ, we are assuming that the selected under-fitted model is the 'right' one when there are strong signals. It is expected that under these situations both SCAD and aLasso will do better than Lasso and the shrinkage estimator, a performance hard to beat! In these cases, shrinkage estimation by construction will do better than Lasso only. Table 2 clearly reveals this story. On the other hand, in the presence of weak–moderate signals, the relative performance of under-fitted models becomes very poor since RMSE tends to zero. The shrinkage estimator outperforms Lasso for all values of κ and performs better than under-fitted estimators in realistic situations. Both SCAD and aLasso are usually competitive, and we suggest using either of them if the model is truly sparse. The findings from Table 3 are similar. Based on the simulation data, we suggest using the shrinkage estimation strategy, which provides better results when the selected under-fitted submodel may not be the right

one. On the other hand, it will perform better than the over-fitted model. In this sense, the shrinkage strategy combines two models in an optimal way, a winning strategy!

5. Real data analysis

We now consider two real data analyses based on the strategies discussed in this paper.

Eye data

The eye data set of Scheetz et al. (2006) contains gene expression data about mammalian eye tissue samples. The format is a list containing the design matrix, which represents the data about 120 rats with 200 gene probes, and a response vector with 120 dimensions, which represents the expression level of the TRIM32 gene. Thus, for this data set we have $(n, d) =$

(120, 200). Aldahmani and Dai (2015) analysed this data set, applied some penalty estimation procedures, and found that the Lasso method identifies 24 influential predictors.

Expression data

The expression data is obtained from the microarray study of Lu et al. (2004). This data set contains measurements of the gene expression of 403 genes from 30 human brain samples. The response provided is the age of each patient. Thus, we have $(n, d) = (30, 403)$. Zuber & Strimmer (2011) reported that the Lasso method selects 36 predictors.

With real experiments or studies we have no knowledge of d_1, d_2, or d_3 unless the experimenter has some uncertain prior information (UPI) owing to acquaintance with the study. Assuming no UPI is available, we analyse the data by using Lasso, aLasso, and SCAD methods and then we construct the shrinkage estimation strategy. However, to appraise the performance of the listed estimators, we estimate the relative prediction error by using the bootstrap method. To do so, we bootstrap from each of the data sets to estimate the prediction error, respectively. We draw 500 bootstrap samples of size B with replacement from the corresponding data matrix.

The prediction error based on $\boldsymbol{\beta}_\vartheta^*$ is calculated as follows:

$$\text{PE}\left(\boldsymbol{\beta}_\vartheta^*\right) = \frac{1}{500} \sum \left[\boldsymbol{y} - \boldsymbol{X}_\vartheta \boldsymbol{\beta}_\vartheta^{*(i)}\right]' \left[\boldsymbol{y} - \boldsymbol{X}_\vartheta \boldsymbol{\beta}_\vartheta^{*(i)}\right],$$

where the supersript '(i)' indicates that the estimator is at the ith sample of bootstrapping and ϑ is the index of the selected model. Then we calculate the relative PE (RPE) of each estimator with respect to Lasso. Thus, a value of RPE > 1 reflects the superiority of the other methods. We report the values of RPE in Table 4. We also report the the number of variables selected by all three variable selection methods. As expected, Lasso selects more variables as compared to SCAD and aLasso, respectively.

It is evident by the RPE values in Table 4 that the shrinkage estimators are superior for both data sets. Further, aLasso and Lasso perform better than SCAD for the eye data. However, aLasso is superior to Lasso. For the expression data, both SCAD and aLasso are under-performing compared with Lasso.

The results of these data analyses strongly corroborate the findings of the simulation study and suggest using the shrinkage estimation strategy when no UPI is available about the parameter subspace.

6. Conclusion and future outlook

We have investigated the relative performance of a Stein-type shrinkage estimation strategy when submodels are obtained from high-dimensional models. The shrinkage estimator is constructed by combining an over-fitted with an under-fitted model in an optimal way. We have conducted a simulation study to investigate the performance of the suggested shrinkage strategy with respect to three penalty estimators: Lasso, aLasso, and SCAD. The simulation results clearly demonstrate that the shrinkage estimator outshines the over-fitted model estimator, and behaves well when compared with the under-fitted model estimators. We analysed two high-dimensional data sets, and the performance of the shrinkage strategy is striking.

For future work, one may consider the pretest estimation strategy for big data analysis. Using some other weight function to improve the performance of the shrinkage estimator would be a good extension to current work. Further, some theoretical justifications would be useful. In a future study it would be interesting to include penalty estimators that correspond to Bayes procedures based on priors with polynomial tails.

Acknowledgements

We would like to thank Editor in Chief Professor Jiuping Xu and Managing Editor Dr Zongmin Li for their suggestions and encouragement regarding this paper.

Disclosure statement

No potential conflict of interest was reported by the authors.

Funding

The research of the first author, S. Ejaz Ahmed, is supported by the Natural Sciences and Engineering Research Council of Canada (NSERC).

References

Ahmed, S. E. (2014). *Penalty, shrinkage and pretest strategies: Variable selection and estimation.* New York: Springer.

Ahmed, S. E., Doksum, K. A., Hossain, S., & You, J. (2007). Shrinkage, pretest and absolute penalty estimators in partially linear models. *Australian & New Zealand Journal of Statistics, 49*, 435–454.

Ahmed, S. E., Hossain, S., & Doksum, K. A. (2012). LASSO and shrinkage estimation in Weibull censored regression models. *Journal of Statistical Planning and Inference, 142*(6), 1273–1284. Retrieved from http://dx. doi.org/10.1016/j.jspi.2011.12.027

Aldahmani, S., & Dai, H. (2015). Unbiased estimation for linear regression when *nv. International Journal of Statistics and Probability, 4*(3), 61–73 .Retrieved from http://dx.doi.org/10.5539/ijsp.v4n3p61

Armagan, A., Dunson, D. B., & Lee, J. (2013). Generalized double Pareto shrinkage. *Statistica Sinica, 23*(1), 119.

Bhattacharya, A., Pati, D., Pillai, N. S., & Dunson, D. B. (2012). Bayesian shrinkage. arXiv preprint arXiv:1212.6088 Retrieved from http://arxiv. org/abs/1212.6088

Bickel, P. J., Ritov, Y., & Tsybakov, A. B. (2009). Simultaneous analysis of Lasso and Dantzig selector. *Annals of Statistics, 37*, 1705–1732. Retrieved from http://dx.doi.org/10.1214/08-AOS620

Carvalho, C. M., Polson, N. G., & Scott, J. G. (2010). The horseshoe estimator for sparse signals. *Biometrika, 97*, 465–480.

Efron, B., Hastie, T., Johnstone, I., & Tibshirani, R. (2004). Least angle regression. *Annals of Statistics, 32*(2), 407–499.

Fan, J. & Li, R. (2001). Variable selection via nonconcave penalized likelihood and its oracle properties. *Journal of the American Statistical Association, 96*(456), 1348–1360.

Frank, I., & Friedman, J. (1993). A statistical view of some chemometrics regression tools (with discussion). *Technometrics, 35*, 109–148.

Hansen, B. E. (2013). The risk of James-Stein and lasso shrinkage. Retrieved from http://www.ssc.wisc.edu/~bhansen/papers/lasso.pdf

Huang, J. & Ma, S. (2008). Adaptive Lasso for sparse high-dimensional regression models. *Statistica Sinica*, 1603–1618.

Kim, Y., Choi, H., & Oh, H. S. (2008). Smoothly clipped absolute deviation on high dimensions. *Journal of the American Statistical Association, 103*(484), 1665–1673.

Leng, C., Lin, Y., & Wahba, G. (2006). A note on the Lasso and related procedures in model selection. *Statistica Sinica, 16*, 1273–1284. Retrieved from http://www3.stat.sinica.edu.tw/statistica/oldpdf/A16n410.pdf

Lu, T., Pan, Y., Kao, S. Y., Li, C., Kohane, I., Chan, J., & Yankner, B. A. (2004). Gene regulation and DNA damage in the ageing human brain. *Nature, 429*(6994), 883–891.

Scheetz, T. E., Kim, K. Y. A., Swiderski, R. E., Philp, A. R., Braun, T. A., Knudtson, K. L., ...Sheffield, V. C. (2006). Regulation of gene expression in the mammalian eye and its relevance to eye disease.

Proceedings of the National Academy of Sciences, 103(39), 14429–14434.

Schelldorfer, J., Bühlmann, P., & van de Geer, S. (2011). Estimation for high dimensional linear mixed effects models using l_1-penalization. *Scandinavian Journal of Statistics, 38*(2), 197–214. Retrieved from http://dx.doi.org/10.1111/j.1467-9469.2011.00740.x

Tibshirani, R. (1996). Regression shrinkage and selection via the Lasso. *Journal of the Royal Statistical Society. Series B (Methodological), 58*(1), 267–288. Retrieved from http://statweb.stanford.edu/~tibs/lasso/lasso.pdf

Tibshirani, R., Saunders, M., Rosset, S., Zhu, J., & Knight, K. (2005). Sparsity and smoothness via the fused lasso. *Journal of the Royal Statistical Society: Series B (Statistical Methodology), 67*(1), 91–108. Retrieved from http://dept.stat.lsa.umich.edu/~jizhu/pubs/Tibs-JRSSB05.pdf

Tran, M. N. (2011). The loss rank criterion for variable selection in linear regression analysis. *Scandinavian Journal of Statistics, 38*(3), 466–479.

Wang, H., & Leng, C. (2007). Unified LASSO estimation by least squares approximation. *Journal of the American Statistical Association, 102*(479), 1039–1048. Retrieved from http://dx.doi.org/10.1198/016214507000000509

Yuan, M., & Lin, Y. (2006). Model selection and estimation in regression with grouped variables. *Journal of the Royal Statistical Society: Series B (Statistical Methodology), 68*(1), 49–67.

Zhang, C. H. (2010). Nearly unbiased variable selection under minimax concave penalty. *Annals of Statistics, 38*, 894–942.

Zhang, C. H., & Zhang, S. S. (2014). Confidence intervals for low-dimensional parameters in high-dimensional linear models. *Annals of Statistics, 76*, 217–242.

Zhao, P., & Yu, B. (2006). On model selection consistency of Lasso. *Journal of Machine Learning Research, 7*, 2541–2563.

Zou, H. (2006). The adaptive lasso and its oracle properties. *Journal of the American Statistical Association, 101*(476), 1418–1429. Retrieved from http://dx.doi.org/10.1198/016214506000000735

Zuber, V., & Strimmer, K. (2011). High-dimensional regression and variable selection using CAR scores. *Statistical Applications in Genetics and Molecular Biology, 10*(1), Article 34, 27pp. Retrieved from http://dx.doi.org/10.2202/1544-6115.1730

Seeking relationships in big data: a Bayesian perspective

Nozer D. Singpurwalla

ABSTRACT

The real purpose of collecting big data is to identify causality in the hope that this will facilitate credible predictivity. But the search for causality can trap one into infinite regress, and thus one takes refuge in seeking associations between variables in data sets. Regrettably, the mere knowledge of associations does not enable predictivity. Associations need to be embedded within the framework of the probability calculus to make coherent predictions. This is so because associations are a feature of probability models, and hence they do not exist outside the framework of a model. Measures of association, like correlation, regression, and mutual information merely refute a preconceived model. Estimated measures of associations do not lead to a probability model; a model is the product of pure thought. This paper discusses these and other fundamentals that are germane to seeking associations in particular, and machine learning in general.

0. Preamble: motivation and viewpoint

The impetus for writing this paper is an article in *Science* by Reshef, Reshef, Finucane, Grossman, McVean, & Sabeti (2011), and the strong reaction that it has spawned by Kinney and Atwal (2014) in *The Proceedings of the National Academy of Sciences*. Given the high visibility that these outlets are endowed with, some discussion clarifying the foundational issues that underlie the said writings seems germane. Both articles pertain to the quantification of the strength of 'association' between variables in large data sets. Whereas the term association has a precise mathematical meaning in the context of probability theory (cf. Esary, Proschan & Walkup, 1967), its use here is colloquial and alludes to dependence. The focus of both articles is a heuristic notion called *equitability*. The former uses Pearson's *correlation* as its core; the latter Shannon's *mutual information*. Whereas the need for pursuing equitability needs to be made more convincing, at least to this author, a closer reading of these articles underscores the importance of fundamentals when discussing associations. The purpose of this paper is to articulate the philosophical and mathematical underpinnings of the notion of dependence; what does it mean to assess it, how best to assess it, and how best to exploit it? The hope is that doing so will make the debates and discussions about seeking relationships in data sets less volatile.

With the above in mind, it is best to present at the outset the seven assertions listed below; these outline the position/viewpoint of this author. This viewpoint is a consequence of a personalistic interpretation of probability in the sense of de Finetti (1938) and Savage (1972).

(1) All probability models are subjectively specified, and they reflect one's disposition to uncertainty, as exemplified by one's attitude to a two-sided bet.

(2) Dependence and association are properties of a probability model, and since probability models are subjectively specified, dependence and associations are judgements.

(3) Observed data can only refute a model; they can never endorse it for perpetuity. In practice one behaves as if the model at hand is the best one to use, until new evidence falsifies it. To quote George Box (1976), 'all models are wrong but some are useful'. Thus any model is waiting to be falsified, and observed data is the main falsifier (cf. Popper, 2014).

(4) Assertions (2) and (3) imply that since dependence and association do not exist outside the framework of a model, seeking associations in the absence of any preconceived notion by merely looking at data is philosophically not tenable.

This means that, when one looks for correlations in data sets, one has at the back of one's mind a linear relationship. Similarly with regression, either a linear or nonlinear relationship lurks in the mind. This viewpoint carries forward when one assesses mutual information, because to do so one needs to estimate a joint density with the histogram as a starting point, and the preconceived notion underlying a histogram is a bivariate uniform distribution.

(5) Like dependence, independence is also a judgment; it implies an absence of learning or the failure of memory. Its mathematical construction entails a hierarchy of assumptions, and these can result in the form of an infinite regress.

(6) Unlike correlation and regression, which encapsulate specific forms of linear and nonlinear relationships, the notion of mutual information is an omnibus measure which can only assert the presence or the absence of an association.

(7) The mere act of seeking relationships in data sets is a limited exercise. In actuality what is needed is predictivity. But prediction needs to be probabilistic, and to

do so one needs to embed all associations within the framework of the probability calculus. This is discussed in Section 4.

Finally, in the context of the topic of this paper on seeking associations, there is one other caveat; it is also discussed in Section 4. Specifically, when assessing dependence using regression based methods, it matters whether the values of the dependent variables are pre-selected, or observed retrospectively.

1. Dependence: a feature of joint distributions

The notions of causality, correlation, information, and regression, play a prominent role in statistics. Their precise definitions are cast in the language of probability. With the advent of big data and machine learning, these notions have gained added prominence. Seeking patterns within variables, and relationships between variables, has now become a full time occupation for some. Whereas pinpointing causality is the holy grail which drives the collection of big data, many have taken heed of the dictum that 'correlation is not causation'. Indeed, causation is an elusive notion that has proven to be a challenge, not only to statisticians, but also to philosophers of science. Yet when one speaks of gaining knowledge from big data sets, one has at the back of one's mind the identification of a *genuine cause* (see Suppes, 1970) that spawns the data. But since the search for a genuine cause can also trigger the problem of an infinite regress, one tends to take refuge in the next best thing, namely an empirical assessment of measures of dependence, like correlation. Because all measures of dependence are properties of a joint probability model, it behooves one to ask: what is a probability model, and where does it come from? This is the topic of the next section.

2. The genesis of a probability model

At some reference time $\tau \geq 0$, consider an analyst ♀ who assesses her uncertainty about an unknown quantity X in light of all the historical information $\mathcal{H}$ that ♀ has at τ, via probability. That is, ♀ needs to specify

$$P_{\female}^{\tau}(X \geq x; \mathcal{H}).$$

Since the dimension of $\mathcal{H}$ is large, conceptually infinite, ♀ seeks simplification by introducing a quantity θ (whose interpretation is given later), and invoking the law of total probability to write

$$P_{\female}^{\tau}(X \geq x; \mathcal{H}) = \int_{\theta} P_{\female}^{\tau}(X \geq x|\theta; \mathcal{H})P_{\female}^{\tau}(\theta; \mathcal{H})\, d\theta,$$

where $P_{\female}^{\tau}(\theta; \mathcal{H})$ encapsulates ♀'s uncertainty about θ in light of $\mathcal{H}$, at time τ. It is called a *prior* for θ. Were ♀ to assume that, given θ, the event $(X \geq x)$ is *independent* of $\mathcal{H}$, then $P_{\female}^{\tau}(X \geq x|\theta; \mathcal{H}) = P_{\female}^{\tau}(X \geq x|\theta)$, and now

$$P_{\female}^{\tau}(X \geq x; \mathcal{H}) = \int_{\theta} P_{\female}^{\tau}(X \geq x|\theta)P_{\female}^{\tau}(\theta; \mathcal{H})\, d\theta.$$

The quantity $P_{\female}^{\tau}(X \geq x|\theta)$ is called a *probability model* for the event $(X \geq x)$, and θ is called the *parameter* of the probability model. The quantity $P_{\female}^{\tau}(X \geq x; \mathcal{H})$ is called the *predictive*

distribution of X, and one endeavours to provide predictive distributions that are trustworthy. To do so, one's choice for a probability model and the prior need to be judicious and meaningful. The notion of independence is articulated above. Note that independence has been defined in the framework of probability. More often than not, independence is conditional; in the above case, $(X \geq x)$ is independent of $\mathcal{H}$, conditional on θ (i.e., were θ to be known).

The parameter θ can be a scalar or a vector whose dimension needs to be much smaller than that of $\mathcal{H}$; otherwise the parameter does not serve a useful purpose. This is because the role of the parameter has been to compress the information about $(X \geq x)$ contained in $\mathcal{H}$. Indeed $\mathcal{H}$ can comprise both qualitative and quantitative information, like previously observed data on $(X \geq x)$.

Thus parameters in probability models can be seen as devices which compress the high dimensional $\mathcal{H}$ to a lower dimensional θ. de Finetti referred to θ merely as a Greek symbol; i.e. an abstract entity which need not have an observable reality. Its role is to impart independence between $\mathcal{H}$ and the event $(X \geq x)$, and also as a device which facilitates the prediction of observables, like X. There are other interpretations of θ, but for now it suffices to say that a statistician's approach to *data compression* is through the introduction of Greek symbols called parameters.

Some of the well-known examples of probability models are the exponential, wherein

$$P_{\female}^{\tau}(X \geq x|\lambda) = \lambda \exp(-\lambda x), \text{ for } \lambda > 0 \text{ and } x \geq 0,$$

and the Weibull, wherein

$$P_{\female}^{\tau}(X \geq x|\lambda, \beta) = \exp(-\lambda x^{\beta}), \text{ for } \lambda, \beta > 0 \text{ and } x \geq 0.$$

In the first case, $\theta = \lambda$ is a scalar, and in the second case, $\theta = (\lambda, \beta)$ is a vector. The best-known and the most commonly used example of a probability model is the normal (or Gaussian), wherein for $\theta = (\mu, \sigma^2)$, with $-\infty < \mu < +\infty$, and $\sigma > 0$

$$P_{\female}^{\tau}(X \geq x|\mu, \sigma) = \int_{-\infty}^{x} \frac{1}{\sqrt{2\pi}\sigma} e^{-[(x-\mu)/\sigma]^2/2}\, dx,$$
$$\times \text{ for } -\infty < x < +\infty.$$

In the context of large data sets, interest is focused on two or more unknown quantities and the relationships between them. For purposes of discussion, consider two unknowns, say X and Y, and their predictive distribution $P_{\female}^{\tau}(X \geq x, Y \geq y; \mathcal{H})$. As before, $\mathcal{H}$ is the historical (or background) information about X and Y possessed by ♀ at time $\tau \geq 0$. Here again, ♀ may choose to introduce a parameter θ, invoke the law of total probability, assume independence of the event $(X \geq x, Y \geq y)$ and $\mathcal{H}$, given θ, and write

$$P_{\female}^{\tau}(X \geq x, Y \geq y|\mathcal{H})$$
$$= \int_{\theta} P_{\female}^{\tau}(X \geq x, Y \geq y|\theta)P_{\female}^{\tau}(\theta; \mathcal{H})\, d\theta. \quad (2.0)$$

The quantity $P_{\female}^{\tau}(X \geq x, Y \geq y|\theta)$ is the joint (bivariate) probability model for the compound event $(X \geq x, Y \geq y)$. Note that whereas the event $(X \geq x, Y \geq y)$ has been judged independent of $\mathcal{H}$ conditional on θ, nothing has yet been said about the dependence or independence of the events $(X \geq x)$ and $(Y \geq y)$. Clearly, whenever $(X \geq x)$ and $(Y \geq y)$ share a θ (or a sub-set of θ), and θ is unknown, they will be unconditionally (in terms of θ) dependent. This form of dependence is called *dependence by mixture*. However, conditional on θ, the events $(X \geq x)$ and $(Y \geq y)$ could be dependent or independent depending on ♀'s judgment. For example, if ♀ judges the events $(X \geq x)$ and $(Y \geq y)$ conditionally (given θ) independent, then the bivariate probability model is

$$P_{\female}^{\tau}(X \geq x, Y \geq y|\theta) = P_{\female}^{\tau}(X \geq x|\theta)P_{\female}^{\tau}(Y \geq y|\theta),$$

where each term on the right is a univariate probability model. If the above judgment of conditional independence is not tenable, then ♀ is faced with the task of specifying a probability model for X and Y which encapsulates dependence. An example is the bivariate exponential distribution of Gumbel wherein, for some $\theta = \sigma, \sigma \in [0, 1]$, and $x, y \geq 0$,

$$P_{\female}^{\tau}(X \geq x, Y \geq y|\theta = \sigma) = e^{-(x+y+\sigma x \cdot y)}. \quad (2.1)$$

Here, the marginals are $P_{\female}^{\tau}(X \geq x|\sigma) = e^{(-x)}$ and $P_{\female}^{\tau}(Y \geq y|\sigma) = e^{(-y)}$, implying that the dependency parameter σ has no role to play with respect to the marginals. Note that when σ is assumed known, and is zero, then the events $(X \geq x)$ and $(Y \geq y)$ are independent; with σ unspecified, they are dependent.

The best-known and the most discussed example of a bivariate probability model is the bivariate normal, with $\theta = (\mu_1, \mu_2, \sigma_1, \sigma_2, \rho)$. Here,

$$P_{\female}^{\tau}(X \geq x, Y \geq y|\theta) = \int_{-\infty}^{x} \int_{-\infty}^{y} f(x, y|\theta) \, dx \, dy,$$

where

$$f(x, y|\theta) = \frac{1}{2\pi \sigma_1 \sigma_2 \sqrt{1 - \rho^2}} \exp \left\{ -\frac{1}{2(1-\rho^2)} \left[\left(\frac{x - \mu_1}{\sigma_1} \right)^2 \right. \right.$$
$$\left. \left. + \left(\frac{y - \mu_2}{\sigma_2} \right)^2 - \frac{2\rho(x - \mu_1)(y - \mu_2)}{\sigma_1 \sigma_2} \right] \right\}. \quad (2.2)$$

3. Measures of association

As mentioned, dependence is a feature of a joint probability distribution, and for purposes of discussion we will centre discussion on the bivariate normal and the bivariate Gumbel distributions. For the former, its $f(x, y|\theta)$ is given by Equation (2.2). For the latter, an analogue of $f(x, y|\theta)$ is the probability density generated by Equation (2.1).

There are several attractive features of the model of Equation (2.2), two of which are closure under marginalization and closure under conditionalization. That is, the marginal of X is also a normal with the parameters μ_1 and σ_1. That is,

$$f(x|\theta) = \frac{1}{\sqrt{2\pi}\sigma_1} \exp \left\{ -\frac{1}{2} \left(\frac{x - \mu_1}{\sigma_1} \right)^2 \right\}, \quad -\infty < x < +\infty,$$

and the conditional of Y given $X = x$ is also a normal, with the parameters $\mu_2 + \rho(\sigma_2/\sigma_1)(x - \mu_1)$ and $\sigma_2^2(1 - \rho^2)$.

Indeed, there are many families of bivariate distributions each possessing its own version of $f(x, y|\theta)$, so the discussion that follows is generic, and is in terms of $f(x, y|\theta)$.

The most commonly used measure of dependence is the Galton–Pearson coefficient of correlation, $\rho(x, y)$. With $f(x, y|\theta)$ specified, $\rho(x, y)$ can always be obtained mathematically. Irrespective of what $f(x, y|\theta)$ is, $|\rho(X, Y)| \leq 1$, and this is its attractive feature. Furthermore, when X and Y are independent, $\rho(X, Y) = 0$. However, $\rho(X, Y) = 0$ does not imply that X and Y are necessarily independent, and this is one of its limitations. An exception is the bivariate normal, for which $\rho(X, Y) = \rho$ of Equation (2.2), and here $\rho = 0$, implies that X and Y are independent. Another limitation of $\rho(X, Y)$ is that it only encapsulates the extent of linear relationship between X and Y. This becomes transparent when one looks at the definition of $\rho(X, Y)$, namely that $\rho(X, Y) \stackrel{\text{def}}{=} \text{Cov}(X, Y)/\sqrt{V(X)V(Y)}$, where $\text{Cov}(X, Y) = \mathscr{E}(X \cdot Y) - \mathscr{E}(X) \cdot \mathscr{E}(Y)$, and $\mathscr{E}$ denotes expectation. The variance of X is $V(X) = \text{Cov}(X, X)$. These properties boil down to the feature that the best-known and commonly used measure of dependence (or association), namely the correlation, is limited in scope. Thus, alternatives to correlation have been considered. Some of these are Kendall's Tau (Kendall, 1938), Spearman's Rho (Spearman, 1904), and the several non-parametric measures of dependence introduced by Lehmann (1966), and further articulated by Barlow and Proschan (1981). We do not pursue these alternatives here.

After correlation, the next best-known measure of a relationship is regression. Specifically, the *regression* of Y on X is $\mathscr{E}(Y|X = x, \theta)$; similarly, $\mathscr{E}(X|Y = y, \theta)$. The regression of Y on X can take several forms, such as *linear* wherein $\mathscr{E}(Y|X = x, \theta) = \alpha + \beta x$ with $\theta = (\alpha, \beta)$, *quadratic* wherein $\mathscr{E}(Y|X = x, \theta) = \alpha + \beta x + \gamma x^2$ with $\theta = (\alpha, \beta, \gamma)$, *cubic*, and so on. Like correlation $\rho(X, Y)$, regression can also be computed theoretically, once $f(x, y|\theta)$ is specified. Thus regression can encapsulate a variety of linear and nonlinear relationships, and is one step up the ladder from correlation for describing relationships.

In the case of the bivariate normal distribution, the regression of Y on X takes the linear form

$$\mathscr{E}(Y|X = x, \theta) = \mu_2 + \rho \left(\frac{\sigma_2}{\sigma_1} \right) (x - \mu_1) \quad (3.1)$$

with $V(Y|X = x, \theta) = \sigma_2^2(1 - \rho^2)$. This means that the average value of Y increases (decreases) linearly in x, depending on whether ρ is $> (<) 0$. Clearly, in the case of the bivariate normal distribution, regression provides little added insight about the relationship between X and Y beyond that which is provided by the correlation ρ. The one interesting feature here is that $V(Y|X = x)$ is independent of x. It is this property which makes the bivariate normal distribution attractive in the context of the standard Kalman filter (cf. Meinhold and Singpurwalla, 1983).

With the bivariate exponential of Gumbel, the regression of Y on X, $\mathscr{E}(Y|X = x, \theta) = (1 + \sigma + \sigma x)/(1 + \sigma x)^2$, which for $\sigma > 0$ is a gracefully decreasing function of x, starting from $(1 + \sigma)$ and tailing off to 0 as x goes to $+\infty$. Here the correlation $\rho(X, Y) < 0$, and depending on the values of the dependency parameter σ, it ranges from $-.4036$ to 0. Here, the regression provides more insight about the relationship between X and Y than the correlation. A similar feature is also exhibited by other bivariate distributions, like the bivariate

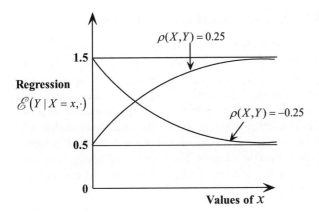

Figure 1. Regression for Gumbel's distribution for positive and negative correlations.

γ is related to the Pearson correlation via the relationship

$$\rho(X, Y) = \sqrt{1 - e^{-2\gamma}}.$$

In general, irrespective of what $f(x, y|\theta)$ is, the quantity $\sqrt{1 - e^{-2\gamma}}$ lies between 0 and 1, and takes the value 0 when X and Y are independent. It takes the value 1 whenever X can be uniquely determined by Y and vice versa. Linfoot (1957) refers to $\sqrt{1 - e^{-2\gamma}}$ as the *informational coefficient of correlation*, and besides the fact that its special case is Pearson's correlation, it has the virtue of invariance. In other words $\sqrt{1 - e^{-2\gamma}}$ does not change if X is replaced by $X' = \varphi_1(X)$ and Y replaced by $\varphi_2(Y)$, for any φ_1 and φ_2. The measure γ is also known as *mutual information*; its invariance was pointed out by Jeffreys (1946).

3.1. Association measures provide insight about models

Assertion (7) of Section 0 makes the claim that the mere act of seeking relationships in data sets is of limited value. Limited, because a knowledge of associations can only provide insight about the nature of a joint distribution that may be entertained. Without further analyses and development, associations on their own do not enable predictivity. Of the three measures of dependence discussed before, correlation is the easiest estimate. Its value indicates the extent to which the two variables in question bear a linear relationship to each other. On its own, correlation does not provide a mechanism for predicting the value of one variable, say Y, knowing the value of X. Mutual information is probably the most difficult measure to compute because it entails the estimation of joint and marginal densities. But, having computed mutual information, all we know is whether underlying variables are dependent or not. Even if mutual information computed from data supports the hypothesis of dependence, one is unable to predict Y knowing a value of X, and vice versa. This suggests that both correlation and mutual information should be viewed as qualitative measures of dependence. Neither can help pinpoint a joint probability model; thus, the main purpose served by these measures is to refute (or not) a contemplated model.

Matters become more attractive when it comes to regression. First, like correlation (but unlike mutual information), regression is easy to estimate. Second, the functional form of regression can provide insight about the joint probability model to entertain. For example, a bivariate normal if the regression is linear, a bivariate Gumbel if it is exponential, and so on. Furthermore, the regression function can serve as a device – albeit naive – for prediction as well. It therefore appears that, when seeking relationships in large data sets, it may be more fruitful to pursue the regression function as opposed to correlation or mutual information.

exponential of Marshall and Olkin (1967) and a second version of Gumbel's bivariate exponential distribution. The specifics about these distributions can be found in Singpurwalla (2006, pp. 89–93).

In the case of Marshall and Olkin's bivariate exponential distribution, when the correlation $\rho(X, Y) = 1/3$, $\mathscr{E}(Y|X = x, \cdot) = 1 - (3/4)e^{-x}$, suggesting that the regression is an exponentially increasing function of x, starting from $1/4$ and tapering off at 1. In the case of the second version of Gumbel's bivariate exponential distribution, when $\rho(X, Y) = 1/4$, the regression of Y on X, when $X = x$, is $(3/2) - e^{-x}$. This is an exponentially increasing function starting from $1/2$ and tapering off at $3/2$. When $\rho(X, Y) = -1/4$, the said regression is $(1/2) + e^{-x}$, which is an exponentially decreasing function starting at $3/2$, and tapering off at $1/2$; see Figure 1.

Moving up the ladder for describing relationships are the distance based measures, of which Shannon's *mutual information* is the best known. A more recent entry in this category is the work of Székely and Rizzo (2009). Mutual information provides a measure of dependence without specifying its nature. It can be interpreted as the gain in information in going from independence to dependence. Since independence suggests an absence of learning, dependence implies knowledge. Consequently, if the notion of information can be quantified, then the difference between information under dependence and information under independence is the gain in knowledge. The quantification of information is due to the work of Shannon (1948). With $f(x, y|\theta)$ specified, and the marginals $f(x|\theta)$ and $f(y|\theta)$ known, Shannon's measure of information leads to the result that the gain in information (knowledge), say γ, is given by the expression

$$\gamma = \int\limits_{x,y} \{ f(x, y|\theta) \log f(x, y|\theta)$$
$$- f(x|\theta)f(y|\theta) \log \left[f(x|\theta)f(y|\theta) \right] \} \, dx dy.$$

Thus γ is the amount of information conveyed to an individual who previously supposed X and Y to be independent by the statement that the joint probability of X and Y is $f(x, y|\theta)$. It may of interest to note that γ provided Kullback and Leibler (1951) with a motivation for defining their famous measure of discrepancy or divergence between two distributions.

On its own, γ is a satisfactory measure of dependence which can be computed once $f(x, y|\theta)$ is specified. However, under certain circumstances, in particular those pertaining to the form of $f(x, y|\theta)$, it can be shown (cf. Linfoot, 1957), that

4. Inference and predictivity

For purposes of discussion, we focus attention on the bivariate case with the bivariate normal as the underlying model. In the absence of any observed data on X and Y, predictivity is achieved via Equation (2.0), once the model and the prior are specified. In the bivariate normal case, $\theta = (\mu_1, \mu_2, \rho, \sigma_1, \sigma^2)$, so that the simultaneous prediction of X and Y is

$$P_{\male\female}^{\tau}(X \geq x, Y \geq y | \mathscr{H}) = \int\limits_{\theta} f(x, y|\theta) P_{\male\female}^{\tau}(\theta; \mathscr{H}) \, d\theta, \quad (4.1)$$

where $f(x, y|\theta)$ is prescribed by Equation (2.2). There are two challenges to implementing Equation (4.1). One is a specification of the prior $P_{\ominus}^{\tau}(\theta; \mathscr{H})$; the second is computing, which entails integration in five dimensions. Given the conceptual character of this paper, neither of these 'operational' matters is discussed.

Data on the variables X and Y can arise under two scenarios, each calling for its own approach to predictivity. We label the two scenarios as *retrospective* and *designed*. Under the former scenario, one obtains n pairs of observations $(x_1, y_1), \ldots, (x_n, y_n)$ as the realizations of two random variables X and Y. This is the kind of data that arises in large data sets. Under the designed scenario, one fixes X at say x_i^* and observes the Y corresponding to x_i^* as y_i, $i = 1, \ldots, n$. Here y_i is the realization of a random variable, whereas x_i^* is not. To summarize, (x_i, y_i), $i = 1, \ldots, n$, is a realization of a random variable (X, Y), whereas with (x_i^*, y_i) it is only y_i that is the realization of a random variable Y when X is set at x_i^*.

Given the data $\underset{\sim}{d} : [(x_1, y_1), \ldots, (x_n, y_n)]$, the posterior distribution of θ is obtained, via the Bayes law, as the proportionality relationship

$$P_{\ominus}^{\tau}(\theta; \underset{\sim}{d}) \propto P_{\ominus}^{\tau}(\theta; \mathscr{H}) \mathscr{L}(\theta; \underset{\sim}{d}),$$

where the likelihood $\mathscr{L}(\theta; \underset{\sim}{d})$, based on Equation (2.2), is

$$\prod_{i=1}^{n} \frac{1}{2\pi\sigma_1\sigma_2\sqrt{1-\rho^2}} \exp\left\{ -\frac{1}{2(1-\rho^2)} \left[\left(\frac{x_i - \mu_1}{\sigma_1}\right)^2 + \left(\frac{y_i - \mu_2}{\sigma_2}\right)^2 - \frac{2\rho(x_i - \mu_1)(y_i - \mu_2)}{\sigma_1\sigma_2} \right] \right\}.$$

With the above in place, the predictive distribution is

$$P_{\ominus}^{\tau}(X \geq x, Y \geq y; \underset{\sim}{d}, \mathscr{H})$$
$$\propto \int_{-\infty}^{x} \int_{-\infty}^{y} \int_{\theta} f(x, y|\theta) P_{\ominus}^{\tau}(\theta; \underset{\sim}{d}) \, d\theta dy dx. \quad (4.2)$$

Continuing in this vein, i.e. with $\underset{\sim}{d}$ at hand, suppose that one wishes to predict Y *conditional* on observing $X = x_{n+1}$, say. That is, one wishes to assess $P_{\ominus}^{\tau}(Y > y|X = x_{n+1}; \underset{\sim}{d}, \mathscr{H})$; this is proportional to

$$\int_{-\infty}^{y} \int_{\theta} f(y|X = x_{n+1}, \theta) P_{\ominus}^{\tau}(\theta; \underset{\sim}{d}) \, d\theta dy,$$

where

$$f(y|X = x_{n+1}, \theta) = \frac{1}{\sigma_2\sqrt{2\pi(1-\rho^2)}}$$
$$\times \exp\left\{ -\frac{1}{2} \left(\frac{y - \mu_2 - \rho\frac{\sigma_2}{\sigma_1}(x_{n+1} - \mu_1)}{\sigma_2\sqrt{(1-\rho^2)}} \right)^2 \right\}.$$

Note that, in the above assessment, X has not been observed as x_{n+1}; rather, it is in the subjunctive mood, meaning 'were X to be observed as x_{n+1}'.

4.1. The scenario leading to linear models

This sub-section pertains to predictivity when X is not random and its value is predetermined. Here $\underset{\sim}{d}^* = [(x_1^*, y_1), (x_2^*, y_2), \ldots, (x_n^*, y_n)]$, and one is interested in predictions about Y when X is set at x_{n+1}^*. To do so, one needs a probability model for Y, with $X = x^*$ acting as a parameter of the model. One possibility would be to consider a family of models called *linear models*, and studied under the (incorrectly) labelled term *regression analysis*. The scenario of having d^* at hand arises in the context of designed or (laboratory) controlled experiments.

We start with the question, what is it that motivates the development of linear models and why the term regression analysis? In other words, what is the genesis of linear models? Our answer to this question is suggested by two features. One is Equation (3.1) pertaining to $\mathscr{E}(Y|X = x, \theta)$, the regression of Y on X. The other is the elementary fact that any random variable Y can be written as the sum of its expectation (assuming that it is finite) and an error whose expectation is 0. That is

$$Y = \mathscr{E}(Y) + \epsilon,$$

where ϵ is the error. Conditioning on $X = x$, we have

$$(Y|X = x) = \mathscr{E}(Y|X = x) + (\epsilon|X = x). \quad (4.3)$$

In the case of the bivariate normal with $\mu_1 = 0$ and $\sigma_1^2 = 1$, $\mathscr{E}(Y|X = x) = \mu_2 + \sigma_2\rho x$, and $V(Y|X = x) = \sigma_2^2\sqrt{1-\rho^2}$. Thus Equation (4.3) becomes, in the bivariate normal case,

$$(Y|X = x) = \mu_2 + \sigma_2\rho x + \epsilon,$$

if ϵ is *assumed* independent of $X = x$. Also $V(\epsilon) = V(Y|X = x) = \sigma_2^2\sqrt{1-\rho^2}$ when X is pre-selected and fixed at x^*, and the above relationship gets written as

$$Y(x^*) = \alpha + \beta x^* + \epsilon, \quad (4.4)$$

where $\alpha = \mu_\alpha$, $\beta = \sigma_\alpha\rho$, and ϵ has a normal distribution with mean 0 and variance $\sigma^2 = \sigma_2^2\sqrt{1-\rho^2}$.

This in turn means that the probability model for Y with x^* as a parameter is a univariate normal with mean $\alpha + \beta x^*$ and variance σ^2.

The relationship of Equation (4.4) can be generalized to a polynomial in x^*, and also to variables other than X, giving us a family of linear models. This could be one way to describe the genesis of linear models and a use of the term regression in their context.

With the above in place, and focusing on the simple linear model of Equation (4.4), the posterior distribution of $\theta = (\alpha, \beta, \sigma^2)$, with $\underset{\sim}{d}^*$ at hand is

$$P_{\ominus}^{\tau}(\theta; \underset{\sim}{d}^*) \propto P_{\ominus}^{\tau}(\theta; \mathscr{H}) \mathscr{L}(\theta; \underset{\sim}{d}^*),$$

where $P_{\ominus}^{\tau}(\theta; \mathscr{H})$ is the prior, and the likelihood

$$\mathscr{L}(\theta; \underset{\sim}{d}^*) = \prod_{i=1}^{n} \frac{1}{\sqrt{2\pi}\sigma} \exp\left\{ -\frac{1}{2} \left(\frac{y_i - \alpha - \beta x_i^*}{\sigma} \right)^2 \right\}.$$

Finally, the predictive distribution of Y with X fixed at x^*_{n+1} is now obtained, at least in principle, as

$$P^\tau_\female(Y \geq y; \underline{d}^*, x^*_{n+1}, \mathscr{H}) \propto \int\limits_{-\infty}^{y} \int\limits_{\theta} \frac{1}{\sqrt{2\pi}\,\sigma}$$

$$\exp\left\{-\frac{1}{2}\left(\frac{y_i - \alpha - \beta x^*_{n+1}}{\sigma}\right)^2\right\} P^\tau_\female(\theta; \underline{d}^*)\, d\theta dy, \quad (4.5)$$

Acknowledgements

The several helpful comments of Michael Edesess and Robert Smythe are gratefully acknowledged. Thanks also go to Boyan Dimitrou, who provided a platform that motivated the writing of this paper.

Disclosure statement

No potential conflict of interest was reported by the author.

Funding

The work reported in this article was supported by a grant from the City University of Hong Kong [Project No. 9380068].

References

Barlow, R. E., & Proschan, F. (1981). *Statistical theory of reliability and life testing: probability models.* Silver Spring, MD: To Begin With.

Box, G. E. (1976). Science and statistics. *Journal of the American Statistical Association, 71*(356), 791–799.

de Finetti, B. (1938). Sur la condition d'"équivalence partielle". *Actualités Scientifiques et Industrielles, 739*, 5–18.

Esary, J. D., Proschan, F., & Walkup, D. W. (1967). Association of random variables, with applications. *The Annals of Mathematical Statistics, 38*(5), 1466–1474. Retrieved from https://projecteuclid.org/download/pdf1/euclid.aoms/1177698701

Jeffreys, H. (1946). An invariant form for the prior probability in estimation problems. *Proceedings of the Royal Society A, Mathematical and Physical Sciences, 186*, 453–461. Retrieved from http://www.jstor.org/stable/97883

Kendall, M. G. (1938). *A new measure of rank correlation. Biometrika, 30*(1–2), 81–93. Retrieved from http://dx.doi.org/10.1093/biomet/30.1-2.81

Kinney, J. B., & Atwal, G. S. (2014). Equitability, mutual information, and the maximal information coefficient. *Proceedings of the National Academy of Sciences, 111*(9), 3354–3359.

Kullback, S., & Leibler, L. R. (1951). On information and suffiency. *The Annals of Mathematical Statistics, 22*, 79–86.

Lehmann, E. L. (1966). Some concepts of dependence. *The Annals of Mathematical Statistics, 37*, 1137–1153.

Linfoot, E. (1957). An informational measure of correlation. *Information and Control, 1*(1), 85–89.

Marshall, A. W., & Olkin, I. (1967). A multivariate exponential distribution. *Journal of the American Statistical Association, 62*(317), 30–44.

Meinhold, R. J., & Singpurwalla, N. D. (1983). Understanding the Kalman filter. *The American Statistician, 37*(2), 123–127. http://dx.doi.org/10.1080/00031305.1983.10482723Retrieved from

Popper, K. (2014). *The logic of scientific discovery.* London: Routledge.

Reshef, D. N., Reshef, Y. A., Finucane, H. K., Grossman, S. R., McVean, G., Turnbaugh, .. Sabeti, P.C. (2011). Detecting novel associations in large data sets. *Science, 334*(6062), 1518–1524. Retrieved from http://dx.doi.org/10.1126/science.1205438

Savage, L. J. (1972). *The foundations of statistics.* New York: Dover.

Shannon, C. (1948). A mathematical theory of communication. *Bell System Technical Journal, 27*, 379–423.

Singpurwalla, N. D. (2006). *Reliability and risk: a Bayesian perspective.* West Sussex: Wiley.

Spearman, C. (1904). The proof and measurement of association between two things. *The American Journal of Psychology, 15*(1), 72–101.

Suppes, P. (1970). *A probabilistic theory of causation.* Amsterdam: North-Holland.

Székely, G. J., & Rizzo, M. L. (2009). Brownian distance covariance. *The Annals of Applied Statistics, 3*(4), 1236–1265. Retrieved from http://dx.doi.org/10.1214/09-AOAS312

Designing a data-driven leagile sustainable closed-loop supply chain network

Abdollah Babaeinesami ⓘ, Hamid Tohidi and Seyed Mohsen Seyedaliakbar

ABSTRACT

Nowadays, there is a great deal of interest in applying sustainability concepts for logistics and supply chain management. This paper proposes a new multi objective model in the area of closed loop supply chain problem integrated with lot sizing by considering lean, agility and sustainability factors simultaneously. In this regard, responsiveness, environmental, social and economic aspects are regarded in the model in addition to the capacity and service-level constraints. Most importantly, strategic and operational backup decisions are developed to increase the resiliency of the system against disruption of the facilities and routes simultaneously. In the following, a new hybrid metaheuristic algorithm comprised a parallel Multi-Objective Particle Swarm Optimization (PMOPSO) algorithm and a multi objective social engineering optimizer (MOSEO) is developed to deal with large size problems efficiency. To ensure about the effectiveness of the proposed hybrid algorithm, the results of this algorithm are compared with a Non-dominated Sorting Genetic Algorithm (NSGA-II).

1. Introduction

In today's competitive market, supply chain management (SCM) should take into consideration the responsivness of their system to increase the customer satisfaction (Fathollahi-Fard, Ranjbar-Bourani, Cheikhrouhou, & Hajiaghaei-Keshteli, 2019a; Fathollahi-Fard, Govindan, Hajiaghaei-Keshteli, & Ahmadi, 2019b; Ghasemi, Khalili-Damghani, Hafezolkotob, & Raissi, 2017; Isaloo & Paydar, 2020; Jalil, Hashmi, Asim, & Javaid, 2019; Pan et al., 2019). Remanufacturing as the process of collecting used products from the users, plays an important role in the economic and environmental aspects of a closed loop supply chain (CLSC) (As' Ad, Hariga, & Alkhatib, 2019; Ghasemi, Khalili-Damghani, Hafezalkotob, & Raissi, 2020; Kannan, Sasikumar, & Devika, 2010; Mehranfar, Hajiaghaei-Keshteli, & Fathollahi-Fard, 2019; Nezhadroshan, Fathollahi-Fard, & Hajiaghaei-Keshteli, 2020; Soleimani & Govindan, 2015; Shamsi, Mahdavi, & Paydar, 2020; Torkaman, Ghomi, & Karimi, 2017). Designing a CLSC can be useful for both the governments and companies by providing profits alongside considering social benefits (Abdi, Abdi, Fathollahi-Fard, & Hajiaghaei-Keshteli, 2019; Cheraghalipour, Paydar, & Hajiaghaei-Keshteli, 2018, 2019; Fathollahi-Fard, Hajiaghaei-Keshteli, Tian, & Li, 2020a; Shalke, Paydar, & Hajiaghaei-Keshteli, 2018). Setting a balance between economic, environmental and social goals in a system is the main goal of a sustainable manufacturing system (Fahimnia, Sarkis, Dehghanian, Banihashemi, & Rahman, 2013; Govindan, Jafarian, & Nourbakhsh, 2015; Hasanov, Jaber, & Tahirov, 2019; Mokhtari & Hasani, 2017). Based on aforementioned points environmental factors are important factor of a sustainable system, thus considering transportation networks and production have a great impact on environment. In this regard, integration of strategic and operational decisions can increase the capabilities of the

supply chain network design (SCND) in a competitive atmosphere to manage the system more efficiency (Abdi et al., 2019; Ghasemi, Khalili-Damghani, Hafezalkotob, & Raissi, 2019; Hajiaghaei-Keshteli et al., 2010; Hajiaghaei-Keshteli, Sajadifar, & Haji, 2011; Habibi-Kouchaksaraei, Paydar, & Asadi-Gangraj, 2018; Safaei, Roozbeh, & Paydar, 2017; Safaei, Farsad, & Paydar, 2018). In a CLSC, determining the best set of routees between the destinations can reduce the traveling costs and times. Production-inventory management is another important problem in the CLSC reducing the production costs by setting the number of production batches and number of items to be preserved for the next periods (Chalmardi & Camacho-Vallejo, 2019; Hosseini-Motlagh, Nouri-Harzvili, Johari, & Sarker, 2020; Safaeian, Fathollahi-Fard, Tian, Li, & Ke, 2019).

On the other hand, natural and man-made calamities can cause considerable damages to a SCs and threat the continuity of the business. In this regard, several strategies have been developed to reduce the possible damages of the disasters and prepare the SC system against the unwanted actions. This type of strategies can be categorized into two main groups including operational decisions and strategic decisions. The operational decisions happen instantly after a disruption begins. The strategic decisions take place before a disruption occurrence fortifying the SCND against disruption. In this regard, business continuity plan is a useful management tool to provide a framework and identify the internal and external factors affecting the SC under disruption (Cardoso, Barbosa-Póvoa, Relvas, & Novais, 2015; Ciccullo, Pero, & Caridi, 2017; Mohammaddust, Rezapour, Farahani, Mofidfar, & Hill, 2017; Rohaninejad, Sahraeian, & Tavakkoli-Moghaddam, 2018).

In this paper, we consider Lean, Agile and sustainable manufacturing strategies simultaneously for a CLSC problem in which strategic and tactical decisions are integrated. In addition, this study introduces strategic and operational decions to face with disruption risks. Most importantly, a hybrid metaheuristic is established by the benefits from a recent and well-known metaheuristic. The main contributions of this study are described as follows:

(1) Designing a new leagile sustainable CLSC problem under partial facility disruption considering location-allocation, lot sizing, and shortage and routeing decisions simultaneously.
(2) Applying an M/M/c queue system to reduce the congestion of system, shipment time and related costs by taking into consideration the alternative routees.
(3) Considering storage and service-level constraints in a CLSC problem under partial facility disruption.
(4) Applying strategic and operational decisions to increase the resiliency of the system against disruptions.
(5) Applying a new hybrid metaheuristic algorithm to efficiency solve the problem.

The rest of this paper is organized as follows: Section 2 reviews the relevant works related to scope of CLSC with different suppositions. Section 3 describes the statement of the proposed problem and establishes the developed model. Section 4 innovates the robust possibilistic formulation as the uncertain version of our model. Section 5 illustrates the solution algorithms and our hybrid metaheuristic. Section 6 provides an extensive analysis and comparison among algorithms. Finally, Section 7 concludes the paper and suggests the future remarks.

2. Literature review

Academically, Location, allocation, routeing and inventory decisions are regarded in various types of SC problems (Fathollahi-Fard et al., 2020a; Soleimani & Govindan, 2015; Vahdani & Mohammadi, 2015). Lot sizing is regarded in some studies of CLSC besides the other strategic and tactical decisions of the system (Golmohamadi, Tavakkoli-Moghaddam, & Hajiaghaei-Keshteli, 2017). Pan, Tang, and Liu (2009) studied a lot sizing problem in CLSC with removal of returned products and applied a dynamic programming algorithm to handle the problem. In addition, Soleimani and Govindan (2015) stated that CLSC problem is an NP-hard problem. They designed an integrate CLSC problem consisting of location, inventory and shipment decisions and applied a hybrid metaheuristic algorithm to solve their problem. Kannan et al. (2010) formulated a model for CLSC problem by taking into account the production, shipping, reproduction and recycling decisions in the structure of the model and implemented the proposed model in the battery industry as a real case. They used a genetic algorithm to solve the problem. Torkaman et al. (2017) compared the performance of a simulated annealing (SA) algorithm with a heuristic approach to solve a multi- product production planning problem with sequence dependent set up times in a CLSC and showed the superiority of SA to solve the large-sized instances. As' Ad et al. (2019) developed a CLSC problem in which raw material procurement, transportation and lot-sizing decisions were integrated. They assumed two different strategy for raw material providing and applied an iterative search algorithm to solve the problem. Hasanov et al. (2019) proposed a four level CLSC problem by determining the order

quantities and inventory level of the system and assumed that a part of the demand is met from remanufacturing items. They proved that higher remanufacturing rate leads to less manufacturing costs.

Combining CLSC with sustainable development goals to contribute on the environmental and social sustainability is an active topic in the last decade. For example, Fahimnia et al. (2013) assessed the effect of greenhouse gas pricing on the forward and backward flow of a CLSC and used a case study to show the applicability of model. Govindan et al. (2015) included environmental issues of all of the SC parts besides economic factors and used a hybrid approach to deal with multi objective problem. Mokhtari and Hasani (2017) proposed a SC model with two objective functions. Their model determined production and inventory level, transportation mode and back order level. They applied a fuzzy goal programming method to reduce the related costs and environmental effects of the system concurrently. Chalmardi and Camacho-Vallejo (2019) developed a SCND problem and considered the social and environmental aspects alongside with economic objectives in the problem. In the proposed model the government plays the role of leader and the manager of the company plays the role of follower and a simulation annealing (SA) based algorithm is applied to solve the problem.

Most notably, the risk management is one of the main factors of the agile production system enhancing the responsiveness by regarding immunity of system (Ciccullo et al., 2017; Fard, Gholian-Jouybari, Paydar, & Hajiaghaei-Keshteli, 2017). In this regard, multiple sourcing is one of the prevalent strategies to face with disasters. In multi multiple sourcing each retailor can be assigned to more than one node. Mohammaddust et al. (2017) designed a lean and responsive nonlinear model for SC problem and considered different type of backup strategies to face with risk of system, they applied a regression approximation method to linearize the model. Rohaninejad et al. (2018) studied a multi-echelon SCND with unreliable facilities and assumed the facilities can be 'hardened'. They applied different approximation algorithms to solve large size problems.

Considering the overcrowding caused by differences between the processing rate of servers and arrival rate of the incoming flow in facilities, queuing approach can be a useful tool to reduce the congestion of the system as lean strategy. Ghobadi, Arkat, and Tavakkoli-Moghaddam (2019) highlighted the importance of queue system in reducing the service time and enhancing the customer satisfaction. Vahdani, Tavakkoli-Moghaddam, Modarres, and Baboli (2012) applied queue system for a bi-objective SC problem including total costs and unforeseen transportation costs and used a robust optimization (RO) approach to face with uncertain parameters. Saeedi, Mohammadi, and Torabi (2015) developed an uncertain model for a CLSC problem and tried to set a balance between queue costs and other costs of system to determine the capacity of facilities. At last but not least, Vahdani and Mohammadi (2015) formulated an uncertain SC problem and used queue system to decrease the processing time.

Stochastic programming methods are a prevalent method to deal with uncertain parameters when experts know the distribution of random data. However, in the absence of enough data to guess the probability distribution of parameters robust optimization (RO) is a suitable approach and enable the decision makers (DM) to obtain trustable solutions (Habibi-Kouchaksaraei et al., 2018; Isaloo & Paydar, 2020; Safaei et al., 2018). As one of the important recent works, Sadghiani, Torabi, and Sahebjamnia (2015) proposed a retail SCND model with operational and disruption risks and deployed a possibilistic-robust method to handle the vagueness of parameters. Kim, Do Chung, Kang, and Jeong (2018) applied robust method to deal with uncertain recycle product and customer demand for a CLSC and showed the efficiency of this method to deal with uncertainty. Hajipour, Tavana, Di Caprio, Akhgar, and Jabbari (2019) proposed a CLSC problem by taking into consideration the radio frequency identification to reduce the lead time, social and environmental objective functions simultaneously. They applied stochastic programming to face with the uncertainty of the model.

More recently, Aydin (2020) have extended a mixed integer linear programming model to a multi-echelon supply chain network, and also considered multi-capacity levels for each facilitation. In spite of identifying numbers and the location of facilities, the model is able to identify the level of optimal capacity for each facility. This study is novel as it takes environmental impacts in the supply chain into consideration. Ayvaz and Görener (2020) present an integer linear programming model for production/distribution network. The increasing importance of network accountability in recent years, has developed a tendency toward designing a logistic network. Additionally, Djatna and Amien (2020) have expanded a mixed integer linear programming model; they have presented a multi-objective genetic algorithm based on a priority-based coding method in order to solve the model, and used two different weighting method to assign weights to the model's objectives and obtain Pareto optimal solutions. Kuvvetli and Erol (2020), investigated designing a network in a custom-build supply chain in which the manner of locating distributors and dedicating customers to these distributors is taken into account. They assumed the demand pattern as dependent on the lead time and investigated the transaction between logistic costs and the lead time. Finally, they solved the problem using a solution algorithm based on Lagrange's method. Another application of Lagrangian theory in this research area was introduced by Fathollahi-Fard et al. (2020a) who proposed a CLSC for water distribution network and formulated it by a two-stage stochastic programming and solved it by a an adaptive algorithm for the case study of the west Azerbaijan province. Furthermore, Aćimović, Mijušković, and Rajić (2020) expanded a mixed integer linear programming model to the supply chain and to solve the problem, they offered a steady-state genetic algorithm according to priority-based coding method. For the purpose of adding more uncertain suppositions, Abdi et al. (2019) developed a CLSC with stochastic parameters like demand, returned products and prices and production costs. Mohtashami, Aghsami, and Jolai (2020) presented an integer linear programming model in order to design reverse logistic networks in which repair and reconstruction options are considered simultaneously. Regarding the fuzzy logic in CLSCs, Safaeian et al. (2019) consider an order allocation by multiple objectives including the total cost, quality and prices of the products and customer's satisfaction. They tried to find an interaction between these goals by the use of non-dominated sorting genetic

algorithm. Hosseini-Motlagh et al. (2020) investigated the impact of dependence between demands and returns in reverse logistic networks. They took two models into consideration: one with returns independent from demands, and one with returns dependent to demands. Results indicated the proper operation of the proposed model. De and Giri (2020) proposed a conceptual framework for decision making which include process monitoring, decisions, financial aspects and operation assessment, considering the differences related to strategic, tactical and operational levels. At last but not least, Mehranfar et al. (2019) developed an integrated CLSC with carbon tax supposition and applied a hybrid whale optimization algorithm to solve it.

Based on the aforementioned works, the studies show that there are some gaps in the context of CLSC that are described as follows:

(1) Previous studies do not consider the integration of location-allocation, lot sizing, inventory and routing decisions in a CLSC problem.
(2) Considering a quick response system (and other agility metrics) to increase the responsiveness of a CLSC problem.
(3) Considering Lean and agile production strategies to support the social and environmental objectives of a CLSC problem.
(4) Considering the concurrent disruption of facilities and routes in a CLSC problem.
(5) Considering back up storage, back up supplier, multi allocation and alternative route decision as the operational and strategic decisions to increase the resiliency of the system against partial disruption risks.
(6) Considering storage and service-level constraints in a CLSC problem under partial disruption risks.
(7) Proposing a data-driven modeling to increase the agility level of the manufacturing system.

3. Problem description

In the most of the CLSC problems with location-allocation decision, the potential locations are predetermined. In real domain, the candidate nodes are determined by the discretion of the DMs. Thus, we develop a data-driven modelling in which the candidate nodes are determined based on proximity to local clients to increase the service level and agility of the SC system. In the proposed CLSC problem, the suppliers send required items through Production-Distribution Centers (PDCs) to the retailers. The retailers are responsible for collecting and sending returned products to RCs. Vehicle's routee begins from a PDC and after visiting the retailers, vehicle returns to its departing PDC. The scrapped items will be sent back to the retailers, after remanufacturing process in the Recycling Centers (RCs). PDCs receive their required materials from suppliers based on their dollar value. The strategic and operational decisions of the model to reduce the damages of the disasters include: satisfying the demand of retailers through more than one PDC/RC (multi allocation), assigning more than one supplier to PDCs, assigning back up stores to PDCs/RCs, applying a M/M/c queue system to reduce the waiting time of machines in routes due to disruption effects.

The main assumptions applied to design a novel CLCS model are described:

(1) The positions of supplier and retailers are known (Abdi et al., 2019).

(2) RCs can only be established at locations where PDCs are open (Safaeian et al., 2019).

(3) Reproduced items have the same quality of new produced items (Govindan et al., 2015).

(4) Opening PDC or an RC in a region results potential risks due to facility disruptions (De & Giri, 2020).

(5) Vehicles spend more time on some routees because of traffic caused by disruptions (Fathollahi-Fard, Hajiaghaei-Keshteli, & Tavakkoli-Moghaddam, 2020b; Fathollahi-Fard et al., 2019a).

Figure 1 demonstrates the structure of proposed model. The notations used in the model are demonstrated as follows:

Indices

p, p'	products $p = \{1, 2, \ldots, P\}$
i, j	PDCs$i = \{1, 2, \ldots, I\}, j = \{1, 2, \ldots, J\}$,
r, q	RCs$r = \{1, 2, \ldots, R\}, q = \{1, 2, \ldots, Q\}$,
t	time periods$t = \{1, 2, \ldots, T\}$,
h	potential locations$h = \{1, 2, \ldots, H\}$,
w, u	retailers $w = \{1, 2, \ldots, W\}$, $u = \{1, 2, \ldots, U\}$,
s	Suppliers$s = \{1, 2, \ldots, S\}$,
a, b	Nodes
v	vehicles$v = \{1, 2, \ldots, V\}$
Z	Total retailers and potential centers

Parameters

Dem_p^t	Demand of product (p) in period (t)
Dem_{pw}^t	Retailer's demand for product (p)
FS_{psi}	Constant order cost for raw material (p) requested by PDC (i) to supplier (s)
Inc_{pi}	Holding cost of product (p) in PDC (i)
US_{sip}	Transportation cost for raw material (p) requested by PDC (i) from supplier (s)
Prc_{pi}	Production cost of product (p) in PDC (i)
Rpc_{pr}	Reproduction cost of product (p) in RC (r)
$CPDC_i$	Opening cost of PDC (i)

CRC_r	Opening cost of RC(r)
$disc_{ab}$	Shipment cost between the node (a) and the node (b)
dis_{ab}	Distance of node (a) and node (b)
Woc_p	Relative importance of product (p)
φ_{1p}	The amount of product (p) to be reproduced
φ_{0p}	The amount of raw material for product (p)
$\rho1_{ip}$	The production capacity for product (p) in PDC (i) due to disruption
$\rho2_i$	The coefficient determining the PDC (i) capacity due to disruption
$\rho3_r$	The coefficient determining the RC (r) capacity due to disruption
$Sercap_i$	Production capacity of PDC (i)
$Pemi_{pi}$	Amount of emitted Co_2 for production of a single product (p) in PDC (i)
$RPemi_{pr}$	Amount of emitted Co_2 for reproduction of a single product (p) in RC (r)
$Remi_v$	Amount of emitted Co_2 by vehicle (v) per unit of distance traveled
$bocs_{pt}$	Shortage cost of product (p) in period (t)
$Maco_v$	Fixed cost of vehicle (v) usage
NPI_i	Number of injured people due to disruption occurred in PDC (i)
φ_1	The number of injured people range in PDC (i) due to disruption
φ_2	The number of injured people range in RC (r) due to disruption
$Icap_i$	Maximum capacity for store of PDC (i) to hold inventories
$Mcap_v$	Maximum capacity for vehicle (v) to ship products
VUN_p	The amount of space required per unit of product (p)
VUN_{1p}	The amount of space required per unit of reproduction (p)
$Icap_i$	Total capacity of PDC (i) to keep products

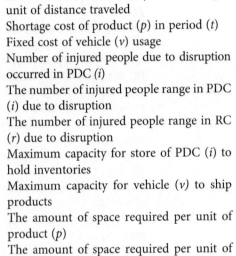

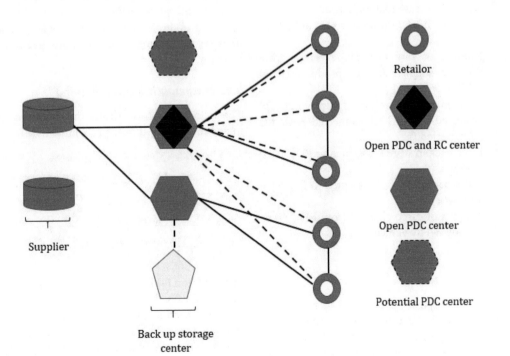

Figure 1. The structure of proposed CLSC network.

$Icap_r$	Total capacity of RC (r) to keep products
BN	Big number
αs	Service level
$Fpdc_i$	Back up facility cost to fortify and expand the storage capacity of PDC (i)
Frc_r	Back up facility cost to fortify and expand the storage capacity of RC (r)
ss	Amount of space added to warehouse of PDCs and RCs as a resilient strategy
acc_v	Accelerate of vehicle v
rol	Factor determining rolling resistance
Ewe_v	Weight of unused part for vehicle v
$BSPC_p$	Backup supplier assignment cost for product (P)
$Ccpu_v$	Cost of shipping each item trough vehicle v

Decision variables

X_{pit}	Number of products (p) produced at PDC (i) in period (t)
Inv_{pit}	Number of products (p) hold at PDC (i) in period (t)
b_{pit}	Shortage of product (p) at PDC (i) in period (t)
EXS_{pt}	1; if a backup supplier is assigned to product (p) in period (t); 0 otherwise,
$Rout^t_{abv}$	1; if node (a) and (b) are connected by vehicle (v) in period (t); 0 otherwise,
PO_{hi}	1; if PDC (i) is founded in location (h); 0 otherwise,
RO_{hr}	1; if RC (r) is founded in location (h); 0 otherwise,
RX_{si}	1; if PDC (i) is related to supplier (i); 0 otherwise,
RZ_{sr}	1; if RC (r) is related to supplier (i); 0 otherwise,
AX_{iw}	1; if retailor (w) is related to PDC (i); 0 otherwise,
BX_{wr}	1; if returned items of retailor(w) are shipped to RC (r); 0 otherwise,
X^0_{psit}	Number of raw materials needed received from supplier (s) for products (p) at PDC (i) in period (t)
$\hat{x}^0_{ps'it}$	Number of raw materials received from back up supplier (s') for products (p) at PDC (i) in period (t)
X^1_{pirt}	Total number of returns for products (p) produced at PDC (i) connected with RC (r) in period (t)
$Xpdc_i$	1; if a backup store is assigned to PDC (i); 0 otherwise,
Xrc_r	1; if a backup store is assigned to RC (r); 0 otherwise,
LAO^t_{iwv}	Amount of cargo shipped from PDC (i) to retailor (w) by vehicle (v)

3.1. M/M/c queuing system

In this section a queue system is designed to reduce the driver and depretiation cost of trucks due to waiting time in the PDCs/RCs (i.e. loading and unloading) and routes (i.e. route disruption). Here, the incoming flow of vehicles differs from other possible routees and a Poisson distribution is

applied to calculate their waiting time in RCs. The related notations are:

Parameters

$\theta_{r/i}$	Number of operators at RC (r)/PDC (i)
$\mu_{r/it}$	Operation rate of RC (r)/PDC (i)
φ_3	The added time on shipment due to route blocking caused by disruptions.
Spe	Mean speed of vehicles
$Vcpt$	Mean cost of vehicles per unit time of delay in queue

Decision variables

$\lambda_{r/i}$	Vehicle's Incoming rate to production/reproduction centers
$WT^t_{r/i}$	Amount of time elapsed as delay time in RC (r) or PDC (i)
$Num^t_{wr/i}$	Total allocated vehicles connecting retailors to production/reproduction centers

The required time of vehicles to receive service in a RC/PDC center is calculated:

$$WT^t_{r/i} = \left(\lambda_{r/i}/\mu_{r/it}\right)^{\theta_{r/i}} \mu_{r/it}/(\theta_{r/i}-1)\left(\theta_{r/i}\mu_{r/it}-\lambda_{r/i}\right)^2$$
$$\left[1+\sum_{n=0}^{\theta_{r/i}-1} 1/n!\left(\lambda_{r/i}/\mu_{r/it}\right)^n + 1/(\theta_{r/i}!)\left(\lambda_{r/i}/\mu_{r/it}\right)^n \left(\lambda_{r/i}/\left(\lambda_{r/i}-\mu_{r/it}\right)\right)\right]^{-1} \quad (1)$$

Where the arrival rate $\lambda_{r/i}$ in the CLSC is calculated by:

$$\lambda_{r/i} = \sum_w Num^t_{wr/i} \quad (2)$$

Finally, the Total Waiting Cost (TWC) is calculated by:

$$TWC = \left(\sum_t \sum_p \sum_w \sum_i \left(Spe/dis_{wi} + WT^t_i\right)\varphi_3 Num^t_{wi} AX_{iw}\right.$$
$$\left. + \sum_t \sum_p \sum_w \sum_r \left(Spe/dis_{wr} + WT^t_r\right)\varphi_3 Num^t_{wr} BX_{wr}\right) Vcpt$$
$$(3)$$

According to the Equation (3), the model decides to assign an appropriate PDC/RC center to a retailer with the least waiting time in the routes and PDCs/RCs. In other word, assigning multiple PDCs/RCs to retailors enables the model to assess the shipment time of alternative routes.

3.2. Mathematical programming

The following section shows the proposed multi objective mixed integer non-linear problem (MOMINLP):

$$a_1 = \sum_i PO_{hi}CPDC_i + \sum_r RO_{hr}CRC_r + \sum_t \sum_p b_{pit}bocs_{pt} + \sum_r Xrc_r Frc_r$$
$$+ \sum_i Xpdc_i Fpdc_i + \sum_t \sum_p \sum_s \sum_i \sum_w (Prc_{pi}X_{pit} + Inv_{pit}Inc_{pi})RX_{si}AX_{iw} + \sum_i \sum_s \sum_p FS_{psi}RX_{si}$$
$$+ \sum_t \sum_i \sum_s \sum_p US_{sip}RX_{si}X^0_{psit} + \sum_t \sum_s \sum_i \sum_w \sum_r \sum_p US_{rsp}X^1_{pirt}RX_{sr}BX_{wr}$$
$$+ \sum_t \sum_s \sum_i \sum_w \sum_r \sum_p Rpc_{pr}X^1_{pirt}RZ_{sr}BX_{wr} + \sum_t \sum_{aZ} \sum_{bZ} \sum_v disc_{ab}Rout^t_{abv}$$
$$+ \sum_t \sum_{aZ} \sum_{bZ} \sum_v Maco_v Rout^t_{abv} + + \sum_t \sum_i \sum_s \sum_p BSPC_p \hat{x}^0_{ps'it}EXS_{pt}$$
$$(4)$$

The Equation (4) is designed to calculate the opening costs of PDCs and RCs, the shortage cost, the renting cost of back up store, the production and inventory costs of PDCs by considering the network connection between PDCs, the fix ordering cost of raw materials from suppliers, the shipment cost of items to the retailers, the shipment cost of scraped items from retailers to RCs, the reproduction cost of the scraped items by regarding the network connection between RCs, retailers and suppliers, the shipment cost between nodes, the fixed cost of vehicles usage and the cost of contracting with other back up suppliers.

$$a_2 = \sum_t \sum_i \sum_w \sum_v (Mcap_v - LAO^t_{iwv})Ccpu_v \qquad (5)$$

The Equation (5) minimizes the unused capacity of vehicles during the transportation of the items and its related cost. The optimal utilization of truck carrying capacity reduces the number of round trips to meet the demand of clients. This equation reduces the number of non-added value activities which can be taken into consideration as a Lean routing strategy.

$$MinZ_1 = a_1 + a_2 + TWC \qquad (6)$$

Finally, the Equation (6) calculates the first objective function in which the items are described in the previous sections.

$$MinZ_2 = \sum_t \sum_p \sum_i Pemi_{pi}X_{pit} + \sum_t \sum_p \sum_r RPemi_{pr}X^1_{pirt} + \sum_t \sum_{aZ} \sum_{bZ} \sum_v dis_{ab}Remi_v(acc_v + \sin(a,b) + g\cos(a,b)acc_v rol)Ewe_v Rout^t_{abv} \qquad (7)$$

The Equation (7) depicts the second objective function which is about the environmental effects of CO_2 emissions, including production, reproduction and transportation effects respectively. It should be note that, the third section of Equation (7) calculates the environmental effects of transportation not only based on the traveled distance but also based on the cargo weight and rolling resistance of the road.

$$MinZ_3 = \sum_i PO_{im}NPI_i\varphi_1 + \sum_r RO_{rm}NPI_r\varphi_2 \qquad (8)$$

The Equation (8) shows the third objective function, this objective function minimizes the negative social impacts of establishing production/reproduction centers and aims to reduce the risks of facility disruptions. In continue the constraints of the model are demonstrated and described.

$$\sum_s RX_{si} = PO_{hi} \forall i, h \qquad (9)$$

$$\sum_s RZ_{sr} = RO_{hr} \forall r, h \qquad (10)$$

$$PO_{hi} \le RO_{hr} \forall i, h, r \qquad (11)$$

$$\sum_i PO_{hi} \le 1 \forall h \qquad (12)$$

$$\sum_r RO_{hr} \le 1 \forall h \qquad (13)$$

$$\sum_h PO_{hi} \le 1 \forall i \qquad (14)$$

$$\sum_h RO_{hr} \le 1 \forall r \qquad (15)$$

$$Inv_{pit} + Dem^t_p - Inv_{pit-1} - X^1_{pirt-1} + b_{pit-1} = X_{pit} + b_{pit} \forall p, i, t \qquad (16)$$

$$X^1_{pirt}BX_{wr} = X_{pit}AX_{iw}\varphi_{1p} \forall p, i, t, r, w \qquad (17)$$

$$X^0_{psit}RX_{si} + \hat{x}^0_{ps'it}EXS_{pt} = X_{pit}\varphi_{0p} \forall p, i, t, s \qquad (18)$$

$$\sum_p Inv_{pit}AX_{iw}VUN_p \le Icap_i\rho 2_i PO_{hi} \forall w, i, t, h \qquad (19)$$

$$\sum_w \sum_i \sum_p Inv_{prt}BX_{wr}VUN_{1p} \le Icap_r\rho 3_r RO_{hr} \forall r, t \qquad (20)$$

$$\sum_a \sum_b Rout^t_{abv} = 1 \forall v, t \qquad (21)$$

$$\sum_w Dem^t_{pw}AX_{iw} \le X_{pit} \forall p, i, t \qquad (22)$$

$$M_{wvt} - M_{uvt} + (Nre + Rout^t_{wuv}) \le Nre - 1 \forall w, u, t, v \qquad (23)$$

$$\sum_{bZ} Rout^t_{abv} = \sum_{aZ} Rout^t_{bav} \forall a, b, t, v \qquad (24)$$

$$\sum_i \sum_w Rout^t_{iwv} \le 1 \forall v, t \qquad (25)$$

$$\sum_u Rout^t_{wuv} + \sum_u Rout^t_{iuv} - AX_{iw} \le 1 \forall v, i, t, w \qquad (26)$$

$$\sum_i AX_{iw} \ge 1 \forall w \qquad (27)$$

$$\sum_r BX_{wr} \ge 1 \forall w \qquad (28)$$

$$Rout^t_{ijv} = 0 \forall j, i, t, v \qquad (29)$$

$$\sum_w \sum_v LAO^t_{wuv} - \sum_p Dem^t_{pu} = \sum_w \sum_v LAO^t_{uwv} \forall u, t, v \qquad (30)$$

$$LAO^t_{wuv} \le Rout^t_{wuv}BN \forall u, w, t, v \qquad (31)$$

$$\sum_p \sum_u Dem^t_{pu}Rout^t_{wuv} \le \sum_u (1 - Rout^t_{wuv})BN + LAO^t_{wuv}$$
$$\le Mcap_v$$
$$+ (1 - Rout^t_{wuv})BN \forall p, v, t, w \qquad (32)$$

$$\left(\sum_p X_{pit}/Mcap_v\right) \le Num^t_{wr/i} \forall i, t, v, r, w \qquad (33)$$

$$\left(\sum_i b_{pit}/Dem^t_p\right)Woc_p \le 1 - \alpha s \forall p, t \qquad (34)$$

$$Icap_i = Icap_i(1 - Xpdc_i) + (Icap_i + ss)(Xpdc_i) \forall i \qquad (35)$$

$$Icap_r = Icap_r(1 - Xrc_r) + (Icap_i + ss)(Xrc_r) \forall r \qquad (36)$$

The Equations (9) and (10) indicate that each open PDC and RC must be assigned to one supplier. The Constraint (11) ensures that an RC can be established where a PDC is open. The Equations (12) and (13) gurantee that at most one of PDC and RC centers can be established in a candidate place. The Equations (14) and (15) implies that at most one candidate place must be assigned to a PDC and RC respectively. The Equation (16) shows the production-inventory balance constraint of the products. In this equation, some orders that cannot be satisfied on time are allowed to be backlogged. The Equations (17) and (18) calculates the amount of raw material and reproduction items by considering the relations between each supplier, PDC and retailer as a network system. The Equation (18) demonstrates that a PDC is able to receive its raw material through the main supplier or the backup supplier. The constraint (19) and (20) Are associated with the capacity of storage in PDCs and RCs. In the both of equations, the capacity of the centers may change due to disruption. The Equation (21) indicates that every route is assigned to a vehicle. The constraint (22) shows the minimum amount of production for a PDC to meet the demand of a retailer. The constraint (23) removes the sub-tours and ensures that each route is comprised one PDC and some retailor. The Equation (24) is associated with flow protection and indicates that when a vehicle visits a place, the vehicle should leave that place within an equal time period. The constraint (25) states that maximum one PDC can exists in a route. The constraint (26) describes that a retailor should be allotted to a PDC if there is a connection between them by vehicle. The Equations (27) and (28) indicate that at least one PDC and RC can be connected to a retailer. These equations show the multi allocation nature of the problem which improves the resiliency and leanness of the system by increasing the routing options. In other word, designing a routing problem with various decisions can reduce the number of trips and provide a wider area of routing. The Equation (29) ensures that there is no route between PDCs. The Equation (30) indicates that the load of a vehicle varies by visiting a retailor on it's route. The constraint (31) describes that the load of a vehicle remains constant when the vehicle does not meet the retailer u. The constraint (32) shows the minimum and maximum limitation of loads for a vehicle to visit the retailers. The constraint (33) determines how many vehicles are needed to ship the returned items from retailor (w) to RC (r). The constraint (34) is about the service level of the system by determining the percentage of orders that are not satisfied. The Equations (35) and (36) calculates the capacity of PDCs and RCs by taking into consideration the backup storage decisions.

4. Robust possibilistic approach

Since some parameters have an uncertain and instable nature and due to lack of historical data, these parameters are set based on expert's judgment and these uncertain parameters are taken into account as trapezoidal fuzzy numbers:

$$\widetilde{Dem}_p^t, \widetilde{Dem}_{pw}^t, \widetilde{\rho 2}_i, \widetilde{\rho 3}_r, \widetilde{Pemi}_{pi}, \widetilde{RPemi}_{pr}, \widetilde{Remi}_v, \widetilde{\varphi}_1, \widetilde{\varphi}_2, \widetilde{\varphi}_3$$

Here, a possibilistic chance-constrained programming (PCCP) is addressed to handle the uncertain constraints. The DM is able to determine a least degree of confidence for uncertain constraints as a safety margin to satisfy each uncertain constraint. Next, the possibility (Pos) and

necessity (Nec) measures are utilized as fuzzy measures. In this regard, the possibility measure specifies the optimistic possibility related with uncertain event and the necessity measure demonstrates the lowest possibility uncertain parameter according to attitude of the DM. Yet, it is a risk averse strategy to use the necessity measure by considering the DM opinion. Here, a model is developed satisfying the possibilistic chance-constraints with the least level of confidence.

$$
\begin{aligned}
Minw_1 &= Ay + Bx \\
Minw_2 &= x \\
Minw_3 &= Kx \\
S.t\ Cx &= 0 \\
\\
Dx &\leq Ly \\
Kx &\leq h \\
Qx &\geq My \\
Gy &\leq 1 \\
y(0,1), x &\geq 0
\end{aligned}
\tag{39}
$$

where C, D, K, Q, G and L represents the coefficient matrices, and x is related continuous and y signify the binary variables. Also, vectors A, B, K, h and M can be regarded as fixed and unit production costs, social effects, capacity constraint and demand of retailers to close the example to the intended model. We consider A, B, h and M as inexact parameters. Here, the summarized format the basic PCCP model is addressed:

$$
\begin{aligned}
MinE[w_1] &= E[\tilde{A}]y + [\tilde{B}]x \\
MinE[w_2] &= x \\
MinE[w_3] &= Kx \\
S.t\ Cx &= 0 \\
\\
Dx &\leq Ly \\
Nec\left(Kx \leq \tilde{h}\right) &\geq \alpha \\
Nec\left(Qx \geq \tilde{M}y\right) &\geq \beta \\
Gy &\leq 1 \\
y(0,1), x &\geq 0
\end{aligned}
\tag{40}
$$

Here, α and β sets the least satisfaction degree of PCCP based on DM opinions. Regarding the trapezoidal possibility distributions of uncertain parameters, model (41) shows the crisp format of previous model:

$$
\begin{aligned}
MinE[w_1] &= \left(A_{(1)} + A_{(2)} + A_{(3)} + A_{(4)}/4\right)y + \left(B_{(1)} + B_{(2)} + B_{(3)} + B_{(4)}/4\right)x \\
MinE[w_2] &= x \\
MinE[w_3] &= Kx \\
S.t\ Cx &= 0 \\
\\
Dx &\leq Ly \\
Kx &\leq h_{(3)}(1-\alpha) + h_{(4)}\alpha \\
Qx &\geq (M_{(3)}(1-\beta) + M_{(4)}\beta)y \\
Gy &\leq 1 \\
y(0,1), x &\geq 0
\end{aligned}
\tag{41}
$$

In the presented model reaching robust solutions is not guaranteed because the model doesn't involve expected value in the objective function. The uncertain format of model based on proposed method is described:

$MinE[w_1] + \xi(w_{1(max)} - E[w_1]) + \eta 1(h_{(4)} - h_{(3)}(1-\alpha) - h_{(4)}\alpha) + \eta 2y(M_{(4)} - M_{(3)}(1-\beta) - M_{(4)}\beta)$

$MinE[w_2] = x + \eta'1(h_{(4)} - h_{(3)}(1-\alpha) - h_{(4)}\alpha) + \eta'2y(M_{(4)} - M_{(3)}(1-\beta) - M_{(4)}\beta)$

$MinE[w_3] = Kx + + \eta''1(h_{(4)} - h_{(3)}(1-\alpha) - h_{(4)}\alpha) + \eta''2y(M_{(4)} - M_{(3)}(1-\beta) - M_{(4)}\beta)$

$S.t \ Cx = 0$

$Dx \leq Ly$

$Kx \leq h_{(3)}(1-\alpha) + h_{(4)}\alpha$

$Qx \geq (M_{(3)}(1-\beta) + M_{(4)}\beta)y$

$Gy \leq 1$

$y(0,1), x \geq 0, 0.5 \leq \alpha, \beta \leq 1$

$$(42)$$

Where $w_{1(max)}$ can be stated as:

$$w_{1(max)} = A_{(4)}y + B_{(4)}x \quad (43)$$

In the presented model the expected value of uncertain parameters, the penalty cost of deviation from expected value and the total penalty costs of constraints deviations are regarded. $\xi, \eta 1 and \eta 2$ determine penalties for deviation and constraint violations, respectively. This approach considers minimum confidence level which can be changed based on the DM's preferences and prepare the model against changes of uncertain parameters. Also, resilient strategies are added to the model to increase the reliability of system. The robust possibilistic mathematical model is proposed in Electronic Supplementary Materials F1. The first objective function has less uncertain parts because of two reasons. In one hand, no fuzzy parameter exists in Equation (40). In addition, there is no need to include the difference between expected value of the objective function for this equation. However, the first objective function is affected by uncertain parameters existed in the constraints. The rest of model is as the before mentioned model in Section 3.4.

5. Proposed solution approach

The solution approach of this problem includes two main steps, in the first step a fuzzy C-mean clustering method is applied to determine the potential centers to locate PDCs/ RCs based on proximity to the local customers. In the second phase, the results of previous step are imported to the proposed model of Section 3.4. The presented model is NP-hard since it is comprised of location, lot sizing and vehicle routing problems as NP-hard problems (Abdi et al., 2019; Bahadori-Chinibelagh, Fathollahi-Fard, & Hajiaghaei-Keshteli, 2019; Fathollahi-Fard et al., 2019a, 2019b; Fathollahi-Fard, Hajiaghaei-Keshteli, & Tavakkoli-Moghaddam, 2018). In addition, considering different conflicting objective functions and proposing a robust possibilistic approach to deal with the uncertainty of the model are the other reasons intensifying the complexity of the model. Thus, a multi objective metaheuristic algorithm is used to solve the model. Figure 2 demonstrates the summary of the presented two-phase algorithm.

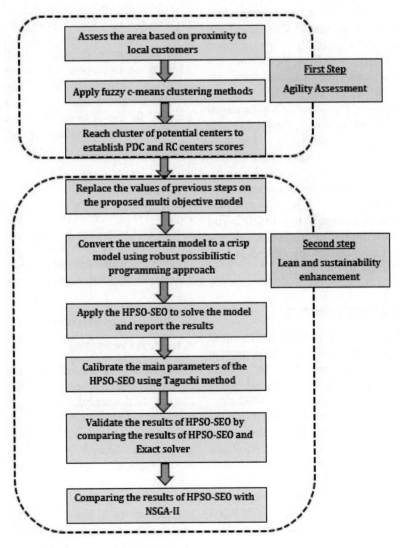

Figure 2. Structure of proposed approach for a league sustainable CLSC.

5.1. Fuzzy c-means clustering method

In this section the location of local customers are categorized into clusters by utilizing the fuzzy c-means clustering method (FCCM). In this study, we desire to partition u customer location into i clusters. Also, let x_u be the vector related to the location of customer u.

5.2. Solution representation

An appropriate solution representation covers all of the potential answers to reach the best answer among them. According to the structure of the model, an order-based solution representation could be a good approach to assess the candidate solutions. In the proposed order-based encoding structure, each chromosome is designed based on the order of the model's component. In this regard, a small-sized problem (i.e. $|h| \times |s| \times |i| \times |r| \times |w| \times |p| \times |v| \times |t| = 5 \times 2 \times 4 \times 2 \times 6 \times 2 \times 3 \times 2$)is proposed to describe the solution representation. As referred to (Fathollahi-Fard et al., 2020b; Fathollahi-Fard, Ahmadi, Goodarzian, & Cheikhrouhou, 2020c; Liu et al., 2020; Safaeian et al., 2019), we have used their encoding scheme and due to page limitation, the matrix of solution representation is not reported here.

Based on their encoding scheme (Fathollahi-Fard et al., 2020c, 2019a), the first chromosome is a $(|1| \times |h|)$ matrix determining the centers to establish PDCs by selecting potential locations randomly. In the first r cells of this chromosome, RCs are allowed to be established. The second and third chromosomes are $(|s| \times |i|)$and$(|s| \times |r|)$ matrixes related to connections between suppliers, PDCs and RCs respectively. The fourth and fifth chromosomes are $(|1| \times |i + w + v - 1|)and(|1| \times |r + v + w - 1|)$ matrixes addressing the order of retailers, PDCs and RCs to be visited by vehicles. In addition, a repair function is designed to alter the generated answers of these chromosomes. The sixth chromosome is a $(|p| \times |t|)$ matrix and calculates the number of produced items during planning horizon, by multiplying the random numbers to the determined production range. The two last chromosomes $(|1| \times |i|)$and$(|1| \times |r|)$ are related to allocation of backup storage centers to PDCs and RCs. Other constraints such as production capacity, storage capacity and service level are regarded by adding penalty function to the main objective functions.

5.3. Parallel version of MOPSO (PMOPSO)

MOPSO produces a Pareto-optimal solution set to make a balance between different objectives. A Pareto optimal solution cannot be conquered or cannot be better without deteriorating at least another objective. In this study a master-slave approach is used to change the MOPSO algorithm to a paralellized version. This method shows its advantages in compariosn with the original PSO from several studies (Soleimani & Govindan, 2015). In this method, the fitness evaluation for each particle is processed independently, the algorithm is decomposed to run the evaluations simultaneously as a parallel system. $v_p(t)$and$x_p(t)$ denote the velocity and the position of each particle respectively based on Equations (44) and (45). Note that $r_1$and $r_2$are random number between zero and one. As such, $c_1$and c_2 are the coefficient of global and local solutions.

$$v_p(t) = wv_p(t-1) + c_1 r_1 \left(x_{pbest} - x_p(t) \right) + c_2 r_2 \left(x_{gbest} - x_p(t) \right) \tag{44}$$

$$x_p(t) = x_p(t-1) + v_p(t) \tag{45}$$

5.4. Social engineering optimizer (SEO)

The SEO is a new single-solution metaheuristic algorithm introduced by Fathollahi-Fard et al. (2018). The SEO showed its high performance in several studies related to routing optimization and supply chain management (Fathollahi-Fard et al., 2019a, 2019b, 2020c). It has a low computational time and has this ability to find the global solution. These justifications motivate our attempt to employ this recent metaheuristic.

In SEO algorithm, the solutions are regarded as different persons with various abilities. The SEO algorithm starts by generating two initial solutions and dividing the solutions to attacker and defender. In this regard, the attacker assesses the abilities of the defender to find the efficient traits of defender.

5.5. Hybrid of PMOPSO & SEO (HPSO-SEO)

From the recent papers, SEO has been applied and revised for different concepts of SCM (Fathollahi-Fard et al., 2020c, 2019b, 2020b). As mentioned in Section 5.4, SEO is a single-solution algorithm with some advantages including short computational time, good intensification phase and finding a tradeoff between diversification and intensification phases. However, population-based algorithms are able to find good solutions (Cheraghalipour et al., 2018, 2019; Feng et al., 2019). Thus, it makes sense to propose a hybrid metaheuristic that benefits from the advantages of a population-based algorithm (PMOPSO) and a single solution algorithm (SEO) simultaneously. In the proposed hybrid algorithm, the results of PMOPSO are provided for the SEO algorithm as the initial solution.

5.6. NSGA-II

NSGA-II comprises of generating initial population, evaluation of members, sorting the results. This operator selects top rank individuals with higher probability. NSGA-II uses crossover to generate solutions similar to the initial chromosomes and mutation to generate more diverse solutions.

6. Results and discussion

6.1. Model validation

In this section, the feasibility of the model and the behavior of the model to reach the optimum value of objective functions are assessed. In this regard, a small-scale deterministic problem (i. e.$|h| \times |s| \times |i| \times |r| \times |w| \times |p| \times |v| \times |t| = 10 \times 2 \times 4 \times 2 \times 6 \times 3 \times 3 \times 10$) is considered and solved by GAMS applying Baron Solver because of nonlinear nature of the presented model. Since the proposed model is comprised of multiple objective functions, we divide the main problem into separate sub-problems based on the method and consider each objective function separately alongside with the constraints. The parameters of the model are determined based on the proposed case of our study as reported in the Table 1. Table 2 demonstrates the optimal decisions of each sub-problem separately. For the first

Table 1. Value of parameters.

Parameters	Values	Parameters	Values
Dem_p^t	$\tilde{U}(50,100)$	Vcpt	$\tilde{U}(5,10)$
Dem_{pw}^t	$\sum_t \sum_p Dem_p^t/w$	$\rho2_i$	$\tilde{U}(0.7,0.9)$
FS_{psi}	$\tilde{U}(15,20)$	$\rho3_r$	$\tilde{U}(0.7,0.9)$
Inc_{pi}	$\tilde{U}(5,7)$	$Sercap_i$	$\tilde{U}(300,600)$
US_{sip}	$\tilde{U}(10,15)$	$Sern_i$	$\tilde{U}(10,15)$
Prc_{pi}	$\tilde{U}(60,90)$	$Pemi_{pi}$	$\tilde{U}(2,5)$
Rpc_{pr}	$\tilde{U}(40,60)$	$RPemi_{pr}$	$\tilde{U}(2,5)$
$CPDC_i$	$\tilde{U}(3000,4000)$	$Remi_v$	$\tilde{U}(3.5,4)$
CRC_r	$\tilde{U}(2500,3500)$	$bocs_{pt}$	$\tilde{U}(20,30)$
$disc_{ab}$	$\tilde{U}(15,20)$	$Maco_v$	$1500 + 0.1 \times Mcap_v$
dis_{ab}	$\tilde{U}(50,300)$	NPI_i	$\tilde{U}(10,20)$
Woc_p	$\tilde{U}(1,3)$	φ_1	$\tilde{U}(1,3)$
φ_{0p}	$\tilde{U}(1.1,1.5)$	φ_2	$\tilde{U}(1,3)$
φ_{1p}	$\tilde{U}(0.2,0.45)$	$Icap_i$	$\tilde{U}(100,450)$
$\rho1_{ip}$	$\tilde{U}(0.7,0.9)$	$Mcap_v$	$\sum_t \sum_p Dem_p^t/v$
VUN_p	$\tilde{U}(2,3)$	$Fpdc_i$	$\tilde{U}(200,400)$
VUN_{1p}	$\tilde{U}(2,3)$	Frc_r	$\tilde{U}(200,400)$
Spe	$\tilde{U}(40,70)$	ss	$\tilde{U}(300,500)$
$Icap_r$	$\tilde{U}(100,450)$	μ_{rt}	$\tilde{U}(1,2.5)$
θ_r	$\tilde{U}(5,10)$	Ewe_v	$\tilde{U}(6,10)$
BN	1,000,000	acc_v	$\tilde{U}(1,3)$
as	$\tilde{U}(0.8,0.95)$	rol	$\tilde{U}(0,1)$
$Ccpu_v$	$\tilde{U}(4,7)$		
φ_3	$\tilde{U}(1.1,1.5)$	$BSPC_p$	$\tilde{U}(20,35)$

Table 2. Optimal decisions for problem instance.

Objective function	Collection route	Optimum number of objective function
Total costs	$s_1 \rightarrow i_1$	8167389
	$s_1 \rightarrow i_2 \rightarrow w_1 \rightarrow w_2 \rightarrow w_3 \rightarrow w_4 \rightarrow r_2 \rightarrow s_1$	
	$s_2 \rightarrow i_4 \rightarrow w_5 \rightarrow w_6 \rightarrow r_4 \rightarrow s_2$	
Environmental effects	$s_1 \rightarrow i_1 \rightarrow w_1 \rightarrow w_2 \rightarrow r_1 \rightarrow s_1$	54731
	$s_1 \rightarrow i_2 \rightarrow w_3 \rightarrow w_4 \rightarrow r_2 \rightarrow s_1$	
	$s_2 \rightarrow i_4 \rightarrow w_5 \rightarrow w_6 \rightarrow r_4 \rightarrow s_2$	
Disruption risks	$s_1 \rightarrow i_1 \rightarrow w_1 \rightarrow w_2 \rightarrow w_3 \rightarrow w_4 \rightarrow r_1 \rightarrow s_1$	43

sub problem, the model tends to decrease the costs of the system and decides to consider back up storage decisions due to high costs of establishing other PDC and RC centers and service-level constraints. For the second sub problem, the model decides to include more number of tours. As a result, each PDC will cover fewer retailers and each RC tackle the remanufacturing of fewer retailers. So, number of carried loads and environmental effects will be decreased. For the third sub problem, establishing PDCs and RCs will increase the disruption risks and model decides to open one center. Notably, this model does not regard the shipping costs.

6.2. Test instances

Since there are not benchmark instances in the literature, different small-sized and large sized deterministic test problems are generated and depicted in Electronic Supplementary Materials F2. The meta-heuristic algorithms are coded in MATLAB software in a personal computer with Core i5 processor and 8GB RAM.

6.3. Benchmarking study

Here, three factors are used to compare the proposed algorithms including: CPU time, Quality of results and the

spacing metric. Equations (46) and (47) are used to analyze the distribution of non- dominated answers.

$$spacing = \sqrt{1/N \sum_{i=1}^{N} (d_i - \bar{d})^2} \qquad (46)$$

$$d_i = \underset{j}{min} \sum_{t=1}^{T} \left| f_t^j - f_t^i \right| \forall i,j \in \{1, \ldots, N\} \qquad (47)$$

Table 3 shows the summary of results reached by conducting small-sized test problems on metaheuristics and BARON solver. The average percentage of relative gap (APRG) measure resulted by conducting each test problem 10 times independently. Here, Equations (48) and (49) are applied to calculate the gap for objective functions aimed to be minimized and maximized. Table 4 demonstrates the differences between metaheuristic methods to deal with large-size test problems, due to complexity of test problems exact method was unable to deal with them.

$$Gap\% = (OFV_{meta} - OFV_{exact})/OFV_{exact} \times 100 \qquad (48)$$

$$Gap\% = (OFV_{meta} - OFV_{pMOPSO})/OFV_{pMOPSO} \times 100 \qquad (49)$$

The results prove the efficiency of HPSO-SEO algorithm compared to NSGA-II to reach near optimum solutions for large-sized instances. Some other analyses related to tuning are not reported here due to encoding scheme.

6.4. Case study

Here, the logistic of main manufacturers of analog and digital equipment and radio transmitters is assessed. The active assembly section of this company receives some parts from a set of suppliers and uses them for the final assembly of more efficient products. The items produced at this facility include high power 100 and 200-Watt transmitters and Remux DVBT2/DVBS2 receivers and PVR (Personal video recorder). Iran is the desired as the case study of this model and logical decisions of problem are determined to reduce the total costs of system besides the environmental and social issues related with the system.

6.4.1 Sensitivity analyses

Here, the robustness of the outcomes reached from proposed method are analyzed for seven small-sized test problems in which parameter's value is determined using Table 1 and created based on the range of trapezoidal fuzzy numbers. The

Table 3. APRG for small-sized test problems in HPSO-SEO and NSGA-II.

	HPSO-SEO			NSGA-II		
	GAP%			GAP%		
Problem number	Obj 1	Obj2	Obj3	Obj 1	Obj2	Obj3
S1	0.01	0.02	0.01	0.03	0.07	0.07
S2	0.094	0.076	0.091	0.17	0.198	0.151
S3	0.25	0.33	0.22	0.42	0.53	0.67
S4	0.43	0.66	0.56	0.84	1.18	1.06
S5	1.05	1.16	0.81	1.66	1.73	1.53
S6	1.48	1.23	1.55	2.17	2.29	1.82
S7	1.73	1.66	1.76	2.52	2.72	2.28
S8	2.05	2.11	2.27	2.94	3.13	2.73
S9	2.56	2.21	2.39	3.34	3.32	3.17
S10	2.74	2.46	2.51	3.51	3.64	3.33

Table 4. APRG for large-sized test problems in HPSO-SEO and NSGA-II.

Problem number	HPSO-SEO VS. NSGA-II GAP%		
	Obj 1	Obj2	Obj3
L1	4.17	4.21	4.31
L2	5.24	5.54	5.17
L3	6.59	6.65	5.91
L4	7.95	7.57	6.89
L5	8.11	8.54	7.35
L6	9.43	9.37	8.36
L7	10.75	10.05	9.47
L8	11.64	11.64	10.74
L9	12.76	12.34	11.94
L10	13.47	13.23	12.38

Table 6. Results of the model for different values of disruption based on $\eta 1 = \eta 2 = 4000000$ and $\xi = 0.8$.

Test problem = S10	The most likely value			
$\varphi_1 = \varphi_2 = \varphi_3$	1.4	1.3	1.2	1.1
$\rho 2_i = \rho 3_r$	0.2	0.4	0.6	0.8
OFV1	31325987	28674389	24872234	22875340
OFV2	184563	187829	199482	204218
OFV3	198	180	171	152
Backup PDC centers	8	7	4	2
Backup RC centers	4	3	2	1

results of Table 5 show the RPP approach reaches better results for various amount of uncertainty for different range of test problems. It is necessary to mention that, for further analysis RPP method is applied to deal with uncertainties ($\eta 1 = \eta 2 = 4000000$ and $\xi = 0.8$).

Table 6 shows the results of model by changing the parameters related with disruption. According to the results, reducing the mentioned parameters increase the OFV_1, OFV_3 and number of backup centers. However, OFV_2 decreases as the value of disruption parameters reduce.

6.4.2. Managerial insights

Conventionally, the sustainable closed-loop supply chain decision-making aims to find the optimal locations of facilities and their capacity with regards to triple lines of sustainability including economic, environmental and social impacts. However, most especially in developing countries (e.g. for our case study in Iran), where the sustainable supply chain management is a challengeable issue, a simplified approach cannot deliver satisfactory all outcomes in an uncertain environment under lean and agility concepts which are rarely considered in this research area.

This study deployed a novel multi-objective optimization model as an MOMINLP based on a location, routing and inventory planning to formulate a sustainable CLSC in a fuzzy environment based on the robust optimization. Practicality requires the lean and agility concepts to improve the flexibility and resiliency aspects of sustainable CLSC. Efficiency needs a robust and efficient metaheuristic to manage this complex problem computationally. Hence, a hybrid metaheuristic based on the social engineering and particle swarm optimization algorithms is developed.

Most importantly, the viability of a centralized CLSC optimization under uncertainty with financial, environmental and social concerns is demonstrated by the results. At first, a deterministic model is developed and accordingly, an FCCM model is applied to deal with uncertainty.

Based on the results, the first practical insight refers to the shifting the CLSC management to the sustainable CLSC management with flexibility and resiliency conceptually. It also provides an introduction for the design of closed-loop option and reverse logistics. The use of multiple echelons for the collecting, recycling and remanufacturing creates the strong potential for added value across the system.

The rest of managerial insight refers to the dynamic sensitivity of the algorithms to find a well-tuned level of controlling parameters as illustrated in Table 6. This fact strongly encourages further application and development of high-performance algorithms such as HPSO-SEO as a new hybrid extension to the SEO as illustrated in Tables 3 and 4.

7. Conclusion

In this paper, a novel data-driven league sustainable CLSC model to find a compromise solution between economic, environmental and social objective functions, was proposed. The main contributions of this study include: simultaneously addressing routing, inventory, lot sizing, reproduction and location-allocation decisions besides the capacity constraints; Considering economic, green, lean, agility and social factors concurrently; Regarding the strategic and operational decisions to decrease the impacts of disruption; proposing a robust possibilistic programming approach to deal with uncertainty; applying the FCCM to select the potential location for establishing production, distribution and reproduction centers based on proximity to the local retailers and applying the HPSO-SEO algorithm to solve large-sized instances with high performance.

To cope with these contributions, this study develops a model based on the lean manufacturing to support the environmental aspects of the model. In addition, including agile manufacturing strategies is aligned with the aim of increasing the resiliency of the system against disruption risks. Next, the performance of the proposed metaheuristic algorithms is compared with an exact solver in case of quality and the processing time. The results prove the superiority of HPSO-SEO algorithm in case of quality and spacing metrics while the CPU time of NSGA-II is shorter. Afterward, the

Table 5. The results of provided solutions.

Test problem	PCCP 0.7			PCCP 0.8			PCCP 0.9			RPP		
	OFV1	OFV2	OFV3	OFV1	OFV2	OFV3	OFV1	OFV2	OFV3	OFV1	OFV2	OFV3
S1	8554379	50442	27	8353675	50456	25	8253567	50326	22	8106345	49857	19
S2	8577623	53799	30	8397653	53793	30	8263456	53762	28	8123450	52462	23
S3	8689750	57769	54	8489654	57662	53	8389657	57654	50	8296792	56432	47
S4	15162432	63591	59	14163124	63587	58	13145678	63556	56	12234598	62341	53
S5	17341322	75643	73	16345675	75632	73	15324562	75543	71	14432567	74321	68
S6	19213865	86753	86	18213564	86674	85	17221356	86543	82	16754327	85392	77
S7	20963755	93467	91	19963453	93435	91	18954432	93221	86	17543667	92344	81

introduced case of this study shows the applicability of model in real situations.

To analyze the model more exactly, some sensitivity analyses are implemented to analyze the behaviour of the model under different situations. Based on all results of comparison and sensitivities, the managerial insights are found and discussed at the end of last section. The results reveal that there is a direct relationship between social risks and transportation cost and inverse relationship between inventory cost and social risks. More efficiently, shipment cost increases the total cost and decreases the environmental effects. The results of increasing inventory cost are conversely. To this end, this study applied a queuing system to decrease the elapsed time of trucks to load/unload the cargo at the centers and lapsed time due to road blocking. Disruption also has significant effect on the economic aspect of the problem and damages caused by disruption increase the total costs of the system.

To address the future directions of this research, considering other aspects of leagility, resiliency of the system, and perishability of the products is suggested for future research. At last but not least, the application of the developed hybrid approach in other CLSC optimization problems and the development of other heuristic algorithms such as red deer algorithm (Fathollahi-Fard et al., 2020b) are interesting topics for continuations of this paper.

Disclosure statement

No potential conflict of interest was reported by the authors.

ORCID

Abdollah Babaeinesami ⓘD http://orcid.org/0000-0001-6526-9949

References

Abdi, A., Abdi, A., Fathollahi-Fard, A. M., & Hajiaghaei-Keshteli, M. (2019). A set of calibrated metaheuristics to address a closed-loop supply chain network design problem under uncertainty. *International Journal of Systems Science: Operations & Logistics*, 1–18. https://doi.org/10.1080/23302674.2019.1610197

Aćimović, S., Mijušković, V., & Rajić, V. (2020). The impact of reverse logistics onto green supply chain competitiveness evidence from Serbian consumers. *International Journal of Retail & Distribution Management*, 213, 426–441.

As' Ad, R., Hariga, M., & Alkhatib, O. (2019). Two stage closed loop supply chain models under consignment stock agreement and different procurement strategies. *Applied Mathematical Modelling*, 65, 164–186.

Aydin, N. (2020). Designing reverse logistics network of end-of-life-buildings as preparedness to disasters under uncertainty. *Journal of Cleaner Production*, 256, 120341.

Ayvaz, B., & Görener, A. (2020). Reverse logistics in the electronics waste industry. In *Waste management: Concepts, methodologies, tools, and applications* (pp. 1664–1680). IGI Global, Istanbul, Turkey.

Bahadori-Chinibelagh, S., Fathollahi-Fard, A. M., & Hajiaghaei-Keshteli, M. (2019). Two Constructive Algorithms to Address a Multi-depot Home Healthcare Routing Problem, *IETE Journal of Research*, https://doi.org/10.1080/03772063.2019.1642802

Cardoso, S. R., Barbosa-Póvoa, A. P., Relvas, S., & Novais, A. Q. (2015). Resilience metrics in the assessment of complex supply-chains performance operating under demand uncertainty. *Omega*, 56, 53–73.

Chalmardi, M. K., & Camacho-Vallejo, J. F. (2019). A bi-level programming model for sustainable supply chain network design that considers incentives for using cleaner technologies. *Journal of Cleaner Production*, 213, 1035–1050.

Cheraghalipour, A., Paydar, M. M., & Hajiaghaei-Keshteli, M. (2018). A bi-objective optimization for citrus closed-loop supply chain using Pareto-based algorithms. *Applied Soft Computing*, 69, 33–59.

Cheraghalipour, A., Paydar, M. M., & Hajiaghaei-Keshteli, M. (2019). Designing and solving a bi-level model for rice supply chain using the evolutionary algorithms. *Computers and Electronics in Agriculture*, 162, 651–668.

Ciccullo, F., Pero, M., & Caridi, M. (2017). Exploring the hidden potential of product design to mitigate supply chain risk. *International Journal of Electronic Customer Relationship Management*, 11(1), 66–93.

De, M., & Giri, B. (2020). Modelling a closed-loop supply chain with a heterogeneous fleet under carbon emission reduction policy. *Transportation Research Part E: Logistics and Transportation Review*, 133, 101813.

Djatna, T., & Amien, G. (2020). Bi-objective freight scheduling optimization in an integrated forward/reverse logistic network using non-dominated sorting genetic algorithm-II. *Decision Science Letters*, 9(1), 91–106.

Fahimnia, B., Sarkis, J., Dehghanian, F., Banihashemi, N., & Rahman, S. (2013). The impact of carbon pricing on a closed-loop supply chain: An Australian case study. *Journal of Cleaner Production*, 59, 210–225.

Fard, A. F., Gholian-Jouybari, F., Paydar, M. M., & Hajiaghaei-Keshteli, M. (2017). A bi-objective stochastic closed-loop supply chain network design problem considering downside risk. *Industrial Engineering & Management Systems*, 16(3), 342–362.

Fathollahi-Fard, A. M., Ahmadi, A., Goodarzian, F., & Cheikhrouhou, N. (2020c). A bi-objective home healthcare routing and scheduling problem considering patients' satisfaction in a fuzzy environment. *Applied Soft Computing*, 93, 106385.

Fathollahi-Fard, A. M., Govindan, K., Hajiaghaei-Keshteli, M., & Ahmadi, A. (2019b). A green home health care supply chain: New modified simulated annealing algorithms. *Journal of Cleaner Production*, 240, 118200.

Fathollahi-Fard, A. M., Hajiaghaei-Keshteli, M., & Tavakkoli-Moghaddam, R. (2018). The social engineering optimizer (SEO). *Engineering Applications of Artificial Intelligence*, 72, 267–293.

Fathollahi-Fard, A. M., Hajiaghaei-Keshteli, M., & Tavakkoli-Moghaddam, R. (2020b). *Red deer algorithm (RDA): A new nature-inspired meta-heuristic.* Soft Computing. doi:10.1007/s00500-020-04812-z

Fathollahi-Fard, A. M., Hajiaghaei-Keshteli, M., Tian, G., & Li, Z. (2020a). An adaptive Lagrangian relaxation-based algorithm for a coordinated water supply and wastewater collection network design problem. *Information Sciences*, 512, 1335–1359.

Fathollahi-Fard, A. M., Ranjbar-Bourani, M., Cheikhrouhou, N., & Hajiaghaei-Keshteli, M. (2019a). Novel modifications of social engineering optimizer to solve a truck scheduling problem in a cross-docking system. *Computers & Industrial Engineering*, 137, 106103.

Feng, Y., Zhang, Z., Tian, G., Fathollahi-Fard, A. M., Hao, N., Li, Z., ... Tan, J. (2019). A novel hybrid fuzzy grey TOPSIS method: Supplier evaluation of a collaborative manufacturing enterprise. *Applied Sciences*, 9(18), 3770.

Ghasemi, P., Khalili-Damghani, K., Hafezalkotob, A., & Raissi, S. (2019). Uncertain multi-objective multi-commodity multi-period multi-vehicle location-allocation model for earthquake evacuation planning. *Applied Mathematics and Computation*, 350, 105–132.

Ghasemi, P., Khalili-Damghani, K., Hafezalkotob, A., & Raissi, S. (2020). Stochastic optimization model for distribution and evacuation planning (A case study of Tehran earthquake). *Socio-economic Planning Sciences*, 71, 100745.

Ghasemi, P., Khalili-Damghani, K., Hafezolkotob, A., & Raissi, S. (2017). A decentralized supply chain planning model: A case study of hardboard industry. *The International Journal of Advanced Manufacturing Technology*, 93(9–12), 3813–3836.

Ghobadi, M., Arkat, J., & Tavakkoli-Moghaddam, R. (2019). Hypercube queuing models in emergency service systems: A state-of-the-art review. *Scientia Iranica. Transaction E, Industrial Engineering*, 26 (2), 909–931.

Golmohamadi, S., Tavakkoli-Moghaddam, R., & Hajiaghaei-Keshteli, M. (2017). Solving a fuzzy fixed charge solid transportation problem using batch transferring by new approaches in meta-heuristic. *Electronic Notes in Discrete Mathematics*, 58, 143–150.

Govindan, K., Jafarian, A., & Nourbakhsh, V. (2015). Bi-objective integrating sustainable order allocation and sustainable supply chain network strategic design with stochastic demand using a novel robust hybrid multi-objective metaheuristic. *Computers & Operations Research, 62*, 112–130.

Habibi-Kouchaksaraei, M., Paydar, M. M., & Asadi-Gangraj, E. (2018). Designing a bi-objective multi-echelon robust blood supply chain in a disaster. *Applied Mathematical Modelling, 55*, 583–599.

Hajiaghaei-Keshteli, M., & Sajadifar, S. M. (2010). Deriving the cost function for a class of three-echelon inventory system with N-retailers and one-for-one ordering policy. *The International Journal of Advanced Manufacturing Technology, 50*(1-4), 343–351 doi:10.1007/s00170-009-2486-9

Hajiaghaei-Keshteli, M., Sajadifar, S. M., & Haji, R. (2011). Determination of the economical policy of a three-echelon inventory system with (R, Q) ordering policy and information sharing. *The International Journal of Advanced Manufacturing Technology, 55* (5–8), 831–841.

Hajipour, V., Tavana, M., Di Caprio, D., Akhgar, M., & Jabbari, Y. (2019). An optimization model for traceable closed-loop supply chain networks. *Applied Mathematical Modelling, 71*, 673–699.

Hasanov, P., Jaber, M. Y., & Tahirov, N. (2019). Four-level closed loop supply chain with remanufacturing. *Applied Mathematical Modelling, 66*, 141–155.

Hosseini-Motlagh, S.-M., Nouri-Harzvili, M., Johari, M., & Sarker, B. R. (2020). Coordinating economic incentives, customer service and pricing decisions in a competitive closed-loop supply chain. *Journal of Cleaner Production, 255*, 120241.

Isaloo, F., & Paydar, M. M. (2020). Optimizing a robust bi-objective supply chain network considering environmental aspects: A case study in plastic injection industry. *International Journal of Management Science and Engineering Management, 15*(1), 26–38.

Jalil, S. A., Hashmi, N., Asim, Z., & Javaid, S. (2019). A de-centralized bi-level multi-objective model for integrated production and transportation problems in closed-loop supply chain networks. *International Journal of Management Science and Engineering Management, 14*(3), 206–217.

Kannan, G., Sasikumar, P., & Devika, K. (2010). A genetic algorithm approach for solving a closed loop supply chain model: A case of battery recycling. *Applied Mathematical Modelling, 34*(3), 655–670.

Kim, J., Do Chung, B., Kang, Y., & Jeong, B. (2018). Robust optimization model for closed-loop supply chain planning under reverse logistics flow and demand uncertainty. *Journal of Cleaner Production, 196*, 1314–1328.

Kuvvetli, Y., & Erol, R. (2020). Coordination of production planning and distribution in closed-loop supply chains. *Neural Computing & Applications, 124*, 1–19.

Liu, X., Tian, G., Fathollahi-Fard, A. M., & Mojtahedi, M. (2020). Evaluation of ship's green degree using a novel hybrid approach combining group fuzzy entropy and cloud technique for the order of preference by similarity to the ideal solution theory. *Clean Technologies and Environmental Policy, 22*(2), 493–512.

Mehranfar, N., Hajiaghaei-Keshteli, M., & Fathollahi-Fard, A. M. (2019). A novel hybrid whale optimization algorithm to solve a production-distribution network problem considering carbon emissions. *International Journal of Engineering, 32*(12), 1781–1789.

Mohammaddust, F., Rezapour, S., Farahani, R. Z., Mofidfar, M., & Hill, A. (2017). Developing lean and responsive supply chains: A robust model for alternative risk mitigation strategies in supply chain designs. *International Journal of Production Economics, 183*, 632–653.

Mohtashami, Z., Aghsami, A., & Jolai, F. (2020). A green closed loop supply chain design using queuing system for reducing environmental impact and energy consumption. *Journal of Cleaner Production, 242*, 118452.

Mokhtari, H., & Hasani, A. (2017). A multi-objective model for cleaner production-transportation planning in manufacturing plants via fuzzy goal programming. *Journal of Manufacturing Systems, 44*, 230–242.

Nezhadroshan, A. M., Fathollahi-Fard, A. M., & Hajiaghaei-Keshteli, M. (2020). A scenario-based possibilistic-stochastic programming approach to address resilient humanitarian logistics considering travel time and resilience levels of facilities. *International Journal of Systems Science: Operations & Logistics*, 1–27. https://doi.org/10.1080/23302674.2020.1769766.

Pan, C., Zhai, J., & Wang, Z. L. (2019). Piezotronics and piezo-phototronics of third generation semiconductor nanowires. *Chemical reviews, 119*(15), 9303–9359 doi:10.1021/acs.chemrev.8b00599

Pan, Z., Tang, J., & Liu, O. (2009). Capacitated dynamic lot sizing problems in closed-loop supply chain. *European Journal of Operational Research, 198*(3), 810–821.

Rohaninejad, M., Sahraeian, R., & Tavakkoli-Moghaddam, R. (2018). Multi-echelon supply chain design considering unreliable facilities with facility hardening possibility. *Applied Mathematical Modelling, 62*, 321–337.

Sadghiani, N. S., Torabi, S., & Sahebjamnia, N. (2015). Retail supply chain network design under operational and disruption risks. *Transportation Research Part E: Logistics and Transportation Review, 75*, 95–114.

Saeedi, S., Mohammadi, M., & Torabi, S. (2015). A De Novo programming approach for a robust closed-loop supply chain network design under uncertainty: An M/M/1 queueing model. *International Journal of Industrial and Manufacturing Systems Engineerin, 6*(2), 211–228.

Safaei, A. S., Farsad, S., & Paydar, M. M. (2018). Robust bi-level optimization of relief logistics operations. *Applied Mathematical Modelling, 56*, 359–380.

Safaei, A. S., Roozbeh, A., & Paydar, M. M. (2017). A robust optimization model for the design of a cardboard closed-loop supply chain. *Journal of Cleaner Production, 166*, 1154–1168.

Safaeian, M., Fathollahi-Fard, A. M., Tian, G., Li, Z., & Ke, H. (2019). A multi-objective supplier selection and order allocation through incremental discount in a fuzzy environment. *Journal of Intelligent & Fuzzy Systems, 37*(1), 1435–1455.

Shalke, P. N., Paydar, M. M., & Hajiaghaei-Keshteli, M. (2018). Sustainable supplier selection and order allocation through quantity discounts. *International Journal of Management Science and Engineering Management, 13*(1), 20–32.

Shamsi, F., Mahdavi, I., & Paydar, M. M. (2020). A possibilistic programming approach to analyze a closed-loop polyethylene tanks supply chain based on decision tree and discounted cash flow. *International Journal of Management Science and Engineering Management, 15*(2), 106–121.

Soleimani, H., & Kannan, G. (2015). A hybrid particle swarm optimization and genetic algorithm for closed-loop supply chain network design in large-scale networks. *Applied Mathematical Modelling, 39* (14), 3990–4012 doi:10.1016/j.apm.2014.12.016

Torkaman, S., Ghomi, S. F., & Karimi, B. (2017). Multi-stage multi-product multi-period production planning with sequence-dependent setups in closed-loop supply chain. *Computers & Industrial Engineering, 219*, 113602–113613.

Vahdani, B., & Mohammadi, M. (2015). A bi-objective interval-stochastic robust optimization model for designing closed loop supply chain network with multi-priority queuing system. *International Journal of Production Economics, 170*, 67–87.

Vahdani, B., Tavakkoli-Moghaddam, R., Modarres, M., & Baboli, A. (2012). Reliable design of a forward/reverse logistics network under uncertainty: A robust-M/M/c queuing model. *Transportation Research Part E: Logistics and Transportation Review, 48*(6), 1152–1168.

Exploring capability maturity models and relevant practices as solutions addressing information technology service offshoring project issues*

Rosine Salman, Tugrul Daim, David Raffo and Marina Dabic

ABSTRACT

This research investigated Capability Maturity Models (CMMs) / Capability Maturity Model Integration (CMMI) best practices and their effects on managing and mitigating critical issues associated with offshore development. Using a web-based survey, data were collected from 451 Information Technology (IT) and software development firms in the US. The results of the analysis show that IT companies applying CMM/CMMI models have fewer issues associated with IT offshoring. When US IT companies utilizing and incorporating different practices from Team Software Process (TSP) and People CMM into CMMI-DEV/SVC is CMMI for Development and Services (CMMI-DEV/SVC) and CMMI for Acquisition (CMMI-ACQ), they have fewer offshoring issues related to language barriers and cultural differences.

1. Introduction

Offshoring is the outsourcing or/and in-sourcing of Information Technology (IT) work to a third party supplier located on a continent different from that of the client (Rottman & Lacity, 2008). The globalization of resources has resulted in a dramatic increase in offshoring. Although client companies have offshored manufacturing services for decades, the practice of offshoring IT services is still maturing. Offshoring is the transfer of an organizational function to another country, regardless of whether the work is outsourced to a third party company (vendor) or stays within the same company (Bhalla, Sodhi, & Son, 2008; Carmel & Agrawal, 2002b; Kakabadse & Kakabadse, 2002; Trent & Monczka, 2005), whereas Carmel defined offshoring as performing work for clients in one country using workers located in a different country, this work may be outsourced to an offshore third party provider or conducted by wholly or partially owned offshore subsidiaries of the onshore parent company (Carmel & Abbott, 2006).

The offshoring of IT services (primarily in India) represents, at a conservative estimate, 25% of US$ 1 trillion in 2014 global IT services (Kathpalia & Raman, 2014). Gartner reported that the top five Indian IT vendors, namely TCS, Cognizant, Infosys, Wipro and HCl Technologies, grew 13.3% in 2012 to reach US$ 34.3 billion in 2012, exceeding the global IT services industry growth rate of 2%. North American markets currently contribute to roughly 70% of the revenue of Indian IT service companies (Kathpalia & Raman, 2014). Many companies used offshoring strategies hoping to reduce costs (Williams, 1995). On the other hand, contrary to popular perceptions, many companies have had mixed or diverse results. Half of the organizations that shifted processes offshore failed to generate the financial benefits they expected (Ferguson, 2004a; Lacity & Willcocks, 1998, 2001; Lacity, Willcocks, & Feeny, 1996) and 50% of the offshoring contracts by North American companies signed between 2001 and 2004 are likely to fail to meet their goals, according the predictions of both Gartner and the Boston Consulting Group (Aron & Singh, 2005). Gartner and the Boston Consulting Group found that 50% of the offshoring contracts by North American companies fail to meet their expectations (Moe et al., 2013).

2. Literature review

Although offshoring IT is technically possible because any work that can be digitized can be moved to an offshore supplier(s), there are many managerial challenges (Rottman & Lacity, 2008). One common complaint was that overall cost savings were less than anticipated due to the high transaction costs associated with finding suppliers and coordinating and monitoring the work done offshore (Ferguson, 2004b; Golder, 2004). Other common complaints were poor initial quality, late deliveries and personnel issues such as high supplier turnover that interfered with success (Lacity & Rottman, 2008). IT services contain a range of activities, such as: software application development (web design development, e-commerce projects); database administration; software customization; IT calling centers; IT help desk support; software maintenance (remote software maintenance, feature enhancement); and operations and facility management (Lacity & Rottman, 2008). IT service offshoring may either be a one-time limited-duration project or a long-term relationship. Offshoring poses additional challenges compared with domestic outsourcing (Rottman & Lacity, 2006). For example, offshoring is more challenging because of: time-zone differences (Carmel, 2006); the need for more control (Chaudhury & Sabherwal, 2003); cultural differences (Carmel & Tjia, 2005; Prikladnicki et al., 2003); the need to define requirements more rigorously (Chaudhury & Sabherwal, 2003; Gopal et al., 2003); the difficulties in managing dispersed teams (Oshri,

---

*A prior version of this paper was presented at Portland International Conference on Management of Engineering and Technology (Hanna et al. 2014b)

Kotlarsky, & Willcocks, 2008); and politically driven interests between the client and the service provider (Orlikowski, 2002). (Table 1) Capability Maturity Models (CMMs) / Capability Maturity Model Integration (CMMI) "in software engineering and organizational development is a process improvement approach that provides organizations with the essential elements for effective process improvement". CMM/CMMI "can be used to guide process improvement across a project, a division or an entire organization (CMMI Product Team, 2010b)". CMM/CMMI tries to define "the key elements of an effective process and outlines how to improve suboptimal processes, i.e. the evolution from an 'immature' process to a 'mature, disciplined' one" (CMMI Product Team, 2010a, 2010c).

CMMI tools minimize the risks of outsourcing projects of government and industrial companies (Harter, Krishnan, & Slaughter, 2000). Research shows that it has proven to increase productivity and the quality of outsourced projects (Harter et al., 2000). Research studies have consistently shown results regarding improved productivity, increased quality and reductions in cycle time (Curtis, Hefley, & Miller, 2001, 2010; Harter et al., 2000; Herbsleb & Grinter, 1999). CMMI for Acquisition (CMMI-ACQ) helps client companies improve relationships with their suppliers by assisting client companies improve their own processes. Research based on case studies and interviews with experts supports the People-CMM approach as a key tool for managing an organization's total performance, and evidence indicates that People Capability Maturity Model imroves teamwork, communication and knowledge levels (Vakaslahti, 1998). Since its release in 1995, thousands of copies of People CMM have been distributed worldwide and were used by organizations large and small such as IBM, Boeing, BAE Systems, Tata Consultancy Services, Ericsson, Lockheed Martin and QAI (India) Ltd.

The practices of the Team Software Process (TSP) help "create a team of software developers that can build a quality product on time and on budget, and where the team is still functional after the product is built". According to Humphrey (2002), the TSP is designed to build and manage quality software teams. (Humphrey, Davis, & McHale, 2003) attributed this rapid pace of improvement to the organization's prior introduction and adaptation of the TSP. The CMM/CMMI model requires a considerable amount of time, money and effort to implement and often requires a major shift of culture and attitude in the organizations that decide to apply it (Brooks, 1987; Ibbs & Kwak, 2000; Jiang, Klien, Hwang, Huang, & Hung, 2004). One study in the US software sector found that the median time for an organization to move up one level of five-level CMM/CMMI is between 21 and 37 months (Herbsleb, Zubrow, Goldenson, Hayes, & Paulk, 1997b). Over three-quarters of the organizations reported that implementing any Specific Practice (SP) activity took longer than expected. In addition, an organization's culture can be adversely impacted by adding to CMMI rigid bureaucracy and reducing the creativity and freedom of the developers (Jones, 1995). Researchers such as Johansen, Mathiassen, Neilsen and Borbjerg have suggested that CMM/CMMI does not deal effectively with the social aspects of IT organizations. (Johansen & Mathiassen, 1998) argue that CMM/CMMI needs a more managerial focus. Iversen, Nielsen and Nørbjerg (2002) explain that "CMM needs to be supplemented with socially oriented theories in order to address organizational change issues and organizational politics". (Aaen, Arent, Mathiassen, 2001) explain that "the scale and complexity of the organizational change proposed by CMM necessitates a managerial rather than a technical approach".

Although these process improvement approaches were originally developed as methods for the objective evaluation of contractors for military software projects (*outsourcing*) and were not designed with *offshoring* development in mind, they are widely adapted and have received great publicity in the software development industry (Amberg & Wiener, 2005; Biberoglu & Haddad, 2002; Dubey, 2003, Fitzgerald & O'Kane, 1999; Gibson, Goldenson, & Kost, 2006; Jiang et al., 2004; Meyer, 2006). However, the literature also shows that there is limited research and investigation of CMM/CMMI best practices and how they mitigate the issues and challenges of offshoring of IT services and software development projects (Ebert, 2007; Ebert, Murthy, & Jha, 2008; Gopal, Mukhopadhyay, & Krishnan, 2002b; Lasser & Heiss, 2005; Prikladnicki, Audy, Damian, & Oliveira, 2007; Sengupta, Chandra, & Sinha, 2006b).

Maturity models have also been developed or studied for other functions: project management maturity in industrial companies (Spalek, 2015); sustainable operations management (Machado, de Lima, da Costa, Angelis, & Mattioda, 2017); enterprise maturity in production management (Kosieradzka, 2017); portfolio management (Nikkhou, Taghizadeh, & Hajiyakhchali, 2016); project management (de Souza & Gomes, 2015; Tahri & Drissi-Kaitouni, 2015); energy management (Finnerty, Sterling, Coakley, & Keane, in press; Jovanović & Filipović, 2016); integrated management systems (Domingues, Sampaio, & Arezes, 2016); remanufacturing process capability (Butzer, Schötz, & Steinhilper, 2017); learning factories (Enke, Glass, & Metternich, 2017); IT based case management (Koehler, Woodtly, & Hofstetter, 2015); and staged models (Uskarci & Demirörs, 2017). CMM/CMMI models and best practices, to mitigate the issues and challenges of offshoring IT services and software development projects, have not been adequately investigated and most evidence is anecdotal.

Hanna et al (2014a) provided further literature detail used for the development of specific hypotheses. This paper builds upon the prior conference presentation by Hanna et al (2014b).

3. Methodology

Based on the literature review, research questions and hypotheses were formed, the questionnaire was designed and two expert panels were formed: (1) a CMM/CMMI IT service offshoring expert panel and (2) an IT service offshoring expert panel with no CMM/CMMI experience. Testing and validation of the questionnaire were applied with various iterations were performed to get the final version of the questionnaire. Data were collected; then the analysis phase started, followed by results, discussion and interpretation. The following research questions and hypotheses were developed for this research.

Research questions

Q1: What is the impact of client firms adopting CMM/CMMI industry standards on the frequency of issues experienced by client firms when offshoring IT service projects?

Q2: What is the relationship between the CMM/CMMI maturity level achieved and the frequency of issues experienced by client firms when offshoring IT service projects?

Q3: What is the relationship between performing CMM/CMMI industry standard practices and the frequency of issues experienced by client firms when offshoring IT service projects?

Hypotheses

H1. *There is a relationship between adopting CMM/CMMI and the frequency of issues experienced by client firms when offshoring IT service projects.*

Table 1. Forms of outsource and offshore sourcing.

Form	Type of outsourcing	Description
In-sourcing	In-house (Lacity & Willcocks, 1998; Lacity, Willcocks, & Rottman, 2008; Metters, 2007)	The clients handle their own IT services and software development projects on their own premises in their home countries
	Subsidiaries (Lacity et al., 2008; Metters, 2007)	The client builds, owns, staffs and operates facilities in domestic locations in the US (Carmel & Agrawal, 2002b; Trent & Monczka, 2005)
	Domestic captive (Lacity et al., 2008; Metters, 2007)	
	Captive service centres (Beulen, Fenema, & Currie, 2005; Carmel & Beulen, 2005)	Clients provide IT services from their own premises, employees, equipment and facilities in domestic locations (Beulen et al., 2005)
Outsourcing	Outsourcing (Carmel & Agrawal, 2002b)	Firms that outsource only domestically (Carmel & Agrawal, 2002b). An agreement in which one company hands over a part or all of their existing internal activity to another company through a contract (Hanna & Daim, 2009b)
	IT outsourcing (Palvia, 1995)	Contracting part or all of a firm's IT such as data processing, software, communication network, systems personnel or call centres to a third-party vendor (Palvia, 1995)
	Outsourcing with a domestic supplier (Lacity et al., 1996, 2008; Willcocks & Kern, 1998)	Refers to a company contracting out of goods or services that were previously produced internally to a domestic third-party company (Amiti & Wei, 2005; Lacity & Hirschheim, 1993b). The third party can be one or multiple domestic/national vendors or in-state providers (Hoffmann, 1996; McFarlan & Nolan, 1995)
	Outsourcing with multiple domestic suppliers (Hoffmann, 1996; Lacity et al., 1996, 2008; McFarlan & Nolan, 1995; Willcocks & Kern, 1998)	
	Outsourcing with in-state supplier (Lacity et al., 2008)	Onshoring represents outsourcing to a domestic supplier (Laplante, Costello, Singh, Bindiganavile, & Landon, 2004)
	Onshoring (Laplante et al., 2004)	
	Total outsourcing (Lacity & Willcocks, 1998)	Contracting out more than 80% of work to an external domestic provider while retaining management (Lacity & Willcocks, 1998). The transfer of all business functions from the outsourcing company to the outsourcing vendor (Allen & Chandrashekar, 2000)
	Complete outsourcing (Allen & Chandrashekar, 2000)	
	Total in-sourcing (Lacity & Willcocks, 1998)	Execute work internally (Lacity & Willcocks, 1998). The delegation of operations or jobs from production within a business to an internal (but 'stand-alone') entity that specializes in that job (Lacity et al., 1996). In-sourcing is a business decision that is often made to maintain control of critical production or competencies. An alternative use of the term implies transferring jobs to within the country where the term is used, either by hiring local subcontractors or building a facility (Hirschheim & Lacity, 2000)
	In-sourcing – contracting-in (Lacity et al., 1996)	
	Fee-for-service contracts (Bhalla et al., 2008; Carmel & Agrawal, 2002b)	
	Selective outsourcing – smart sourcing – right sourcing (Lacity & Willcocks, 1998)	Outsourcing of selected processes while still executing internally between 20 and 80% of work. The company may outsource to a single or multiple vendors (Lacity & Willcocks, 1998)
	Business Process Outsourcing (BPO) (Halvey & Melby, 2007; Yang et al., 2007)	The biggest difference between outsourcing and BPO is that the BPO third-party vendor providers control all issues related to business processes, human resources and technology (Yang, Kim, Nam, & Min, 2007)
Offshoring: multi-national company	Multinational company outsourcing Consultancy companies (Schwalbe, 2010)	Companies having their headquarters in high-wage countries open subsidiaries in low-wage countries to work on products and services for their domestic and global market
	MultiNational Enterprises (MNEs)	Companies having their headquarters in low-wage countries can open subsidiaries in high-wage countries to serve the local market (Niosi & Tschang, 2009; Schwalbe, 2010)
	Value centres (Trent & Monczka, 2005), Profit value centres (Venkatraman, 1997).	The customer owns and runs the facility as a profit centre, offering services to other international companies (Trent & Monczka, 2005; Venkatraman, 1997)
	'Greenfield' subsidiaries (Niosi & Tschang, 2009)	A form of foreign direct investment where a parent company in a developing country starts a new venture in a developed foreign country from the ground up (Niosi & Tschang, 2009)
	Body-shopping (Majumdar, Simons, & Nag, 2011)	On-shore temporary hiring from a multinational (such as an Indian) firm. Onsite consultancy performed at clients' premises, involving software professionals who act as temporary employees of clients. For international clients, body-shopping keeps work within their home nations and premises. Clients' demand determines how much body-shopping is needed (Majumdar et al., 2011). Normally these services are provided by US domestic subsidiaries of multinational companies (Lacity & Willcocks, 1995)
Offshoring	Near-shore (Laplante et al., 2004)	Relocation of business processes to (classically) lower-cost foreign locations, but in close geographical proximity (e.g. shifting US-based business processes to Canada/Latin America) (Bock, 2008; Carmel, 1999, 2007; Carmel & Abbott, 2006; Laplante et al., 2004)
	Far-shore/Offshore	Near-shoring, far-shoring and offshoring refer to the fact that some of the duties belonging to software projects are sourced out to a lower-wage country (Aspray, Mayadas, & Vardi, 2006). Whether the term used is offshoring or near-shoring seems to be a matter of distance (Carmel & Abbott, 2006). Offshoring is associated with countries being 'far away', referring to a distance of more than 1000 km (i.e. 621 miles) or a few hours flight away (Carmel, 2007; Carmel & Abbott, 2006)
	Dedicated offshore outsourcing (Carmel & Agrawal, 2002b; Palvia, 1995; Trent & Monczka, 2005)	The offshore vendor owning the operation dedicates part of its facility to the customer (Carmel & Agrawal, 2002b; Leiblein et al., 2002; Palvia, 1995; Trent & Monczka, 2005)
	Fully owned facility (Leiblein, Reuer, & Dalsace, 2002)	
	Build–Operate–Transfer (BOT) (Carmel & Agrawal, 2002b; Colombo, 2003; Trent & Monczka, 2005)	BOT forms a hybrid between dedicated and captive facilities. The company forms a strategic alliance with an offshoring vendor to set-up and manage an offshore facility with an option to own the facility after the expiration of a specified period (Bhalla et al., 2008; Carmel & Agrawal, 2002b; Colombo, 2003)
	Strategic alliances/partner-ships (Lacity & Willcocks, 1998)	
	Offshore in-sourcing	The client builds, owns, staffs and operates the offshore facility (Carmel & Agrawal, 2002b; Trent & Monczka, 2005). The company owns and establishes offshore IT centres where foreign technology workers are employees of US based companies and receive the same training, software tools and development process guidelines as their western counterparts (Carmel & Agrawal, 2002b; Rao, 2004)
	Captive model (Trent & Monczka, 2005)	
	Wholly owned offshore Captive centre (Carmel & Agrawal, 2002b)	
	Subsidiary Offshore in-sourcing	
	Global in-sourcing	
Offshore out-sourcing	Offshore outsourcing (Hanna & Daim, 2009b; Michell & Fitzgerald, 1997; Trent & Monczka, 2005)	A contract or agreement with the vendor for his services. The company offshore outsources one or more projects based on a contract(s) for a fixed cost and depending on identified deliverables and time schedules (Hanna & Daim, 2009b; Rivard & Aubert, 2007). The offshore vendor owns, builds, staffs and operates the facility on behalf of the customer (Lacity & Willcocks, 1998; Michell & Fitzgerald, 1997; Trent & Monczka, 2005)
	Global outsourcing	
	International outsourcing (Amiti & Wei, 2005; Carmel & Agrawal, 2002b)	

H2. *There is a relationship between the CMM/CMMI maturity level achieved and the frequency of issues experienced by firms when offshoring IT service projects.*

H3. *There is a relationship between CMM/CMMI practices and the frequency of issues experienced by firms when offshoring IT service projects.*

The hypotheses were derived from the research questions. The first hypothesis aims to test the relationship between adopting industrial standards and the frequency of issues experienced by the client firms when offshoring IT service projects. The second hypothesis is aimed at testing the relationship between the maturity level achieved and the frequency of issues experienced by client firm when offshoring IT service projects. The third hypothesis is intended to test the relationship between adopting industrial standard best practices and the frequency of issues experienced by client firms when offshoring IT service projects.

Web- and email-based surveys are used more because it is easier, less expensive and faster than mail or phone surveys (Reynolds, Woods, & Baker, 2006; Schonlau, Fricker, & Elliott, 2002; Sue & Ritter, 2007). A standard survey instrument (Cooper & Pamela, 2008, Cooper & Schindler,

2006; Graziano & Raulin, 2006; Zikmund, 1999) will help to collect data for analysis utilizing Chi-squared for testing the hypotheses (Dillon & Goldstein, 1984; Hair, Anderson, Tatham, & Black, 1995; Johnson & Wichern, 1992). The Kompass database was used to build the database of 12,000 target IT companies (www.us.kompass.com). At the conclusion of data collection, 316 valid responses were considered for this research; 558 responses were received (a 6.14% response rate), 451 of which were completed responses, 371 responses were from companies that offshored their IT projects and 55 responses were excluded from the analyses (being from companies that used other quality assurance models – in this manner, their results will not affect our data analysis).

4. Results

A growing number of organizations are adopting the Software Engineering Institutes' (SEI's) Capability Maturity Model (CMM) and Capability Maturity Model Integrate (CMMI) to improve their IT service and software development process. CMM/CMMI became an industry standard based on industry best practices and features industry standard appraisal methods

Table 2. Summary of H1.1 – Adopting CMMI for DEV/SVC and offshoring issues.

Hypothesis 1.1			
'There is a relationship between adopting CMMI-DEV/SVC and … '		Status: 'significantly associated'?*	Strength of association
H1.1.1	Over expenditure issue	Yes	0.610
H1.1.2	Poor execution plan, specifically timing and type of work transferred to the supplier issue	Yes	0.707
H1.1.3	Difference in interpretation of project requirements between client company and supplier	Yes	0.659
H1.1.4	Poorly developed and documented requirements by the client company	Yes	0.685
H1.1.5	Poor tracking and managing of requirement changes by the client company	Yes	0.681
H1.1.6	Lack of a full communication plan between the client company and the supplier company	Yes	0.641
H1.1.7	Communication and coordination problems between the client company and the supplier company	Yes	0.703
H1.1.8	Language barriers between the client company and the supplier	No	0
H1.1.9	Time-zone differences between the client company and the supplier	No	0
H1.1.10	Cultural differences between the client company and the supplier	No	0
H1.1.11	Incomplete and unclear contract	Yes	0.617
H1.1.12	Early contract renegotiation and termination	Yes	0.589
H1.1.13	Difference in project management practices between your company and the supplier	Yes	0.639
H1.1.14	Client company unable to measure the performance of the supplier	Yes	0.672
H1.1.15	Supplier technical/security and political issues	No	0
H1.1.16	Insufficient previous experience of the supplier	Yes	0.645
H1.1.17	Lack of supplier standardized working methods	Yes	0.626

*$p = .05/68 = 0.000,7352$ (Bonferroni adjustment).

Table 3. Summary of H1.2 – Adopting CMMI for acquisition and offshoring issues.

Hypothesis 1.2			
'There is a relationship between adopting CMMI for acquisition and … '		Status: 'significantly associated'?*	Strength of association
H1.2.1	Over expenditure issue	Yes	0.769
H1.2.2	Frequency of poor execution plan	Yes	0.609
H1.2.3	Difference in interpretation of project requirements	Yes	0.542
H1.2.4	Poorly developed and documented requirements	Yes	0.532
H1.2.5	Poor tracking and managing of requirement changes	Yes	0.566
H1.2.6	Lack of a full communication plan	Yes	0.545
H1.2.7	Communication and coordination problems	Yes	0.613
H1.2.8	Language barriers	No	0
H1.2.9	Time-zone differences	No	0
H1.2.10	Cultural differences	No	0
H1.2.11	Incomplete and unclear contract issue	Yes	0.498
H1.2.12	Early contract renegotiation and termination issue	Yes	0.642
H1.2.13	Difference in project management practices	Yes	0.474
H1.2.14	Unable to measure the performance of the supplier issue	Yes	0.584
H1.2.15	Supplier security and political issues	No	0
H1.2.16	Insufficient previous experience of the supplier issue	Yes	0.624
H1.2.17	Lack of supplier standardized working methods issue	Yes	0.645

*$p = .05/68 = 0.000,7352$ (Bonferroni's adjustment).

(Dubey, 2003; Olson, 2008). This research examined four CMM/CMMI models: (1) CMMI for Development/Services (DEV/SVC); (2) CMMI for Acquisition (CMMI-ACQ); (3) People CMM; (4) TSP. Little is known regarding how adopting CMM/CMMI influences the frequency of IT offshoring issues experienced by the client companies. This research investigated CMM/CMMI best practices and their effect on managing and mitigating critical issues associated with offshore development. The analysis of hypothesis H1 showed a statistically associated relationship between adopting CMMI for DEV/SVC and CMMI for ACQ models and IT offshoring issues (77%). However, the results did not show a significant relationship, with 25% of the IT offshoring issues being language barriers, time-zone differences, cultural differences and supplier political and security issues. Therefore, this may suggest that, consistent with the literature, IT services and software development offshoring projects pose significant issues and challenges to the client companies in managing these projects (Ebert et al., 2008). In IT service offshoring, delivery occurs under the additional condition of distance between the service supplier and the client in terms of physical distance, time-zone differences or cultural differences. As more geographically dispersed teams are formed, complexity increases (Holmström, Fitzgerald, & Conchuir, 2008; McIvor, 2000; Yalaho & Nahar,

2009). Therefore, there is a need to utilize different methods to mitigate the issues and challenges of offshoring effectively and efficiently.

The analyses of hypotheses H1.1, H1.2, H1.3 and H1.4 showed surprising results (see Tables 2–5). There was a statistical association relationship between adopting People CMM and TSP and language barriers and cultural differences between the client company and the supplier company, whereas these two issues did not show a significance when adopting CMMI for DEV/SVC and CMMI for ACQ, which are mostly adopted by IT offshoring companies. This may suggest that there is a need to utilize and incorporate different practices from TSP and People CMMI along with CMMI for DEV/SVC and CMMI for ACQ to mitigate the issues of language barriers and cultural differences effectively and efficiently. On the other hand, the analysis of hypothesis H2 showed a statistical significance between adopting CMMI for DEV/SVC and CMMI for ACQ maturity levels achieved and IT offshoring issues (77%) (Tables 6–8). Table 9 shows a summary of the status of hypothesis 3 investigating the relationship between adopting CMM/CMMI industry standards best practices and the frequency of IT offshoring issues experienced. To explain the statistical results, a possible hypothetical scenario is developed based on the company background and the targeted goal. Adopting CMM/

Table 4. Summary of H1.3 – Adopting People CMM and IT offshoring issues.

Hypothesis 1.3			
'There is a relationship between adopting People CMM and … '		Status: 'significantly associated'?*	Strength of association
H1.3.1	Over expenditure issue	No	0
H1.3.2	Poor execution plan	Yes	.307
H1.3.3	Difference in interpretation of project requirements	Yes	.427
H1.3.4	Poorly developed and documented requirements by client company	Yes	.382
H1.3.5	Poor tracking and managing of requirement changes	Yes	.342
H1.3.6	Lack of a full communication plan	Yes	.499
H1.3.7	Communication and coordination problems	Yes	.453
H1.3.8	Language barriers between the client and supplier	Yes	.387
H1.3.9	Time-zone differences between the client company and the supplier	No	0
H1.3.10	Cultural differences between the client company and the supplier	Yes	.413
H1.3.11	Incomplete and unclear contract issue	Yes	.335
H1.3.12	Early contract renegotiation and termination issue	No	0
H1.3.13	Difference in project management practices	No	0
H1.3.14	Unable to measure the performance of the supplier	No	0
H1.3.15	Supplier technical/security and political issues	No	0
H1.3.16	Insufficient previous experience of the supplier issue	Yes	.314
H1.3.17	Lack of supplier standardized working methods issue	Yes	.296

*p = .05/68 = 0.000,7352 (Bonferroni's adjustment).

Table 5. Summary of H1.4 – Adopting TSP and IT offshoring issues.

Hypothesis 1.4			
'There is a relationship between adopting TSP and … '		Status: 'significantly associated'?*	Strength of association
H1.4.1	Over expenditure	No	0
H1.4.2	Poor execution plan	Yes	0.304
H1.4.3	Difference in interpretation of project requirements	Yes	0.384
H1.4.4	Poorly developed and documented requirements	Yes	0.304
H1.4.5	Poor tracking and managing of requirement changes	Yes	0.324
H1.4.6	Lack of a full communication plan	Yes	0.464
H1.4.7	Communication and coordination problems	Yes	0.424
H1.4.8	Language barriers	Yes	0.517
H1.4.9	Time-zone differences	No	0
H1.4.10	Cultural differences	Yes	0.492
H1.4.11	Incomplete and unclear contract issue	Yes	0.303
H1.4.12	Early contract renegotiation and termination issue	Yes	0.304
H1.4.13	Difference in project management practices	No	0
H1.4.14	Unable to measure the performance of the supplier issue	No	0
H1.4.15	Supplier security and political issues	No	0
H1.4.16	Insufficient previous experience of the supplier issue	No	0
H1.4.17	Lack of supplier standardized working methods issue	No	0

*p = .05/68 = 0.000,7352 (Bonferroni's adjustment).

Table 6. H2.1 – CMMI-DEV/SVC Maturity Level (ML) achieved and IT offshoring issues.

Hypothesis 2.1

'There is a relationship between the CMMI-DEV/SVC ML achieved and … '		Status: 'significantly associated'?*	Strength of association
H2.1.1	Over expenditure issue	Yes	0.769
H2.1.2	Poor execution plan, specifically timing	Yes	0.609
H2.1.3	Difference in interpretation of project requirements	Yes	0.542
H2.1.4	Poorly developed and documented requirements	Yes	0.532
H2.1.5	Poor tracking and managing of requirement changes	Yes	0.566
H2.1.6	Lack of a full communication plan	Yes	0.545
H2.1.7	Communication and coordination problems	Yes	0.613
H2.1.8	Language barriers between client and supplier	No	0
H2.1.9	Time-zone differences	No	0
H2.1.10	Cultural differences	No	0
H2.1.11	Incomplete and unclear contract issue	Yes	0.498
H2.1.12	Early contract renegotiation and termination issue	Yes	0.642
H2.1.13	Difference in project management practices	Yes	0.474
H2.1.14	Unable to measure the performance of supplier	Yes	0.584
H2.1.15	Supplier technical/security and political issues	No	0
H2.1.16	Insufficient previous experience of supplier	Yes	0.624
H2.1.17	Lack of supplier standardized working methods	Yes	0.645

*p = .05/51 (17*3) = 0.000,980,39 (Bonferroni's adjustment).

Table 7. H2.2 – CMMI-ACQ ML achieved and IT offshoring issues.

Hypothesis 2.2

'There is a relationship between adopting CMMI-ACQ ML achieved and … '		Status: 'significantly associated'?*	Strength of association
H2.2.1	Over expenditure issue	Yes	0.769
H2.2.2	Poor execution plan	Yes	0.609
H2.2.3	Difference in interpretation of project requirements	Yes	0.542
H2.2.4	Poorly developed and documented requirements	Yes	0.532
H2.2.5	Poor tracking and managing of requirement changes	Yes	0.566
H2.2.6	Lack of a full communication plan	Yes	0.545
H2.2.7	Communication and coordination problems	Yes	0.613
H2.2.8	Language barriers between client company and supplier	No	0
H2.2.9	Time-zone differences	No	0
H2.2.10	Cultural differences	No	0
H2.2.11	Incomplete and unclear contract issue	Yes	0.498
H2.2.12	Early contract renegotiation and termination	Yes	0.642
H2.2.13	Difference in project management	Yes	0.474
H2.2.14	Unable to measure performance of supplier	Yes	0.584
H2.2.15	Supplier technical/security and political issues	No	0
H2.2.16	Insufficient previous experience of the supplier issue	Yes	0.502
H2.2.17	Lack of supplier standardized working methods	Yes	0.498

*p = .05/51 (17*3) = 0.000,980,39 (Bonferroni's adjustment).

Table 8. H2.3 – People-CMM maturity level achieved and IT offshoring issues.

Hypothesis 2.3

'There is a relationship between adopting People-CMM ML achieved and the … '		Status: 'significantly associated'?†*
H2.3.1	Over expenditure issue	No
H2.3.2	Poor execution plan	No*
H2.3.3	Difference in interpretation of project requirements	No*
H2.3.4	Poorly developed and documented requirements by the client company issue	No*
H2.3.5	Poor tracking and managing of requirement changes by client company issue	No*
H2.3.6	Lack of a full communication plan issue	No*
H2.3.7	Communication and coordination problems	No*
H2.3.8	Language barriers between the client company and the supplier issue	No*
H2.3.9	Time-zone differences	No*
H2.3.10	Cultural differences	No*
H2.3.11	Incomplete and unclear contract issue	No*
H2.3.12	Contract renegotiation and termination issue	No*
H2.3.13	Difference in project management practices between client and supplier	No
H2.3.14	Unable to measure the performance of the supplier issue	No*
H2.3.15	Supplier technical/security and political issues	No*
H2.3.16	Insufficient previous experience of the supplier issue	No*
H2.3.17	Lack of supplier standardized working methods	No*

†Small sample of 36 valid cases – results may differ with more data.
*p = .05/51 (17*3) = 0.000,980,39 (Bonferroni's adjustment);
Note: The investigation of hypothesis H3 showed that the more frequently did an IT offshoring company routinely perform CMM/CMMI industry standard practices, the fewer issues with IT offshoring did they report (see Table 9). The analysis showed a significant relationship between CMM/CMMI industry standard practices and the IT offshoring issues (92%).

Table 9. H3.1 – Results of the practices and IT offshoring issues.

Hypothesis	Issues and CMM/CMMI practices	Status: 'significantly associated'?*	Strength of association
H3.1	Issue 1: Over expenditure and CMM/CMMI practices PR1 to PR6		
H3.1.1	PR1: Establishes and maintains a project plan as the basis for managing the project	Yes	0.611
H3.1.2	PR2: Establishes and maintains the overall project plan	Yes	0.692
H3.1.3	PR3: Estimates the project's effort and cost for work products and tasks based on estimation rationale	Yes	0.651
H3.1.4	PR4: Establishes and maintains the project's budget and schedule, milestones, constraints, dependencies	Yes	0.591
H3.1.5	PR5: Monitors offshoring supplier project progress and performance (effort, and cost) as defined in the contract	Yes	0.606
H3.1.6	PR6: Manages invoices submitted by the supplier	Yes	0.541
H3.2	Issue 2: Differences in interp-retation of project requirements between the client and the supplier and CMM/CMMI practices PR7 to PR9		
H3.2.1	PR7: Develops an understanding with offshoring supplier on the meaning of requirements	Yes	0.451
H3.2.2	PR8: Validates requirements to ensure that the resulting product performs as intended in the end user's environment	Yes	0.525
H3.2.3	PR9: Obtains commitment to requirements from project participants	Yes	0.446
H3.3	Issue 3: Poorly developed and documented requirements by the client company and CMM/CMMI practices PR10 and PR11		
H3.3.1	PR10: Stakeholder needs, expectations, constraints and interfaces are collected and translated into customer requirements	Yes	0.561
H3.3.2	PR11: Maintains bidirectional traceability among requirements and work products	Yes	0.651
H3.4	Issue 4: Poor tracking and managing of requirement changes by client company and PR12 to PR14		
H3.4.1	PR12: Manages changes to requirements as they evolve during the project.	Yes	0.640
H3.4.2	PR13: Ensures that project plans and work products remain aligned with requirements	Yes	0.614
H3.4.3	PR14: Customer interface manager leads the team in estimating and documenting the impact of every change in requirement and works with the Configuration Control Board (CCB) to get approval for changes to those requirements	Yes	0.657
H3.5	Issue 5: Lack of a full communication plan between the client and the supplier and PR15 to PR19		
H3.5.1	PR15: Establishes and manages the coordination and collaboration between the project and relevant stakeholders	Yes	0.655
H3.5.2	PR16: Team members track actual results and performance against plans on a weekly basis. Team members track progress against individual plans on a daily basis	Yes	0.693
H3.5.3	PR17: Develops a documented plan to be used to communicate group commitments and to coordinate and track work performed	Yes	0.646
H3.5.4	PR18: Team managers are responsible for coordination across all project teams	Yes	0.677
H3.5.5	PR19: Communication and coordination practices are institutionalized to ensure they are performed as managed processes	Yes	0.635
H3.6	Issue 6: Communication and coordination problems between the client and the supplier and CMM/CMMI practices PR20 to PR23	Strength of Association	
H3.6.1	PR20: Representatives of the client company project's software engineering group work with representatives of the supplier engineering groups to monitor and coordinate technical activities and resolve technical issues	Yes	0.515
H3.6.2	PR21: Selects team roles, including the role of supplier interface manager, who is the liaison between the team and the supplier company representative, and is responsible for requirements change management	Yes	0.411
H3.6.3	PR22: Communicates quality issues and ensures the resolution of non-compliance issues with the staff and managers	Yes	0.601
H3.6.4	PR23: Establishes and maintains a documented policy for conducting its communication and coordination activities	Yes	0.549
H3.7	Issue 7 (language barriers), Issue 8 (time-zone differences) and Issue 9 (cultural differences) between the client and the supplier and CMM/CMMI practices PR24 to PR29		
H3.7.1a–c	PR24: Client company ensures that the workforce has the skills to share information and coordinate their activities efficiently	Yes (language, Cultural)	.458 –language .411 –Cultural
H3.7.2a–c	PR25: Client company establishes a culture for openly sharing information and concerns across organizational levels as well as among team members	Yes (language, cultural)	.400 – language .395 – cultural
H3.7.3a–c	PR26: Client company establishes project teams as well as their responsibilities, authorities and interrelationships	Yes (language, cultural)	.438 – language .447 – cultural
H3.7.4a–c	PR27: Client company establishes and maintains open and effective project teams' communication and coordination plan	Yes (language, cultural)	.455 – language .465 – cultural
H3.7.5a–c	PR28: Client company team managers are responsible for tracking and resolving inter-group issues	Yes (language, cultural)	.422 – language .326 – cultural
H3.7.6a–c	PR29: Maintains effective workgroups, interpersonal problems are addressed quickly and meetings are managed to ensure that workgroup time is used most effectively	Yes (language, cultural)	.402 – language .367 – cultural
H3.8	Issue 10: Incomplete and unclear contract and CMM/CMMI practices PR30 to PR34		
H3.8.1	PR30: Establishes and maintains a mutual understanding of the contract with selected suppliers and end users	Yes	0.660
H3.8.2	PR31: Stakeholder needs, expectations, constraints and interfaces are collected and translated into customer requirements	Yes	0.581
H3.8.3	PR32: Requirements are refined and elaborated into contractual requirements	Yes	0.537
H3.8.4	PR33: Establishes and maintains formal contract management plan	Yes	0.539
H3.8.5	PR34: Establishes and maintains contractual requirements	Yes	0.490
H3.9	Issue 11: Early contract renegotiation and termination and CMM/CMMI practices PR35 and PR36		
H3.9.1	PR35: Establishes and maintains negotiation plans to use in completing a supplier agreement	Yes	0.453

(Continued)

Table 9. (*Continued*).

Hypothesis	Issues and CMM/CMMI practices	Status: 'significantly associated'?*	Strength of association
H3.9.2	PR36: Insures that agreements with suppliers are satisfied by both the project and the supplier	Yes	0.566
H3.10	Issue 12: Insufficient previous experience of the supplier and CMM/CMMI practices PR37 to PR39		
H3.10.1	PR37: Selects suppliers based on an evaluation of their ability to meet specified requirements and established criteria	Yes	0.520
H3.10.2	PR38: Client Company identifies and qualifies potential suppliers	Yes	0.537
H3.10.3	PR39: Selects suppliers using a formal evaluation	Yes	0.655
H3.11	Issue 13: Unable to measure performance of the supplier and CMM/CMMI practices PR40 to PR48		
H3.11.1	PR40: Establishes and maintains quantitative objectives to address quality and process performance, based on customer needs and business objectives	Yes	0.486
H3.11.2	PR41: Manages the project using statistical and other quantitative techniques to determine whether or not the project's objectives for quality and process performance will be satisfied	Yes	0.507
H3.11.3	PR42: Performs root cause analysis of selected issues to address deficiencies in achieving the project's quality and process performance objectives	Yes	0.470
H3.11.4	PR43: Manages corrective actions to closure when the project's performance or results deviate significantly from the plan	Yes	0.520
H3.11.5	PR44: Periodically reviews the project's progress, performance and issues experienced	Yes	0.537
H3.11.6	PR45: Reviews the project's accomplishments and results at selected project milestones	Yes	0.489
H3.11.7	PR46: Establishes and maintains records of quality assurance activities	Yes	0.580
H3.11.8	PR47: Monitors the actual project performance and progress against the project plan	Yes	0452
H3.11.9	PR48: Ensures that the supplier agreement is satisfied before accepting the acquired product	Yes	0.465
H3.12	Issue 14: Supplier technical/security and political issues and CMM/CMMI practices PR49 to PR51		
H3.12.1	PR49: Selects supplier technical solutions to be analysed and analysis methods to be used	Yes	0.400
H3.12.2	PR50: Conducts technical reviews with the supplier as defined in the supplier agreement	Yes	0.446
H3.12.3	PR51: Evaluates and categorizes each identified issue using defined risk categories and determines its relative priority	Yes	0.305
H3.13	Issue 15: Difference in project management practices between the client and the supplier and CMM/CMMI practices PR52 to PR56		
H3.13.1	PR52: Selects suppliers based on an evaluation of their ability to meet specified requirements and established criteria	Yes	0.491
H3.13.2	PR53: Identifies and qualifies potential suppliers	Yes	0.547
H3.13.3	PR54: Selects, monitors, and analyses supplier processes	Yes	0.607
H3.13.4	PR55: Selects suppliers using a formal evaluation	Yes	0.607
H3.13.5	PR56: Establishes and maintains a usable set of organizational process assets, work environment standards, and rules for teams	Yes	0.538
H3.14	Issue 16: Poor execution plan, specifically timing and type of work transferred to the supplier, and CMM/CMMI practices PR57 to PR60		
H3.14.1	PR57: Establishes and maintains the offshoring strategy	Yes	0.507
H3.14.2	PR58: Establishes and maintains the plan for performing offshoring	Yes	0.507
H3.14.3	PR59: Determines the type of acquisition for each product	Yes	0.476
H3.14.4	PR60: Plan transition to operations	Yes	0.443
H3.15	Issue 17: Lack of supplier standarized working methods and CMM/CMMI practices PR61 to PR64		
H3.15.1	PR61: Evaluates supplier technical solutions (designs) to confirm that contractual requirements continue to be met	Yes	0.634
H3.15.2	PR62: Selects suppliers based on an evaluation of their ability to meet specified requirements and established criteria	Yes	0.614
H3.15.3	PR63: Selects, monitors, and analyses supplier processes	Yes	0.658
H3.15.4	PR64: Selects suppliers using a formal evaluation	Yes	0.707

*$p = .05/64 = 0.000,781,25$ (Bonferroni's adjustment).

Table 10. A hypothetical scenario.

Company	Goal	Industrial CMM/CMMI best practices and maturity level
1: US IT offshoring client companies that want to mitigate management problems when offshoring	Mitigate overexpenditure due to hidden costs incurred by the client company	• A project plan is established and maintained as the basis for managing the project (CMMI ACQ, CMMI DEV, CMMI SVC, ML2). • Establish and maintain the overall project plan. (CMMI DEV, CMMI SVC, ML2). • Estimate the project's effort and cost for work products and tasks based on estimation rationale (CMMI ACQ, CMMI DEV, CMMI SVC, ML2). • Establish and maintain the project's budget and schedule, milestones, constraints, dependencies (CMMI ACQ, CMMI DEV, CMMI SVC, ML2) • Monitor supplier project progress and performance (effort, and cost) as defined in the contract (CMMI ACQ, CMMI DEV, CMMI SVC, ML2). • Manage invoices submitted by the supplier (CMMI ACQ, ML2).

CMMI models and performing multiple CMM/CMMI practices may help in mitigating the IT offshoring issues (Table 10).

5. Conclusions and limitations

This research contributes to the existing body of knowledge on the offshoring of IT services from the client management perspective. The key findings can be summarized as follows.

Finding 1: US IT companies applying CMM/CMMI models have fewer issues associated with IT offshoring.

Finding 2: When US IT companies utilize and incorporate different practices from TSP and People CMM into CMMI-DEV/SVC and CMMI-ACQ, they have fewer offshoring issues related to language barriers and cultural differences.

Finding 3: US IT companies applying CMM/CMMI models did not mitigate the offshoring issues of: (1) time-zone difference between the client company and the supplier company; or (2) supplier security and political issues.

Finding 4: US IT companies achieving higher maturity levels of CMMI have fewer issues associated with IT offshoring compared with lower maturity levels.

Finding 5: US IT companies routinely performing industry practices have fewer issues associated with IT offshoring.

While our research made contributions, it had limitations. This study was restricted to US IT offshoring services companies. Conducting this study in another country would help to make the results more generalizable. This research focused on only four CMM/CMMI models tested. It would be interesting to expand the survey beyond the adopted CMM/CMMI models to other quality standards models. Another limitation related to research design was that only a limited set of relationships (correlations) were tested. This research focused on companies that applied one of the four CMM/CMMI models and conducted additional analysis of companies that adopted multiple CMM/CMMI models, which (1) would reduce the robustness of the claims one could make on the current analyses and (2) deviates from a pure application of the scientific method.

Disclosure statement

No potential conflict of interest was reported by the authors.

References

Aaen, I., Arent, J., Mathiassen, L., O., & N. (2001). A conceptual map of software process improvement. *Scandinavian Journal of Information Systems, 13,* 8–12.

Allen, S., & Chandrashekar, A. (2000). Outsourcing services: The contract is just the beginning. *Business Horizons, 43,* 25–34.

Amberg, M., & Wiener, M. (2005). *Lessons learned in IT offshoring.* Proceedings of ISOneWorld and Convention, Enabling Executive IS Competencies. Las Vegas Nevada, USA: Information Institute.

Amiti, M., & Wei, S. (2005). Fear of service outsourcing. *Economic Policy, 20,* 308–347.

Aron, R., & Singh, J. (2005). Getting offshoring right. *Harvard Business Review, 83,* 135–154.

Aspray, W., Mayadas, F., & Vardi, M. (2006). *Globalization and offshoring of software, a report of the ACM job migration task force.* Association for Computing Machinery (ACM). Available on line at http://oldwww.acm.org/globalizationreport/pdf/fullfinal.pdf.

Beulen, E., Fenema, P. V., & Currie, W. (2005). From application outsourcing to infrastructure management: Extending the offshore outsourcing service portfolio. *European Management Journal, 23,* 133–144.

Bhalla, A., Sodhi, M. S., & Son, B. (2008). Is more offshoring better? An exploratory study of western companies offshoring IT-enabled services to S.E. *Asia Journal of Operations Management, 26,* 322–335.

Biberoglu, E., & Haddad, H. (2002). A survey of industrial experiences with CMM and the teaching of CMM practices. *Journal of Computing Sciences in Colleges, 18,* 143–152.

Bock, S. (2008). Supporting offshoring and nearshoring decisions for mass customization manufacturing processes. *European Journal of Operational Research, 184,* 490–508.

Brooks, E. P. (1987). No silver bullet essence and accidents of software engineering. *IEEE Computing, 20,* 10–19.

Butzer, S., & Schötz, S., Steinhilper, R. (2017). Remanufacturing process capability maturity model. *Procedia Manufacturing, 8,* 715–722.

Carmel, E. (1999). *Global software teams: Collaborating across borders and time zones.* Upper Saddle River, NJ: Prentice Hall.

Carmel, E. (2006). Building your information systems from the other side of the world: How infosys manages time zone differences. *MIS Quarterly Executive, 5,* 43–53.

Carmel, E. (2007). Why 'nearshore' means that distance matters. *Communications of the ACM, 50,* 40–46.

Carmel, E., & Abbott, P. (2006). *Configurations of global software development: Offshore versus nearshore.* Proceedings of the 2006 International Workshop on Global Software Development for the Practitioner. Shanghai, China: ACM.

Carmel, E., & Agrawal, R. (2002b). The maturation of offshore sourcing of information technology work. *MIS Quarterly Executive, 20,* 65–78.

Carmel, E., & Beulen, E. (2005). *Governance in offshore outsourcing relationships. Offshore outsourcing of information technology work,* Cambridg, UK., Cambridg University Press.

Carmel, E., & Tjia, P. (2005). *Offshoring information technology: Sourcing and outsourcing to a global workforce.* Cambridge: Cambridge University Press.

Chaudhury, V., & Sabherwal, R. (2003). Portfolios of control in outsourced software development projects. *Information Systems Research, 14,* 291–314.

CMMI Product Team. (2010a). CMMI for Acquisition. *In:* 1.3, V. (ed.). Pittsburgh, PA: Software Engineering Institute, Carnegie Mellon University.

CMMI Product Team. (2010b). CMMI for Development, CMMI-DEV, V1.3. Pittsburgh, PA: Carnegie Mellon, Software Engineering Institute (SEI).

CMMI Product Team. (2010c). CMMI for Services, CMMI-SVC, V1.3. Pittsburgh, PA: Carnegie Mellon Software Engineering Institute (SEI).

Colombo, M. G. (2003). Alliance form: A test of the contractual and competence perspectives. *Strategic Management Journal, 24,* 1209–1229.

Cooper, D., & Pamela, S. (2008). *Business research methods.* NY: Irwin, McGraw-Hill.

Cooper, D., & Schindler, P. (2006). *Business research methods.* NY: Irwin, McGraw-Hill..

Curtis, B., Hefley, W., & Miller, S. (2001). People capability maturity model (P-CMM). In 2nd Version. Pittsburgh, PA: Software Engineering Institute, Carnegie Mellon University.

Curtis, B., Hefley, W., & Miller, S. (2010). *People CMM: A framework for human capital management.* New York, NY: Addison-Wesley.

Dillon, W., & Goldstein, M. (1984). *Multivariate analysis.* NY NY: John Wiley and Sons.

Domingues, P., & Sampaio, P., Arezes, P. M. (2016). Integrated management systems assessment: A maturity model proposal. *Journal of Cleaner Production, 124,* 164–174.

Dubey, P. (2003). *The voyage east: An executives' guide to offshore outsourcing.* New York, NY: iUniverse.

Ebert, C. (2007). *Optimizing supplier management in global software engineering.* Internaltional Conference of Global Software Engineering (ICGSE). Munich, Germany: IEEE.

Ebert, C., Murthy, B. K., & Jha, N. N. (2008). *Managing risks in global software engineering: Principles and practices.* IEEE International Conference on Global Software Engineering. Bangalore: IEEE.

Enke, J., Glass, R., & Metternich, J. (2017). Introducing a maturity model for learning factories. *Procedia Manufacturing, 9,* 1–8.

Ferguson, E. (2004a). Impact of offshore outsourcing on CS/IS curricula. *Journal of Computing Sciences in Colleges, 19,* 68–77.

Ferguson, R. B. (2004b). Bringing it home again: Hidden offshoring costs frustrate IT. *e-Week* [Online], 21.

Finnerty N., Sterling, R., Coakley, D., & Keane, M. M. (In press). An energy management maturity model for multi-site industrial organisations with a global presence. *Journal of Cleaner Production 167*, 1232–1250.

Fitzgerald, B., & O'Kane, T. (1999). A longitudinal study of software process improvement. *Software IEEE, 16*, 37–45.

Gibson, D., Goldenson, D. R., & Kost, K.. (2006). *Performance results of CMMI-based process improvement*. Pittsburgh, PA: Carnegie Mellon, Software Engineering Institute.

Gopal, A., Mukhopadhyay, T., & Krishnan, S. (2002b). The role of software processes and communication in offshore software development. *Communications of the ACM, 45*, 193–200.

Gopal, A., Sivaramakrishnan, K., Krishnan, M., & Mukhopadhyay, T. (2003). Contracts in offshore software development: An empirical analysis. *Management Science, 49*, 1671–1683.

Golder, A. (2004). Companies unhappy with results in 50% of IT deals. *Supply Management, 9*, 10.

Graziano, A., & Raulin, M. (2006). *Research Methods*. Boston, MA: Allyn & Bacon.

Hair, J., Anderson, R., Tatham, R., & Black, W. (1995). *Multivariate data analysis*. New Jersey: Prentice Hall.

Halvey, J. K., & Melby, B. M. (2007). *Business process outsourcing: Process, strategies, and contracts*. Ny NY: Wiley.

Hanna, R., & Daim, T. (2009b). Managing offshore outsourcing in the software industry. *Technology Analysis & Strategic Management Journal, 21*, 881–897.

Hanna, R., Raffo, D., & Daim, T. U. (2014a). Managing issues of IT service offshore outsourcing projects. In T. U. Daim, R. Neshati, R. Watt,& J. Eastham (Eds.), *Technology development* (pp. 197–208). New York, NY: Springer.

Hanna, R., Raffo, D., & Daim, T. U. (2014b). Managing issues through the lifecycle of IT service offshoring projects. In *2014 proceedings of PICMET '14: Infrastructure and service integration* (pp 523–529). IEEE.

Harter, D. E., Krishnan, M. S., & Slaughter, S. A. (2000). Effects of process maturity on quality, cycle time, and effort in software product development. *Management Science, 46*, 451–466.

Herbsleb, J, & Grinter, R. (1999). *Splitting the organization and integrating the code: Conway's law revisited*. International Conference on Software Engineering (ICSE99). Los Angeles, CA: ACM/IEEE.

Herbsleb, J. D., Zubrow, D., Goldenson, D. R., Hayes, W., & Paulk, M. (1997b). Software quality and the capability maturity model. *Communication of the ACM, 40*, 30–40.

Hirschheim, R., & Lacity, M. (2000). The myths and realities of information technology insourcing. *Communications of the ACM, 43*, 99–107.

Hoffmann, T. (1996). JP Morgan to save $50 million via outsourcing pact. *Computer World, 30*, 10.

Holmström, O. H., Fitzgerald, B., & Conchuir, O. (2008). Two-stage offshoring: An investigation of the irish bridge. *MIS Quarterly, 32*, 257–279.

Humphrey, W. S. (2002). *Winning with software: An executive strategy. How to transform your software group into a competitive asset*.Reading, MA: Addison-Wesley.

Humphrey, W., Davis, N., & McHale, J. (2003). Relating the Team Software Process (TSP) to the capability maturity model for software (SW-CMM). Pittsburgh, PA: Software Engineering Institute, Carnegie Mellon.

Ibbs, C. W., & Kwak, Y. H. (2000). Assessing project management maturity. *Project Management Journal, 31*, 32–43.

Iversen, J. H., Nielsen, P. A., & Nørbjerg, J. (2002). Problem diagnosis in SPI. In *Improving software organizations: From principles to practice* L. Mathiassen, J. Pries-Heje, O. Ngwenyama (Eds.). Boston, MA: Addison Wesley.

Jiang, J., Klien, G., Hwang, H-G., Huang, J., & Hung, S-Y. (2004). An exploration of the relationship between software development process maturity and project performance. *Information & Management, 41*, 279–288.

Johansen, J., & Mathiassen, L. (1998). *Lessons learned in a national SPI effort*. Proceedings of EuroSPI '98, Nov. 16-18 (pp. 5–17). Gothenburg, Sweden: EuroSPI.

Johnson, R., & Wichern, D. (1992). *Applied multivariate statistical analysis*. Prentice Hall: Prentice Hall.

Jones, T. (1995). Managing the behavior of people working in teams: Applying the project management method. *International Journal of Project Management, 13*, 47–53.

Jovanović, B., & Filipović, J. (2016). ISO 50001 standard-based energy management maturity model – proposal and validation in industry. *Journal of Cleaner Production, 112*, 2744–2755.

Kakabadse, A., & Kakabadse, N. (2002). Trends in outsourcing: Contrasting USA and Europe. *European Management Journal, 20*, 189–198.

Kathpalia L., Raman R. (2014, February 20). The Road Ahead for the Indian IT and ITES: Industry Considering its Service Offerings, Domestic Market and Technology Trends, *Journal of Theoretical and Applied Information Technology*, 60 (2).

Koehler, J., Woodtly, R., Hofstetter, J. (2015). An impact-oriented maturity model for IT-based case management. *Information Systems, 47*, 278–291.

Kosieradzka, A. (2017). Maturity model for production management. *Procedia Engineering, 182*, 342–349.

Lacity, M. C., & Hirschheim, R. A. (1993b). *Information systems outsourcing: Myths, metaphors, and realities*. New York, NY: John Wiley & Sons Inc.

Lacity, M., & Rottman, J. W. (2008). *Offshore outsourcing of IT work: client and supplier perspectives* (Technology. Work and Globalization). New York Palgrave, Macmillan.

Lacity, M. C., & Willcocks, L. P. (1995). Interpreting information technology sourcing decisions from a transaction cost perspective: Findings and critique. *Accounting, Management and Information Technologies, 5*, 203–244.

Lacity, M. C., & Willcocks, L. P. (1998). An empirical investigation of information technology sourcing practices: Lessons from experience. *MIS Quarterly, 22*, 363–408.

Lacity, M. C., Willcocks, L. P., & Feeny, D. F. (1996). The value of selective IT sourcing. *MIT Sloan Management Review, 37*, 13–25.

Lacity, M. C., & Willcocks, L. (2001). *Global Information technology outsourcing: In search of business advantage*. John Wiley & Sons Ltd.

Lacity, M., Willcocks, L., & Rottman, J. W. (2008). Global outsourcing of back office service: Lessons, trends, and enduring challenges. *Strategic Outsourcing: An International Journal, 1*, 13–34.

Laplante, P. A., Costello, T., Singh, P., Bindiganavile, S., & Landon, M. (2004). Who, what, why, where, and when of IT outsourcing. *IT Professional, 6*, 19–23.

Lasser, S., & Heiss, M. (2005). *Collaboration maturity and the offshoring cost barrier: The tradeoff between flexibility in team composition and cross-site communication effort in geographically distributed development projects*. IEEE International Professional Communication Conference IPCC. Limerick, Ireland: IEEE.

Leiblein, M. J., Reuer, J. J., & Dalsace, F. (2002). Do make or buy decisions matter? The influence of organizational governance on technological performance. *Strategic Management Journal, 23*, 817–833.

Machado, C. G., de Lima, E. P., da Costa, S. E. G., Angelis, J. J., Mattioda, R. A. (2017). Framing maturity based on sustainable operations management principles. *International Journal of Production Economics, 190*, 3–21.

Majumdar, S., Simons, K., & Nag, A. (2011). Body shopping versus offshoring among indian software and information technology. *Information Technology and Management, 12*, 17–34.

McFarlan, F. W., & Nolan, R. L. (1995). How to manage an IT outsourcing alliance. *Sloan Management Review, 36*, 9–23.

McIvor, R. (2000). A practical framework for understanding the outsourcing process. *Supply Chain Management: An International Journal, 5*, 22–36.

Metters, R. (2007). A typology of offshoring and outsourcing in electronically transmitted services. *Journal of Operations Management, 26*, 198–211.

Meyer, B. (2006). *The unspoken revolution in software engineering Computer, 39*, 121–123.

Michell, V., & Fitzgerald, G. (1997). The IT outsourcing market-place: Vendors and their selection. *Journal of Information Technology, 12*, 223–237.

Moe, N. B., Šmite, D., Hanssen, G. K., & Barney, H. (2013). From offshore outsourcing to insourcing and partnerships: four failed outsourcing attempts. *Empirical Software Engineering*, 1–34.

Nikkhou, S., Taghizadeh, K., & Hajiyakhchali, S. (2016). Designing a portfolio management maturity model (Elena). *Procedia - Social and Behavioral Sciences, 226*, 318–325.

Niosi, J., & Tschang, T. (2009). The strategies of Chines and Indian software multinationals: Implications for internationalization theory. *Industrial and Corporate Change, 18*, 269–294.

Olson, T. 2008. Using Baldrige performace criteria to strengthen CMMI measurable results. INDIA CMMI Conference. Lean Solution Institute, INC. (LSI).

Orlikowski, W. J. (2002). Knowing in practice: Enacting a collective capability in distributed organizing. *Organization Science, 13,* 249–273.

Oshri, I., Kotlarsky, J., & Willcocks, L. P. (2008). Managing dispersed expertise in IT offshore outsourcing, lessons from Tata consultancy services. *MIS Quarterly Executive, 6,* 53–65.

Palvia, P. (1995). A dialectic view of information systems outsourcing: Pros and cons. *Journal of Information Processing and Management, 38,* 265–267.

Prikladnicki, R., Audy, J., Damian, D., & Oliveira, T. (2007). *Distributed software development: Practices and challenges in different business strategies of offshoring and onshoring.* International Conference on Global Software Engineering (ICGSE). Munich, Germany: IEEE.

Prikladnicki, R., Audy, J., & Evaristo, R. (2003). Global software development in practice lessons learned. *Software Process Improvement and Practice, 8,* 267–281.

Rao, M. T. (2004). Key issues for global it sourcing: Country and individual factors. *Information Systems Management, 21,* 16–21.

Reynolds, R., Woods, R., & Baker, J. D. (2006). *Handbook of research on electronic surveys and measurements.* Hershey, PA, USA: Idea Group Inc.

Rivard, S., & Aubert, B. (2007). *Information technology outsourcing.* New York, NY: M.E Sharpe.

Rottman, J. W., & Lacity, M. (2006). Proven practices for effectively offshoring IT work. *Sloan Management Review, 47,* 56–63.

Rottman, J. W., & Lacity, M. (2008). A US client's learning from outsourcing IT work offshore. *Information Systems Frontiers, 10,* 259–275.

Schonlau, M., Fricker, R., & Elliott, M. (2002). *Conducting research surveys via e-mail and the web.* California: RAND Distribution Services.

Schwalbe, K. (2010). *Information technology project managment.* Boston, MA: Cengage Learning.

Sengupta, B., Chandra, S., & Sinha, V. (2006b). *A research agenda for distributed software development.* Proceedings of the 28th International Conference on Software Engineering, May 20-28. Shanghai, China: ACM New York.

de Souza, T. F., & Gomes, C. F. S. (2015). Assessment of maturity in project management: A bibliometric study of main models. *Procedia Computer Science, 55,* 92–101.

Spalek, S. (2015). Establishing a conceptual model for assessing project management maturity in industrial companies. *International Journal of Industrial Engineering: Theory, Applications and Practice, 22,* 301–313.

Sue, V., & Ritter, L. (2007). *Conducting online surveys.* California: Sage Publication.

Tahri, H., & Drissi-Kaitouni, O. (2015). New design for calculating Project Management Maturity (PMM). *Procedia - Social and Behavioral Sciences, 181,* 171–177.

Trent, R. J., & Monczka, R. M. (2005). Achieving excellence in global sourcing. *MIT Sloan Management Review, 47,* 24–32.

Uskarci, A., & Demirörs, O. (2017), Do staged maturity models result in organization-wide continuous process improvement? Insight from employees. *Computer Standards & Interfaces, 52,* 25–40

Vakaslahti, P. (1998). Process improvement frameworks – a small case study with people capability maturity model. *Software Process Improvement and Practice, 3,* 225–234.

Venkatraman, N. (1997). Beyond outsourcing: Managing IT resources as a value center. *Sloan Management Review, 38,* 51–64.

Willcocks, L. P., & Kern, T. (1998). IT outsourcing as strategic partnering: The case of the UK Inland Revenue. *European Journal of Information Systems, 7,* 29–45.

Williams, T. (1995). A classified bibliography of recent research relating to project risk management. *European Journal of Operational Research, 85,* 18–38.

Yalaho, A., & Nahar, N. (2009). The ICT-supported unified process model of offshore outsourcing of software production: Exploratory examination and validation. *International Journal of Innovation and Technology Management, 6,* 59–96.

Yang, D.-H., Kim, S., Nam, C., & Min, J.-W. (2007). Developing a decision model for business process outsourcing. *Computers & Operations Research, 34,* 3769–3778.

Zikmund, W. (1999). *Business research methods.* Dryden: Harcourt.

The evolution and governance of online rumors during the public health emergency: taking COVID-19 pandemic related rumors as an example

Jiali Yan

ABSTRACT

The outbreak of the infodemic during COVID-19 caused mass panic in society. Studying the evolution law of online rumors in the relatively complete cycle of COVID-19 can improve the pertinence of rumor governance. In this paper, the Python crawler program was used to collect rumor-refuting microblogs. Based on the development of public opinion and the pandemic, it was divided into five stages, including incubation stage, explosion stage, digestion stage, fluctuation stage, and re-digestion stage. Then, the statistical analysis methods ranging from correlation analysis to chi-square analysis and analytical methods like hot trend analysis, stage-based analyses of quantity, hot words and subjects were used to study the dynamic evolution laws of online rumors from the perspective of quantity and content. The research found that online rumors had the rules of periodic evolution of quantity and periodic fluctuation of hot words and subjects, which were in line with the COVID-19 pandemic. Social platforms such as WeChat and Tik Tok were the main places for rumors' generation and propagation. In different stages of rumor transmission, the public mood was staggered repeatedly, and the homogeneous or same rumors would spread repeatedly. Based on the above laws, the corresponding governance strategies were put forward.

1. Introduction

In 11 March 2020, the World Health Organization (WHO) made the assessment that COVID-19 could be characterized as a pandemic (World Health Organization, 2020). Globally, as of 6 August 2021, there have been more than 200 million confirmed cases of COVID-19, including 4.26 million deaths. Moreover, the infodemic has transformed COVID-19 from a worldwide health crisis into a global economic and social crash. Therefore, it is of great importance to clarify the evolution rules of online rumors during the pandemic of COVID-19 in the context of infodemic, in order to find effective rumor governance strategies and ensure the success of pandemic prevention and control.

Ordinarily, rumors are defined as 'unverified and instrumentally relevant information statements in circulation that arise in contexts of ambiguity, danger or potential threat, and that function to help people make sense and manage risk' (DiFonzo & Bordia, 2007). However, in the Chinese context, rumors are more similar to fake news or misinformation. In view of this, this paper used the Python crawler program to collect rumor-refuting microblogs on Sina Weibo based on Chinese context, and explored the dynamic evolution of the quantity and content of rumors.

2. Literature review

2.1. Definition of infodemic

Infodemic is a blend of 'information' and 'epidemic', which typically refers to a rapid proliferation of unconfirmed information related to something such as a crisis (Infodemic 2020). In 2003, the infodemic was coined to describe the phenomenon of mass panic caused by the mixture of facts and rumors in the outbreak of SARS by Rothkopf (2003). The infodemic in public health emergencies will cause mass public panic and have a negative impact on people's physical and mental health, the governance of public health events and even the harmony and stability of society. During COVID-19, especially at the early outbreak, the public was more dependent on getting information from the Internet to cope with the uncertainty. The explosion of online rumors eventually led to the emergence of infodemic (Ball & Maxmen, 2020).

2.2. Related work

During the COVID-19 outbreak, the blowout of online rumors has attracted the attention of many scholars, and plenty of studies have been carried out. Existing researches on COVID-19 related rumors mainly include three categories. (1) Construction of rumor spreading models. Hui, Zhou, Lu, and Li (2020) added the education level of susceptible users to develop a novel epidemic-like model and they found that improving the education level or carrying out short-term training for lower-educators class could effectively curb the spread of rumors. Huang, Chen, and Ma (2020) constructed a two-layer network model including a communication layer and a contact layer to model the spread of information and epidemic respectively. Yin, Lv, Zhang, Xia, and Wu (2020) developed a multiple-information susceptible-discussing-immune (M-SDI) model and considered that Sina Weibo users might participate in related topics after discussion. Such studies mainly focused on the influencing factors of rumor diffusion, and paid less attention to the quantitative and content characteristics of rumors themself with the change of pandemic situation. (2) Evolution and controlling of online rumors and fake news. Wu,

Deng, Wen, Wang, and Xiong (2020) performed a statistical analysis about different features of rumor and anti-rumor accounts, which was helpful in rumor governance. Pulido Rodriguez et al. (2020) compared the circulation of false or scientific-based information on Twitter and Sina Weibo, which provided some meaningful results on overcoming false information. Zhang, Chen, Jiang, and Zhao (2020) described how a piece of information became a rumor through the process of leveling, sharpening, and assimilation and affected people's behaviors and perception based on a purchase craze event of SHL. (3) Development of public opinion and attention. Xie, Tan, and Li (2020) utilized a search index to reflect the degree of public concern and they concluded that Internet monitoring was more efficient in controlling of epidemic and rumors. Gao, Hua, and Luo (2021) analyzed the dynamic trend characteristics of public opinion related to COVID-19 over time and critical factors affecting the public opinion. Han, Wang, Zhang, and Wang (2020) used the LDA model and RF algorithm to extract seven COVID-19-relevant public opinion topics and 13 subtopics and analyzed their temporal-spatial distributions.

To sum up, academic circles have made great achievements in the research on the spread of online rumors during the COVID-19 outbreak. However, the data sources of existing studies (Gao et al., 2021; Han et al., 2020; Wu et al., 2020; Xie et al., 2020) were concentrated from January 2020 to April 2020. As COVID-19 is a virus that will coexist with humans for a long time, it is far from enough to study the spread of online rumors during its outbreak period. In addition, existing studies rarely considered the transmission characteristics of rumors at different stages of the pandemic. However, in the context of infodemic, it is necessary to strengthen the cognition of the correlation between rumor spread and epidemic development.

3. Data acquisition and processing

3.1. Data acquisition

As the most popular platform in China, Sina Weibo has 511 million monthly active users and 224 million daily active users by September 2020. Different from the China Internet Joint Rumor Refuting Platform and Baidu Rumor Refuting Platform, Sina Weibo not only allows official accounts to publish rumor-refuting microblogs, but also allows people to repost, comment and give thumbs up, which can reflect the changes of public concerns based on content mining. Therefore, this paper

took Sina Weibo as the data source, retrieves key words included 'COVID-19', 'novel coronavirus', 'CoV' and so on.

Compared with the traditional manual search and data collection process, web crawler technology has the characteristics of high efficiency and accuracy, which is one of the most important methods to obtain data in the era of big data. In this paper, the crawler program was used to collect rumor-refuting microblogs on Sina Weibo. The acquisition process is shown in Figure 1. 63,373 microblogs from 1 January 2020 to 31 January 2021 were collected, including the blog publishers, blog contents, number of forwarding, number of comments, number of likes and links. The national pandemic data of China (from 16 January 2020 to 31 January 2021) came from the Sina real-time COVID-19 situation dashboard.

When using the advanced filtering function of Sina Weibo, some repeated microblogs in a certain short period of time will be automatically filtered. The data loss will not have any bad effect on the subsequent analysis but will eliminate the role of 'water army' to make the data more representative. At the same time, the author will also eliminate such data in the subsequent data processing process.

3.2. Data processing

After eliminating meaningless microblogs (punctuations or stickers, etc.) and the microblogs with the same or similar contents, 28,509 rumor-refuting microblogs were conserved, with a time rage of 392 days, spanning the whole period of pandemic incubation, large-scale outbreak, fluctuation, and digestion, which could better reflect the overall pattern of propagation characteristics of online rumors about COVID-19 against the background of infodemic.

4. Analysis on the propagation of rumors related to COVID-19 under the infodemic

4.1. Correlation analysis between rumor propagation and pandemic situation

Panic is one of the psychological factors leading to the spread of online rumors. On the contrary, rumors also stimulate the public panic. During the COVID-19 pandemic, the public panic will affect the formation and spread of rumors to a certain extent. It is necessary to study the correlation between rumor spreading and the trend of pandemic development.

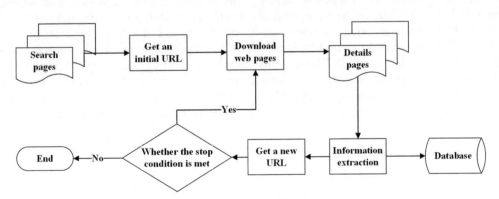

Figure 1. Data collection flowchart.

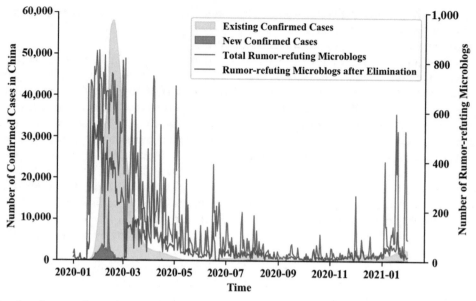

Figure 2. Number of confirmed cases in China and rumor-refuting microblogs.

Table 1. Pearson correlation analysis.

Correlations

		Total Rumor-Refuting Microblogs	Rumor-Refuting Microblogs after Elimination	Existing Confirmed Cases	New Confirmed Cases
Total Rumor-Refuting Microblogs	Pearson Correlation	1	.867**	.633**	.447**
	Sig. (2-tailed)		0.000	0.000	0.000
	N	392	392	377	377
Rumor-Refuting Microblogs after Elimination	Pearson Correlation	.867**	1	.634**	.553**
	Sig. (2-tailed)	0.000		0.000	0.000
	N	392	392	377	377
Existing Confirmed Cases	Pearson Correlation	.633**	.634**	1	.539**
	Sig. (2-tailed)	0.000	0.000		0.000
	N	377	377	377	377
New Confirmed Cases	Pearson Correlation	.447**	.553**	.539**	1
	Sig. (2-tailed)	0.000	0.000	0.000	
	N	377	377	377	377

Correlation is significant at the 0.01 level (2-tailed).

Figure 2 gives the number of microblogs and confirmed cases. In order to further prove the correlation between rumor spreading and pandemic situation, the Pearson correlation analysis has been performed. Table 1 shows that the total number of rumor-refuting microblogs is strongly positively associated with the number of existing confirmed cases and moderately positively correlated with the number of new confirmed cases (r = 0.633, 0.447). Meanwhile, the number of rumor-refuting microblogs after elimination is strongly positively correlated with the number of existing confirmed cases and new confirmed cases (r = 0.634, 0.553). These results reveal that there is a significant positive correlation between the number of rumors and the daily trend of the pandemic, and the periodic evolution law is prominent.

4.2. Stage-based analysis on rumor propagation

In the research of network public opinion, many scholars have divided its evolution process into different stages from the backgrounds of life cycle theory. Based on the four-stage theory (incubation stage, growth stage, mature stage, and declining stage) (Qiao, Gao, Huang, Hou, & Wei, 2015)

and the development characteristics of COVID-19 in China, and taking major time nodes as separation positions, the spread of online rumors related to COVID-19 can be divided into 5 stages including incubation stage, explosion stage, digestion stage, fluctuation stage and re-digestion stage (Figure 3). Although the fluctuation stage can still be divided into incubation stage, explosion stage and digestion stage, the local pandemic and rumors will not bring intense panic and threats like the first large-scale outbreak. Therefore, detailed analyses are not made. However, since COVID-19 is still transmitting globally, the fluctuation of pandemic may recur constantly in the future. If it is not effectively controlled, it is likely to develop into a monstrous disaster. Therefore, it still has research value.

(1) Incubation stage (from 1 January 2020 to 19 January 2020)

On 1 January 2020, Huanan Seafood Wholesale Market made an announcement of suspension because of several cases of unknown pneumonia. Once the announcement was issued, it had triggered the discussion of some netizens.

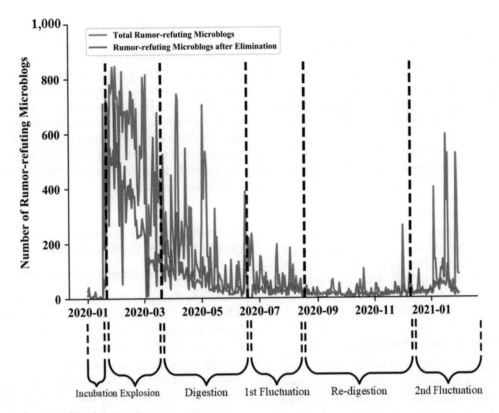

Figure 3. Five stages of rumor propagation.

However, in this stage, the number of existing and new diagnosis rose slowly, and the public, even the government and medical professionals, had insufficient knowledge and attention to the characteristics and transmission of the virus. Therefore, rumors did not spread widely. However, negative emotions such as anxiety and anger have been quietly spread among some individuals, which has buried hidden dangers for rumor controlling in the future.

(2) Explosion stage (from 20 January 2020 to 17 March 2020)

At this stage, the number of microblogs increased rapidly to the peak, and then decreased slowly, but still maintained at a high level. On January 20 2020, Zhong Nanshan confirmed that COVID-19 could be transmitted from person to person. Since January 23 2020, Wuhan had been sealed off. After a series of major events, the public's attention surged sharply with the increasingly serious pandemic situation and strict government instructions. In addition, the Spring Festival travel rush further aroused people's concern. Rumors with negative emotions suddenly full filled the Internet. The complexity and difficulty of rumor governance became more obvious. In the middle and late February, the domestic pandemic situation in China was controlled gradually. Moreover, the government timely disclosed the pandemic information and actively refuted rumors. People knew more about the virus itself, and the spread of online rumors was suppressed. But related rumors were still emerging and spreading because of the long-term trend of COVID-19 pandemic.

(3) Digestion stage (from 18 March 2020 to 16 June 2020)

On March 18 2020, the number of new confirmed cases in Hubei Province, the most affected area, dropped to zero for the first time, illustrating a huge victory in the battle against COVID-19 in China. At the same time, the national economy gradually recovered along with the resumption of work and production. The obvious decrease of number of rumor-refuting microblogs reveals significant digestion of rumors.

(4) 1st fluctuation stage and re-digestion stage (from 17 June 2020 to 16 August 2020, from 17 August 2020 to 7 December 2020)

Since the middle of June 2020, there have been reversal of COVID-19 pandemic caused by overseas imports in China. Beijing and Xinjiang were two prominent sites that suffered most. On June 17, Beijing's emergency response level was upgraded from level 3 to level 2. The recurrence of the pandemic caused the fluctuation of rumors, but both the scope and types of rumors are not comparable with the first outbreak, which did not lead to great social turbulence. On August 16, the number of newly diagnosed cases in Xinjiang dropped to zero for the first time. Since then, the spread of rumors entered the re-digestion stage.

(5) 2nd fluctuation stage (after 8 December 2020)

Since COVID-19 is much easier to spread in winter, clusters of COVID-19 infection occurred in various places like Beijing, Sichuan, Liaoning, Hebei, and Heilongjiang in this stage. On December 8, Zhao, a confirmed patient in Chengdu, caused a huge discussion because her route involved several bars. Then, different medias commented on the personal information leakage incident, detonating the network again. Taking this as a time node, online rumors entered the second fluctuation stage. As shown in Figure 3, in the second fluctuation stage, the number of microblogs is slightly higher than that in the first fluctuation stage, indicating that the spread of rumors is slightly more serious, which may be related to the more obvious fluctuation of pandemic situation in autumn and winter and the approach of Spring Festival.

It can be seen from the stage-based analysis of rumor diffusion that in the first extensive outbreak, the generation and spread of rumor are related to the pandemic situation, the public's cognitive and judgment ability, the government's policy, and information release, etc. When the pandemic fluctuated in a small range, online rumor propagation is mainly related to the severity of the pandemic and the main time nodes such as the Spring Festival because the public know more about COVID-19 with corresponding science popularization education.

4.3. Hot trend analysis of online rumors

In the Internet age, the hot trend represents people's attention and discussion on a topic or character. In this paper, the number of interactions (the sum of the number of forwarding, comments, and likes) of total microblogs without elimination at a certain stage is expressed as the hot trend of rumors. The higher the number of interactions, the more people participate in rumor refutation, and the higher the hot trend. The hot trend chart of rumors is shown in Figure 4. The horizontal axis represents the stage, the vertical axis represents the number of total microblogs, and the bubble size represents the hot trend of rumors. The relationships between the three can directly reflect the public's attention and discussion on COVID-19-related rumors in different stages under the infodemic.

In the explosion stage, not only the number of rumor-refuting microblog is the largest but also the hot trend is the highest, which illustrates that at this stage, the public is aware of the urgency of the pandemic situation, and the demand for information rises significantly. This situation is utilized by people with ulterior motives, and massive rumors are spread on the Internet. At the same time, the government's efforts to refute rumors are also increasing, the public participate in the process of rumor refutation out of the demand for information, and the degree of attention and discussion of rumor has reached the peak.

5. Analysis on hot words of rumors related to COVID-19 under the infodemic

5.1. Stage-based analysis on hot words

In order to further explore the changing pattern of hot spot information and public focus of online rumors with the spread and fluctuation of the pandemic, this paper used Python to extract hot words.

Before processing, the synonyms such as 'Wuhan city' and 'Wuhan' were replaced. 'Jieba' database was used to segment more than 60,000 microblog texts. 'Jieba' supports three kinds of word segmentation modes. This paper adopted the accurate mode suitable for text analysis. The user-defined dictionary was introduced to make specific words such as 'Huanan Seafood Wholesale Market' uncut. The stop words dictionary was utilized to filter redundant words such as 'COVID-19' and 'rumor' to avoid covering up the useful information. The regular expression matches were used to remove punctuations, stickers, and interference content. After corpus cleaning, the numbers of words in each stage are 3,814, 51,066, 30,153, 13,273, 12,132, and 12,510 respectively. According to the formula of high frequency and low frequency words (Xu & Bi, 2019) as follow:

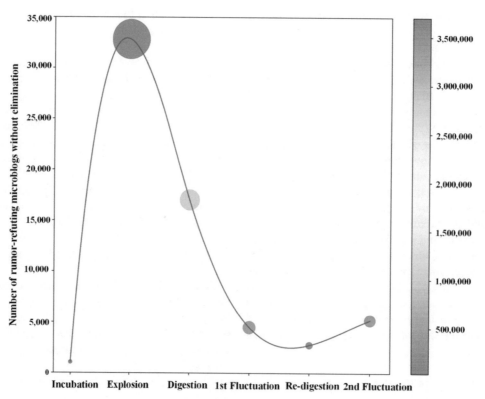

Figure 4. Hot trend chart of online rumors related to COVID-19.

Table 2. Representative hot words in each stage.

Stage	Hot Words
Incubation Stage	Hubei, Wuhan, Huanan Seafood Wholesale Market, Shanghai, Guangzhou, the Sixth Affiliated Hospital of Sun Yat sen University, unknown, SARS, cold, flu, panic, government, China CDC
Explosion Stage	infection, transmission, diagnosis, Shanghai, Beijing, market, village, community, mask, prevention, disinfect, smoking, alcohol, city closure, panic, subway ticket, pet, horrible, love, victory
Digestion Stage	China, US, 5G, UK, conspiracy theory, arson, lab, politician
1st Fluctuation Stage	US, 5G, antenna, nose bridge bar, vaccine, Hubei, Wuhan, Ezhou, Huaiyin park, Jinyintan hospital, Xinfadi, Haidian
Re-digestion Stage	Beijing, Hangzhou, Qingdao, Laishan, Wal-Mart, market, supermarket, hotel, community, refrigeration, meat ware, import, sea food, appear, find, detection
2nd Fluctuation Stage	brine, garlic, vinegar, fireworks, disinfect, tea, throat, retention, express delivery, Spring Festival travel rush, vaccine

$$T = \left[(1 + 8I_1)^{1/2} - 1\right]/2$$

I_1 is the number of words appearing once, T is the critical value of high-frequency and low-frequency words. When the frequency of a word is greater than or equal to T, it is judged as a high-frequency word, otherwise, it is judged as a low-frequency word. Combined with human judgment, 75, 339, 205, 106, 95 and 98 typical hot words with prominent semantic meaning were extracted respectively for analysis. Part of them are shown as Table 2.

In the incubation stage, hot words on behalf of locations such as 'Hubei', 'Wuhan', 'Huanan Seafood Wholesale Market', 'Guangzhou' show that even in the incubation stage, rumors like 'new confirmed cases are found in a city' can emerge. In addition, 'unknown', 'SARS', 'cold', 'flu' and other words indicate that the public is very concerned about the type of the virus at this stage. 'panic', 'government', 'China CDC' and other words show that confusion, fear, and other negative emotions are full of the network environment, and the public is eager for more open and transparent information release.

In the explosion stage, online rumors present the characteristics of complex content and emotional interweaving. 'infection', 'transmission', 'diagnosis' and other words related to new cases and 'Shanghai', 'Beijing', 'supermarket', 'community' and other words meaning locations reflect the public's strong concern about the pandemic situation and trend. Most of the rumors are like 'a new diagnosis is found in a district, community, or supermarket'. Compared with the incubation stage, the content of rumors is more specific, with detailed descriptions of locations and the number of cases. Moreover, rumors about protective measures and virus transmission routes related to words like 'mask', 'prevention', 'disinfection', 'smoking', 'alcohol', 'city closure', 'subway ticket', 'pet' and so on also account for a high proportion, which are often be added with names of experts like Zhong Nanshan to increase the credibility. From the perspective of public sentiment, there are not only negative words such as 'panic', 'horrible', and 'serious', but also positive words such as 'fight', 'victory', and 'love'. The interweaving of positive and negative emotions makes the public have a strong emotional confrontation, leading to improper behaviors such as discrimination, driving up prices and burying alive pets.

In the digestion stage, the situation of domestic pandemic continued to improve, but foreign countries were still at a perilous point. At the same time, the public's attention also shifted from home to abroad. Overseas rumors such as '5G mobile networks spreads COVID-19' and 'novel coronaviruses can be killed by injecting disinfectant into the body' have been widely discussed on the Internet. Therefore, it is necessary to prevent the import of rumors from misleading the national public.

According to hot words in the 1st fluctuation stage, the content of online rumors can be summarized into 3 points. (1) First, overseas rumors such as 'vaccine changes human gene', 'nose bridge bar is the antenna of 5G' corresponding to the words like 'vaccine', 'nose bridge bar' still attract the attention of Internet users. If not prevented and controlled, they would inevitably radiate to China and cause adverse effects. (2) Second, through the artificial interpretation of high-frequency words such as 'Hubei', 'Wuhan', 'Xiaogan', 'Ezhou', it is found that most of the rumors are ' a mutant virus appears in Wuhan', 'a person in Xiaogan of Hubei died of COVID', which indicates that the initial pandemic site is often used repeatedly by rumormongers to create rumors. With the help of the public's painful memories and uneasiness, they spread rapidly and widely. (3) Third, because of the emergence of the pandemic situation in Beijing and Xinjiang, rumors about new confirmed cases have appeared simultaneously, interfering with the pandemic prevention and anti-pandemic work.

The hot words in the re-digestion stage can be divided into three categories: (1) 'Beijing', 'Hangzhou', 'Qingdao', 'Laishan', 'Wal-Mart' and other words indicating exact locations; (2) 'market', 'supermarket', 'hotel', 'community' and other words indicating vague locations; (3) 'refrigeration', 'meat ware', 'import', 'seafood' and so on. Combined with manual recognition, the content of rumors in the re-digestion stage can be summarized as ' the nucleic acid test of a certain food in a supermarket/market is positive' or 'there are overseas imported cases in a hotel/community'. The reason for this is that the pandemic in China has entered the most stable stage in its history, and there are relatively few indigenous cases in China, while the number of imported cases increase.

In the 2nd fluctuation stage, rumors about protective measures come into sight again because of the resurgent pandemic. Rumors like '99.9% of novel coronaviruses can be killed by tea in ten minutes', 'novel coronaviruses can stay latent in the throat for 4 days' have been forwarded by many netizens. In addition, taking advantage of the approaching Spring Festival, some people make use of people's psychological motivation to seek self-consolation to fabricate rumors such as 'express delivery outage', 'Spring Festival transportation will be cancelled', 'COVID-19 vaccinations can be booked online', 'people can receive pandemic subsidies with social insurance cards', etc., which hinder the pandemic prevention work.

Based on previous analyses, we can reach the following conclusions. First of all, the segmented changes of public opinion affect the subjects and contents of rumors to a certain extent. Secondly, the homogeneous or same rumors reconstruct the content and continue to spread in a new way (e.g. 'eating garlic can prevent COVID-19' and 'drinking garlic water can kill coronavirus'). For example, the rumor about new infections mentioned above will change the detailed content from the entry point of local confirmed cases and overseas imports at different stages of the pandemic. In addition, the public mood is staggered repeatedly. When the pandemic situation is serious or fluctuating, most of people are negative. Through the timely guidance of the government and experts, people become optimistic and confident. Besides, WeChat, Tik Tok and other keywords indicates that people tend to seek psychological approval on social platforms, which are the main places for rumors' generation and propagation.

5.2. Stage-based analysis of rumor subjects

In order to further analyze the periodic evolution law of rumor subjects, according to the hot words analysis of each stage and the actual rumor content, rumor subjects are shown in Table 3. A total of 947 typical hot words were classified and labeled with a single topic, and the frequency and percentage of various words in different stages of rumor development were counted. SPSS was used to make chi-square analysis and residual analysis of rumor topics and stages, as shown in Table 4.

In general, rumors about protective measures and treatment (268, 28.3%) and the current situation of COVID-19 (267, 28.2%) are the most widely spread topics, such as 'wearing multilayer masks to prevent New Coronavirus', 'Jinlong district has new cases' and so on. Rumors about source, transmission, and symptoms of the virus (145, 15.3%) and derivative social events (147, 15.5%) such as

Table 3. Different subjects of rumors and their representative words.

Theme of Rumors	Representative Hot Words
Source, Transmission and Symptoms of the Virus	SARS, source, lab, nature, pet, subway ticket, clothing, fever, cough
Protective Measures and Treatment	mask, smoking, antibiotic, self testing, anti-static clothing, diagnostic kit, specific medicine, vaccine, plasma
The Current Situation of COVID-19	infection, transmission, diagnosis, accumulation, suspected, multiple cases, asymptomatic infection, market, supermarket, hotel, cold chain, refrigeration
Overseas Rumors	US, UK, India, conspiracy theory, 5G, arson, signal tower, nose bridge bar, antenna, Facebook
Derivative Social Events	heresy, Shi Zhengli, Li Wenliang, doctors, medical staff, bid up prices, Spring Festival travel rush, express delivery

Table 4. Cross table analysis of rumor subjects and stages.

Chi-Square Tests

		Source, Transmission and Symptoms of the Virus	Protective Measures and Treatment	The Current Situation of COVID-19	Overseas Rumors	Derivative Social Events	Total
Incubation Stage	Count	29	28	12	2	4	75
	Expected Count	11.5	21.2	21.1	9.5	11.6	75.0
	Adjusted Residual	5.9	1.8	−2.4	−2.7	−2.5	
Explosion Stage	Count	61	124	73	21	60	339
	Expected Count	51.9	95.9	95.6	43.0	52.6	339.0
	Adjusted Residual	1.7	4.2	−3.4	−4.5	1.4	
Digestion Stage	Count	29	50	50	64	42	235
	Expected Count	36.0	66.5	66.3	29.8	36.5	235.0
	Adjusted Residual	−1.5	−2.8	−2.7	7.7	1.1	
1st Fluctuation Stage	Count	12	26	36	18	14	106
	Expected Count	16.2	30.0	29.9	13.4	16.5	106.0
	Adjusted Residual	−1.2	−0.9	1.4	1.4	−0.7	
Re-digestion Stage	Count	8	12	55	11	9	95
	Expected Count	14.5	26.9	26.8	12.0	14.7	95.0
	Adjusted Residual	−2.0	−3.6	6.8	−0.3	−1.7	
2nd Fluctuation Stage	Count	6	28	41	4	18	97
	Expected Count	14.9	27.5	27.3	12.3	15.1	97.0
	Adjusted Residual	−2.6	0.1	3.3	−2.7	0.9	
Total	Count	145	268	267	120	147	947

$\chi^2 = 187.089$, df = 20, p = 0.000

'woolen coats are easy to adsorb the virus' and 'bodies of a hospital in Wuhan are left unattended' are comparatively popular rumor topics. Overseas rumors (120,12.7%) spread relatively less, but they also deserve attention, such as 'injecting disinfectant into the human body can kill the virus'.

According to chi-square test, at the 95% confidence level, there is a significant correlation between rumor subjects and stages (p-value = 0.000), which illustrates that the distribution of rumor topics is different in different stages of rumor evolution. According to the normalized residual value after correction, the formula is as follows:

$$AR = \frac{O_{ij} - E_{ij}}{\sqrt{\left[n_{i+} \times n_{+j} \times n_{++}^{-1} \times (1 - n_{i+} \times n_{++}^{-1}) \times \left(1 - n_{+j} \times n_{++}^{-1}\right) \right]}}$$

$$E_{ij} = \frac{n_{i+} + n_{+j}}{n_{++}}$$

O_{ij} represents the count in cell (i, j). E_{ij} represents the expected count in cell (i, j). n_{i+} represents the number of observations in line i. n_{+j} represents the number of observations in column j. n_{++} represents the total number of observations. When the absolute value of AR is greater than 3, the difference between the count and the expected count is statistically significant. It can be seen that in the incubation stage, rumors about source, transmission, and symptoms of the virus (AR = 5.9) are the hottest, which is in line with the psychology that people are extremely concerned about the virus itself when it first appears. In the explosion stage, rumors about protective measures and treatment (AR = 4.2) are the most attractive. People are anxious about their lives and health due to the spread of the virus, so they are easy to believe such rumors to get psychological compensation. In the digestion stage, overseas rumors (AR = 7.7) become the most intensive topic of rumors. In the re-digestion stage and 2nd fluctuation stage, rumors about the current situation of COVID-19 (AR = 6.8, AR = 3.3) occupy the primary position, which indicates that the people are eager for the end of the pandemic, but the cold chain food and overseas imports pose a threat to domestic stability in China. Relatively speaking, rumors about the current situation of COVID-19 (AR = −3.4) and overseas rumors (AR = −4.5) in the explosion stage, and rumors about protective measures and treatment (AR = −3.6) in the re-digestion stage are less. Although the theme of rumor has different emphases in different stages, there are also periodic fluctuations.

6. Governance strategies

COVID-19 is a major examination of the national governance system and governance capacity, and the infodemic is the examination of the public's scientific literacy and the system of rumor governance. With the development of we-media era, anonymous online remarks make people with ulterior motives wantonly fabricate and spread rumors, threatening the long-term stability of society. With the updating of social media, the boundary of information transmission has been broken. Every public health emergency in the future will inevitably face the test of infodemic. Therefore, in combination with the evolution laws of online rumors, this paper proposes strategies to deal with rumors during COVID-19 under the infodemic.

First, based on the periodic evolution of quantity and periodic fluctuation of hot words and subjects, we can predict the number and content trend of rumors, and quickly and effectively curb the generation and spread of rumors. Relevant government departments should predict the number and theme of online rumors based on the pandemic trend, public demand, and key time nodes, and improve the sensitivity of refuting and controlling rumors. For example, overseas rumors are easy to attract the attention of netizens in the digestion stage. Therefore, authoritative institutions should perceive in advance, issue early warnings on rumor refuting platforms and social media, and admonish the public not to believe rumors, so as to achieve the purpose of taking preventive measures and improve the effectiveness of online rumor control.

Second, since netizens are willing to participate in rumor refutation due to the information demand in the explosion stage, we should carry out publicity and education activities to expand the rumor refuting group. The government and the media should seize this opportunity to jointly carry out various rumor refutation publicity and education activities, attract more people to join the rumor refutation group, and widely improve the public's scientific literacy and the ability of rumor refutation, to reduce the possibility of rumor spread.

Third, use the leverage principle to fight a protracted war of rumor governance. Lever principle is one of the basic mechanical principles of physics, which refers to prying a heavier object with less force at a place far from the fulcrum. Later, it gradually expanded to financial management and other fields. Relevant departments and platforms should pay attention to recurring rumors, fully recognize the essence of their contents, and use the leverage principle to strengthen the governance of such rumors to effectively curb re-dissemination. For example, deal with the rumor makers seriously and strictly, label rumors in time, etc.

Fourth, based on the agenda-setting theory, we should eliminate the negative emotions in the Internet, and promote the positive energy of the Internet. In the era of social media, interest recommendation algorithms trap Internet users in the information cocoon room, and personal emotions will continue to expand with the echo room effect. Therefore, it is particularly important to understand and control the emotions of Internet users. Agenda-setting theory means that the public's attention can be shifted, focused, or ignored under the guidance of the media. Mainstream media should timely understand public concerns and emotional trends, guide netizens to correct emotional counseling, at the same time, lead everyone to fully understand the pandemic dynamics, pay attention to pandemic risks, treat Internet rumors and pandemic changes with a rational and objective attitude, and create a harmonious and civilized network environment.

Fifthly, government departments, expert teams, rumor refuting platforms and social platforms should make full use of the characteristics that rumors are easy to appear on social platforms to build a normalized and integrated dynamic rumor refuting mechanism. Government departments and expert teams are responsible for timely disclosure and release of authoritative information, openness and transparency of the pandemic control process, and active science popularization. Rumor refuting platforms, such as the China Internet Joint Rumor Refuting Platform, should collect and sort out information released by the government and experts, clarify online rumors in real time, and reduce negative effects. Social platforms should be open to the government departments, expert teams and rumor refuting platforms, and the official account, small programs and other sectors should be able to roll up rumor-refuting information around the clock to control rumors from the source.

7. Conclusion

This research used the Python crawler to collect more than 60,000 rumor-refuting microblogs related to COVID-19. Based on the network public opinion's stage theory, pandemic situations, and major events, it exploded the evolution rules of online rumors in a complete period under the background of infodemic, which made up for the lack of time in previous studies. Moreover, using statistical analysis, text analysis and other technologies, from the point of quantity and content, fine-grained analyses were carried out, which further enriched the related research by combining public sentiment and rumor sources. Finally, aiming at the evolution of COVID-19 related rumors under the infodemic, this paper put forward the corresponding rumor control strategies, which were conducive to maintaining public health and social stability. In the follow-up research, it may be possible to apply text classification and topic mining technologies to further analyze the subjects of online rumors.

Disclosure statement

No potential conflict of interest was reported by the author(s).

References

Ball, P., & Maxmen, A. (2020). Battling the infodemic. *Nature, 581*(7809), 371–374.

DiFonzo, N., & Bordia, P. (2007). *Rumor psychology: Social and organizational approaches.* American psychological association. Washington, DC: American Psychological Association.

Gao, Y., Hua, H., & Luo, J. (2021). Analyzing public opinion on COVID-19 through different perspectives and stages. *Apsipa Transactions On Signal And Information Processing, 10,* e8.

Han, X., Wang, J., Zhang, M., & Wang, X. (2020). Using social media to mine and analyze public opinion related to COVID-19 in China. *International Journal Of Environmental Research And Public Health, 17,* 27888.

Huang, H., Chen, Y., & Ma, Y. (2020). Modeling the competitive diffusions of rumor and knowledge and the impacts on epidemic spreading. Applied Mathematics And Computation, 388, 125536

Hui, H., Zhou, C., Lu, X., & Li, J. (2020). Spread mechanism and control strategy of social network rumors under the influence of COVID-19. *NONLINEAR DYNAMICS, 101*(3SI), 1933–1949.

Infodemic. (2020). Oxford English Dictionary. London: Oxford University Press. Retrieved August 9, 2021, from https://oed.com/view/Entry/88407009

Pulido Rodriguez, C., Villarejo Carballido, B., Redondo-Sama, G., Guo, M., Ramis, M., & Flecha, R. (2020). Untold false news around COVID-19 circulated less on sina weibo than on twitter. how to overcome false information? *International And Multidisciplinary Journal Of Social Sciences-Rimcis, 9*(2SI), 107–128.

Qiao, J., Gao, Z. H., Huang, Y. R., HOU, Y. Y., & Wei, X. C. (2015). *Analysis on life cycle of network public opinion.* Paper presented at the Analysis on Life Cycle of Network Public Opinion, Beijing,China.

Rothkopf, D. J. (2003). When the buzz bites back. Retrieved March 24, 2021, from http://www1.udel.edu/globalagenda/2004/student/readings/infodemic.html

World Health Organization. (2020). Listings of WHO's response to COVID-19. Retrieved August 9, 2021, from https://www.who.int/news/item/29-06-2020-covidtimeline

Wu, Y., Deng, M., Wen, X., Wang, M., & Xiong, X. (2020). Statistical analysis of dispelling rumors on sina weibo. *Complexity, 2020,* 3176593.

Xie, T., Tan, T., & Li, J. (2020). An extensive search trends-based analysis of public attention on social media in the early outbreak of COVID-19 in China. *Risk Management And Healthcare Policy, 13,* 1353–1364.

Xu, K., & Bi, Q. (2019). Selection of sub high-frequency keywords and its application in co-word analysis (in Chinese). *Information Studies: Theory & Application, 42*(5), 148–152.

Yin, F., Lv, J., Zhang, X., Xia, X., & Wu, J. (2020). COVID-19 information propagation dynamics in the Chinese Sina-microblog. *Mathematical Biosciences And Engineering, 17*(3), 2676–2692.

Zhang, L., Chen, K., Jiang, H., & Zhao, J. (2020). How the health rumor misleads people's perception in a public health emergency: Lessons from a purchase craze during the COVID-19 outbreak in China. *International Journal Of Environmental Research And Public Health, 17,* 721319.

An empirical study of data warehouse implementation effectiveness

Nayem Rahman

ABSTRACT
A data warehouse implementation involves a huge financial undertaking on the part of a business organization. Business organizations maintain an enterprise data warehouse to get access to the most accurate and up-to-date information concerning their business. That information needs to be available at the right time to enable organizations to make strategic business decisions. This article discusses the findings of an empirical study of data warehouse implementation effectiveness. The motivation behind conducting this study was to identify the variables that are influential. In this study eight variables were taken as predictive variables and four as response variables. The findings of the study show that certain variables have a significant influence on the response variables for data warehousing success. IT professionals, academicians and researchers might find these findings beneficial.

1. Introduction

The capability of IT infrastructures is strongly correlated with the agility (Lu & Ramamurthy, 2011) and performance (Mithas et al., 2011; Goncalves et al., 2015) of an organization. A data warehouse is one of the major IT infrastructures (Weill et al., 2002) of business organizations. The data warehouse plays a prominent role in providing strategic business information. Business executives use this information to achieve competitive advantage. With the advent of personal computers and the Internet, business organizations are embracing huge amounts of data that has business value. All large companies and most medium size companies maintain an enterprise data warehouse (EDW) to hold both historical and current data. This data is used by reporting tools, business intelligence (BI), and data mining tools to make strategic and tactical business decisions.

In order for business organizations to make strategic and tactical business decisions, the data warehouse needs to provide business information in a timely manner. The data warehouse must meet service level agreements (SLAs) set up with the analytical community. A data warehouse must provide improved analysis to support the reporting needs of an organization. The DW team must deliver a data warehouse environment that is stable and returns query results within a short period of time – from seconds to a few minutes. It must ensure quality data so that executives can make reliable business decisions. A data warehouse receives data from numerous sources (operational databases). Given that data comes to EDW from external sources, data latency occurs. A successful data warehouse tries to minimize data latency as much as possible. Here, the goal should be to ensure the timeliness of data availability in the data warehouse so that business executives can make decisions at the right time.

In order to fulfill business needs such as data quality, improved analysis and reporting capability, data availability

with reduced latency, and meeting SLAs, several organizational and technical factors must be considered when implementing a data warehouse. A data warehousing project needs to have a clear set of objectives to be successful. There need to be champions from management, customers, and data warehouse architects to support data warehousing projects. Building a data warehouse poses many technical challenges (Rahman, 2013; Rahman, 2014). The data warehouse architects need to ensure that there is a well understood technical plan to ensure successful system development and information delivery capability.

In order to have a successful data warehouse, it is important to have a solid working relationship between user groups and the data warehouse project staff and team. To ensure data quality, it is thought that integrated metadata plays a key role (Sen & Jacob, 1998; Shankaranarayanan & Even, 2006). The data warehouse project managers' experience is considered one of the key factors in the design and development of an effective data warehouse. In a project's life cycle there will be many known and unforeseen design, technical, and resources-related challenges that arise during the course of the project (Kharbanda & Pinto, 1996; Rundensteiner et al., 2000). A project manager without significant prior experience could find it difficult to overcome the obstacles encountered or adopt the right course of action at the right time.

The users' functional requirements need to be well understood to deliver quality data successfully in the data warehousing environment. User requirements that are not well understood might result in delivering defective applications in the production environment. Fixing issues with an application after it landed in production might result in many issues including missing SLAs, customer dissatisfaction and costly fixes (Keil & Carmel, 1995). Data integration is another area which needs to be thought through carefully to ensure quality data in the data warehouse. As noted earlier, data comes into EDW from numerous sources. If not all the data can be stored in the data warehouse, the incompleteness of the data will cause the user community to lose faith in the data warehouse information.

Maintaining a stable, scalable, and efficient data warehouse depends on how it is built from the standpoints of data architecture (Leitheiser, 2001), data modeling (Rahman et al., 2012), and extract, transform, and load (ETL) programming. The data warehouse is a shared environment. Maintaining a stable data warehousing environment is essential given numerous applications running in a data warehouse. If an application that is skewed landed in a production environment it might significantly degrade the performance of other applications by using up all the computing resources or making the data warehousing environment unstable and even unavailable (Cataldo & Herbsleb, 2013).

There many things that need to be considered when making a data warehouse effective. In preceding paragraphs, we gave an account of implementation success criteria and also identified several organizational and technical factors that could impact data warehouse implementation. There is also a long-held belief in the data warehousing industry that these factors contribute to the success of the data warehouse implementation (Huber, 1990). This empirical study investigates if any or all of those factors really contribute to having a successful data warehouse implementation.

2. Theoretical framework and literature review

Previous research on data warehousing focused on design issues (Golfarelli & Rizzi, 2009), data maintenance strategies related to relational view materialization, implementation issues (Rahman & Rutz, 2015), and query performance issues. Several researchers have investigated data warehouse ETL tools and have identified alternative tools (Simitsis et al., 2005). There has also been a good amount of research work that has addressed the issues of data inconsistency and quality (AlMabhouh & Ahmad, 2010; Ballou & Tayi, 1999). To complement the prior research, this author conducted an empirical survey to see what organizational and technical factors have influence on the effective implementation of data warehouses.

A data warehouse is destined to provide reporting and business intelligence solutions (Brohman et al., 2000) for companies trying to stay competitive (Miyamoto, 2015; Rutz et al., 2012; Shin, 2003). The data warehouse also helps business organizations with gathering strategic and timely business information to support corporate strategies (Cooper et al., 2000) to stay competitive and increase revenue. For the last decade, business organizations have been increasingly using data warehouses as the central repositories of their enterprise data. In their study, Wixom & Watson (2001) observed a significant relationship between data warehouse systems and data quality. They also observed a relationship between the strong skill-sets of project team members and implementing data warehouse projects on time. This study made an attempt to revalidate the findings of the last decade.

Gefen et al. (2008) suggest that business familiarity is one of the key factors in software development and that it builds trust with customers. This study attempted to investigate how understanding data warehouse users' requirements plays out in implementing a successful data warehouse project. Parssian et al. (2009) attempted to address the data quality issue in a relational database system. They stated that data quality issues primarily arise from source data, and to address the issue they

came up with a framework to define relevant metrics constituting of a quality profile. This study took data quality issues from the standpoints of lack of system development capability and lack of a process for identifying and resolving data integration issues. The DeLone and McLean (1992) study asserted that system quality, information quality, and user satisfaction are interrelated and interdependent. This study made an attempt to investigate the degree of the relationship between these factors and data warehouse implementation.

Brohman and Parent (2001) conducted an exploratory study to identify the relationship between data modelers' expertise and their impact on data usage in the data warehouse. They found that more technical expertise would increase the reliability of data usage. In our study, we tried to identify the relationship between data analysts' data integration knowledge, processes and effective data warehouse implementation. We also made an attempt to see how project managers' experiences are relevant in the successful implementation of applications in the data warehouse.

Previous studies suggest that in many cases data warehousing projects fail due to lack of sponsors from the management side and lack of partnership with customers. One other reason for project failure is the lack of a clear set of data warehousing project objectives. This study takes these issues into consideration and makes an attempt to see how they impact data warehouse implementation. Previous studies have identified that the key factors for the success of data warehouses are: (1) improved availability of data to meet business needs; (2) improved capability of satisfying analysis and reporting needs; (3) improved data quality for better decision-making; and (4) improved timeliness of information for business users' use (Brohman et al., 2000; Shin, 2003; Wixom & Watson, 2001). In this study we measure the effectiveness these factors in data warehouse implementation.

3. Research questions and variables studied

The research questions were designed to facilitate understanding how successful data warehouses have been in providing reporting environment and business intelligence capabilities. How much value have they delivered to customers, the analytical community, knowledge workers, and business executives? Do they enable a business organization to achieve competitive advantage? Do they help business organizations make strategic and tactical business decisions? To get answers to these questions the survey was geared towards understanding the deliverables that a data warehouse is supposed to deliver. This study attempts to assess the implementation success of data warehousing in the spirit of the information systems success model developed by DeLone and McLean (2002).

Previous research suggests that managerial decision-making is dependent on the availability of high quality information that is made available in a timely manner (March & Hevner, 2007). Mannino and Walter (2006) suggested the need for research on data timeliness evaluation to determine optimal refresh policy design. Shankaranarayanan and Cai (2006) and Ballou and Tayi (1999) asserted the importance of data quality for better managerial decision-making. Redman (1998) reported the impacts of poor data quality on a typical enterprise such as 'customer dissatisfaction, increased operational cost, less effective decision-making, and reduced ability to make and execute strategy'. In this study, we have devised the following questions to investigate what has been suggested by the above research.

(1) Has the data warehouse improved the availability of information to meet the needs of data warehouse sponsors and customers?

(2) Has the data warehouse improved the capability of satisfying the overall analysis and reporting needs of business organizations?

(3) Has the data warehouse facilitated the improved quality of decisions made by business executives?

(4) Has the data warehouse improved the timeliness of information?

We identify answers to these questions as response variables.

To determine whether a data warehouse can deliver business information and other benefits based on the above questions, certain organizational and technical factors must be in place. We need to ask several questions in this regard. We have identified them as predictive variables. They include the following.

- Do the data warehousing projects follow a clear set of objectives?
- Are there champions to support the data warehousing projects?
- Does the data warehouse have top management support?
- Do the data warehousing project teams have the capability to develop efficient systems and deliver information?
- Do the data warehouse user groups and project teams have sufficiently good working relations and partnership to deliver applications that are efficient and stable, and to satisfy required information needs?

The following predictive variables were identified based on the importance given to them in previous research as key determinants of data warehouse success (AlMabhouh & Ahmad, 2010; Ballou & Tayi, 1999; Cooper et al., 2000; Idris & Ahmad, 2011; Isik et al., 2013; Keil & Carmel, 1995; Leitheiser, 2001; O'Donnell et al., 2012; Rahman et al., 2011, 2012, 2014; Redman, 1998; Schlegel et al., 2013; Weli, 2014):

- Data warehouses receive data from heterogeneous sources and hence data warehouse refresh identified by timestamp is necessary. Data definitions also need to be stored. Does the data warehouse maintain and manage integrated metadata for that purpose?
- Does the data warehousing team have strong data warehousing project management experience?
- Do the project teams understand the users' functional requirements?
- Is there any process for identifying and resolving data integration issues in the data warehouse?

There are 13 questions involved in this survey. All these questions are closed-ended. The respondents were asked to fill out responses on a five-point scale – Strongly Agree, Agree, Neither Agree nor Disagree, Disagree, and Strongly Disagree – with score points of 5, 4, 3, 2, and 1, respectively. There are certain advantages of closed-ended questions. Survey responses were easy to code (for example by assigning scores 5, 4, 3, 2, and 1), easy to enter and analyze, had enhanced reliability, had less research bias, and had a high degree of anonymity.

4. Research methodology

A survey was used to collect relevant data. The survey was conducted based on 13 companies. A few of them were large companies and the others were medium sized companies. These companies included manufacturing, banking, health care, and retail businesses. They had huge transactional data to process on a daily basis. The data came from operational data stores to enterprise data warehouses. The data in data warehouses was used to perform analytics based on both current and historical data. Most of these companies had big IT departments and possessed a data warehouse. Data were collected from different stakeholders of the data warehouse including customers, the BI analytical community, systems analysts, application developers, solution architects, quality assurance analysts, database administrators, data analysts, and product managers. Data were collected from one developed country (USA) and two developing countries (Bangladesh and India). Most of the questions were developed to reflect the performance of data warehouses and how these data warehouses influenced the business organizations. This study was designed according to the Information Systems (ISs) success factors model developed by DeLone and McLean (1992, 2002). About 75 questionnaires were distributed among the data warehouse stakeholders in these companies. Fifty-eight respondents participated in the survey.

The questionnaires were distributed in person to some respondents and electronically to others. Survey responses were entered on a spreadsheet (a csv file). The survey questions were categorized into eight predictive variables and four response variables. The variables were assigned coded names along with variable descriptions. The statistical package R (Field et al., 2012) was used to read the csv file and perform correlation and regression analysis, hypothesis testing, generate histograms, and plot graphs.

5. Survey data analysis

Survey data were analyzed using two statistical techniques: correlation analysis and regression analysis. These statistical techniques were used to study the effect on data warehouse system performance, data quality, timeliness of data availability, and fulfillment of customers' reporting and analytical needs. In these, statistical analysis hypothesis tests were conducted. For this purpose, we used the open-source statistical package R. This software is command based and pretty efficient. The survey data were also analyzed with a few descriptive statistics. This is useful for providing some insight into the characteristics of the variables (Shin, 2003).

5.1. Correlation analysis and hypothesis tests

Correlation analysis was conducted to evaluate the relationship between each of the eight predictive variables and four response variables.

Table 1 summarizes the variables studied. There are eight predictive variables (items 2, 3, 5, 7, 8, 9, 11, and 12) and four response variables (items 4, 6, 10, and 13).

5.1.1. Availability of information in the DW

Correlation analysis was performed between each of the eight predictive variables and the response variable 'AvailInfoNeeds' (The DW has improved the availability of Info to meet users' needs) – see Table 1. The analysis shows that two predictive variables have influence on the response variable 'AvailInfoNeeds'. The predictive variable 'ProjChamp' (We have people who champion DW projects) has a strong positive correlation (33%). The p-value is 0.011,05, which is less than the α value of 0.05. The other predictive variable, 'CapSysDevDeliv' (Has capability

Table 1. Response variables (in bold) and predictive variables.

Item	Column (variable)	Interpretation
1	IDNo	Survey response identification (numbered upon receipt and entry)
2	ProjObj	We follow a clear set of Data Warehousing Project Objectives
3	ProjChamp	We have people who champion DW projects
4	**AvailInfoNeeds**	**The DW has improved the availability of Info to meet our needs**
5	CapSysDevDeliv	We have capability to deal with system development & Info Delivery
6	**ImpvRptNeeds**	**The DW has improved the capability of satisfying analysis and reporting needs**
7	UserProjStaffRel	Excellent relationship between user group and DW project staff
8	IntegMetadata	We maintain and manage integrated metadata for the DW
9	ProjMgmtExp	We have strong DW project management experience
10	**ImpvQualDecn**	**The DW has improved the quality of decision-making**
11	UserFuncReq	The project team understands users' functional requirements
12	RslvDataIntgIssue	We have a process for identifying & resolving data integration issues
13	**TimelinessInfoUse**	**The DW has improved the timeliness of information for use**

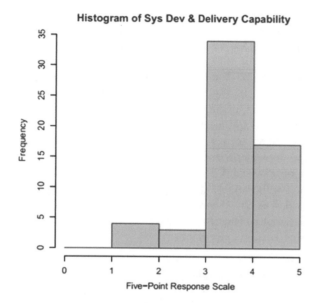

Figure 1. Histogram: X-axis = CapSysDevDeliv; Y-axis = Frequency.

to deal with system development & Info Delivery) has a strong

```
> cor.test(CapSysDevDeliv, ImpvRptNeeds)

        Pearson's product-moment correlation

data:  CapSysDevDeliv and ImpvRptNeeds
t = 5.3547, df = 56, p-value = 1.659e-06
alternative hypothesis: true correlation is not equal to 0
95 percent confidence interval:
 0.3808723 0.7304272
sample estimates:
      cor
0.5819201
```

Figure 2. X = CapSysDevDeliv; Y = ImpvRptNeeds.

positive correlation (39%). The p-value is 0.002,757, which is also less than the α value of 0.05.

In terms of survey responses, 31% of respondents 'Strongly Agree' and 57% of respondents 'Agree' that their data warehouse ensures the availability of information needed by business users. The survey results provide important information about user satisfaction with information delivery by the data warehouse. And correlation analysis reveals that only two predictive variables, 'ProjChamp' (DW project champions) and 'CapSysDevDeliv' (Has capability to deal with system development & Info Delivery), have a strong influence on the response variable 'AvailInfoNeeds'.

Correlation analysis shows that the rest of the predictive variables do not have a strong correlation with the response variables and that the p-values are also greater than 0.05.

5.1.2. Improvement of capability of satisfying analysis and reporting needs by a DW

These time correlation analyses were performed between each of the eight predictive variables and the response variable 'ImpvRptNeeds' (the DW has improved the capability of satisfying analysis and reporting needs) – see Table 1.

The analysis shows that four predictive variables, ProjObj (We follow a clear set of DW project objectives), 'ProjChamp' (We have people who champion DW projects), CapSysDevDeliv (The DW project team has capability to deal with system development & Info delivery), and 'RslvDataIntgIssue' (We have a process for identifying & resolving data integration), have a strong correlation (32, 31, 58, and 31%, respectively) with p-values of 0.015,16, 0.017,65, 0.000,001,659, and 0.014,72, respectively.

Correlation analysis shows that the rest of the predictive variables do not have a strong correlation with the response variables. Here we provide syntax for the correlation analysis of the predictive variable 'CapSysDevDeliv' and the response variable 'ImpvRptNeeds'.

Figure 1 shows a histogram of values of the predictive variable CapSysDevDeliv. Respondents' responses are on a five-point scale: 0 to 1 is for 'Strongly Disagree', 1 to 2 is for 'Disagree', 2 to 3 is for 'Neither Agree nor Disagree', 3 to 4 is for 'Agree', and 4 to 5 is for 'Strongly Agree'. The histogram shows that most of the respondents agreed that the capability for system development and information delivery has an influence on providing an improved capability of satisfying reporting needs. The specification of the null and alternative hypotheses is provided below.

Ho: Cor = 0 [Null Hypothesis: a DW's System Development & Information Delivery capability has no influence on a DW's ability to satisfy analysis and reporting needs.]

Ha: Cor ≠ 0 [Alternative Hypothesis: a DW's System Development & Information Delivery capability does have an influence on a DW's ability to satisfy analysis and reporting needs.]

The hypothesis test shows that the 95% confidence interval for the mean difference is from 0.380,8723 to 0.730,4272. The p-value is smaller than the α of .05 (see Figure 2). The p-value = 0.000,001,659 < α = .05. So **reject** the null hypothesis. There is a strong positive correlation (0.581,9201 or 58%) between a DW's systems development capability and providing for analysis and reporting needs.

Plotting a graph of the two variables from the correlation also confirms a strong positive correlation (see Figure 3).

5.1.3. Improvement of quality decision-making in a DW

Correlation analysis was performed between each of the eight predictive variables and the response variable 'ImpvQualDecn'

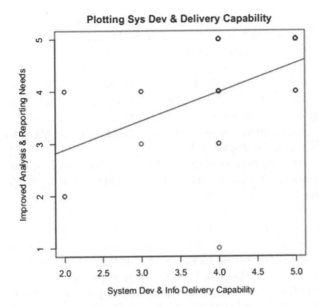

Figure 3. X = CapSysDevDeliv; Y = ImpvRptNeeds.

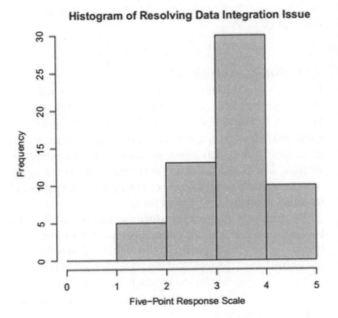

Figure 4. Histogram: X-axis = RslvDataIntgIssu; Y-axis = Frequency.

```
> cor.test(RslvDataIntgIssue, TimelinessInfoUse)

        Pearson's product-moment correlation

data:  RslvDataIntgIssue and TimelinessInfoUse
t = 3.0346, df = 56, p-value = 0.003649
alternative hypothesis: true correlation is not equal to 0
95 percent confidence interval:
 0.1301298 0.5779872
sample estimates:
      cor
0.3757944
```

Figure 5. X = RslvDataIntgIssue; Y = TimelinessInfoUse.

(The DW has improved the quality of decision-making) – see Table 1.

The analysis shows that only two predictive variables are strongly positively correlated with this response variable. The predictive variable 'UserFuncReq' (The project team understands users' functional requirements) has a strong positive correlation (53%) with a p-value of 0.000,6433. About 81% of the respondents 'Agree' or 'Strongly Agree' (on a five-point scale) that understanding users' functional requirements has enabled the improvement of quality decision-making in a data warehouse.

The other predictive variable, 'ProjObj' (We follow a clear set of DW project objectives) also has a strong positive correlation (36%) with a p-value of 0.005,056. About 83% of the respondents 'Agree' or 'Strongly Agree' that a clear set of DW project objectives helps improve quality decision-making using a data warehouse.

The correlation analysis showed that the rest of the predictive variables were not strongly correlated with the response variable.

5.1.4. Improvement of timeliness using DW refresh

In this case, correlation analyses were performed between each of the eight predictive variables and the response variable 'TimelinessInfoUse' (The DW has improved the timeliness of information for use) – see Table 1.

The analysis shows that three predictive variables have a strong influence on the response variable. The predictive variable, 'RslvDataIntgIssue' (We have a process for identifying & resolving data integration issues) has a strong positive correlation (38%) with a p-value of 0.003,649. The predictive variable 'ProjObj' has a strong positive correlation (34%) with a p-value of 0.009,008, and the predictive variable 'UserFuncReq' also has a positive correlation (37%) with a p-value of 0.004,093. The correlation analysis shows that the rest of the predictive variables do not have strong correlation with the response variable.

The details of correlation analysis of predictive variable 'RslvDataIntgIssue' and response variable, 'TimelinessInfoUse' is provided in subsequent sections.

Figure 4 shows a histogram of values of the predictive variable RslvDataIntgIssue. Respondents' responses are shown on a five-point scale: 0 to 1 is for 'Strongly Disagree', 1 to 2 is for 'Disagree', 2 to 3 is for 'Neither Agree nor Disagree', 3 to 4 is for 'Agree', and 4 to 5 is for 'Strongly Agree'. The histogram shows that most of the respondents agreed that the process for identifying and resolving data integration issues has an influence on improving the timeliness of information use. The null and alternative hypotheses are set as below.

Ho: Cor = 0 [Null Hypothesis: Resolving Data Integration Issue has no influence on the timeliness for information use.]

Ha: Cor ≠ 0 [Alternative Hypothesis: Resolving Data Integration Issue does have influence on the timeliness for information use.]

The hypothesis test in the correlation analysis (Figure 5) shows that the 95% confidence interval for the mean difference is from 0.130,1298 to 0.577,9872. The p-value (0.003,649) is significantly less than the α of .05. So **reject** the null hypothesis. There is a strong positive correlation (0.375,7944 or 37%) between the predictive and response variables.

The plotting of the correlation in the graph also shows a strong positive correlation (Figure 6).

The correlation analysis shows that each of the four response variables is influenced by only one or two predictive variables. This is a quite interesting finding. We were under the impression that most of the predictive variables would have a positive correlation with each of the response variables. There is a long-held belief in the IT industry that those predictive variables have implications for the successful implementation of data warehouses.

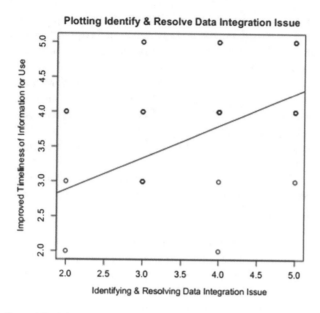

Figure 6. X = RslvDataIntgIssue; Y = TimelinessInfoUse.

```
> summary(lm(RslvDataIntgIssue ~ TimelinessInfoUse))

Call:
lm(formula = RslvDataIntgIssue ~ TimelinessInfoUse)

Residuals:
    Min      1Q  Median      3Q     Max
-1.7996 -0.3404  0.2004  0.2004  1.6596

Coefficients:
                  Estimate Std. Error t value Pr(>|t|)
(Intercept)         1.9627     0.6063   3.237  0.00203 **
TimelinessInfoUse   0.4592     0.1513   3.035  0.00365 **
---
Signif. codes:  0 '***' 0.001 '**' 0.01 '*' 0.05 '.' 0.1 ' ' 1

Residual standard error: 0.7841 on 56 degrees of freedom
  (142 observations deleted due to missingness)
Multiple R-squared: 0.1412,     Adjusted R-squared: 0.1259
F-statistic: 9.209 on 1 and 56 DF,  p-value: 0.003649
```

Figure 7. X = RslvDataIntgIssue; Y = TimelinessInfoUse.

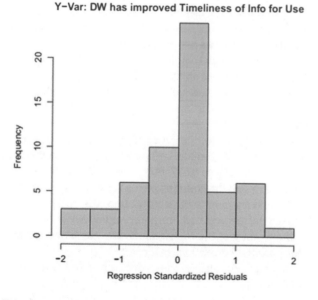

Figure 8. Histogram: regression residuals for TimelinessInfoUse; [X = RslvDataIntgIssue].

5.2. Regression analysis and hypothesis tests

Multiple regression analysis is a very powerful tool used in research for decades. In this study attempts have been made to determine regression relationship between a single X-variable, 'RslvDataIntgIssue', and a Y-variable, 'TimelinessInfoUse'. The null and alternative hypotheses are as below.

$H_0: R^2 = 0$ [Null Hypothesis: Resolving Data Integration has no dependency on the Timeliness of Information Use]

$H_1: R^2 \neq 0$ [Null Hypothesis: Resolving Data Integration does have dependency on the Timeliness of Information Use]

The output indicates that the fitted value is given by $\hat{Y} = 1.9627 + 0.4592 (X_1)$.

Overall Relationship between Predictive and Response variables (Figure 7): The probability of the F-statistic (9.209) for the overall regression relationship is 0.003,649, significantly less than the level of significant of 0.05. We reject the null hypothesis that there is no relationship between the predictive variable and the response variable ($R^2 = 0$). We support the research hypothesis that there is a statistically significant relationship between the set of predictive variables and the response variable. In addition, output also shows that $R^2 = 0.1412$ and adjusted $R^2 = 0.1259$. In this example we see that the adjusted R^2 is 0.1259 which seems reasonable. In real world many cases regression model is being developed with a low R^2. Perhaps it depends on subject matter where it is applied to.

5.2.1. Histogram of residuals

In general, a residual is the difference between the actual value of a response variable (DV) and the value of variable that was predicted by a statistical model. In the context of a regression, a residual is how far a predicted value (as determined by the predictors in the model) is from the actual value of the response variable. This is also called an "error term" (because it represents how much a regression model was in error, in terms of its ability to predict the value of the DV).

The residuals should approximate a normal distribution, because the regression procedure is based on the assumption that the error term is normally distributed. If the errors are not normal, then the results of the regression are not correct.

This is a histogram for the residuals, measured in standard deviations. X-Variable = 'RslvDataIntgIssue' and Y-Variable – 'TimelinessInfoUse'.

Figure 8 shows that the histogram of the residuals is consistent with the assumption of normality.

5.2.2. Residual plot

In a simple linear regression model the residual data is the difference between the observed data of the dependent variable, 'TimelinessInfoUse' and the fitted values. In this experiment we apply R function lm to a formula to describe dependent variable by the independent variable (RslvDataIntgIssue). Then we compute the residual. We also plot the residual against the observed values (Figure 9).

mydata2 = lm(TimelinessInfoUse ~ RslvDataIntgIssue, data=mydata)

plot(mydata2)

In general, values that are close to the horizontal line are predicted well. The points above the line are under-predicted and the ones below the line are over-predicted. The linearity assumption is supported to the extent that the amount of points scattered above and below the line is equal. In this example we can see the values are both below and above the horizontal line which appears to be normal.

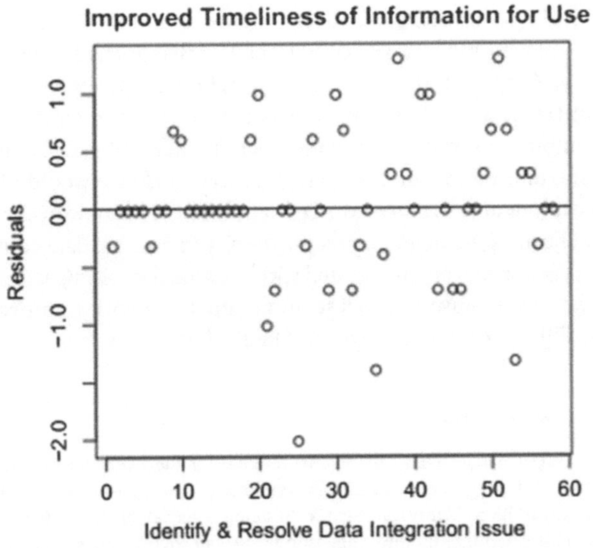

Figure 9. Regression residual plot for TimelinessInfoUse and RslvDataIntgIssue.

5.2.3. Stepwise regression

Stepwise regression methods are sometimes relied upon to determine a set of predictive variables that represent the best set of predictors of a particular response variable. There are steps involved in conducting forward stepwise regression. In this study there were as many as eight predictive variables involved. Out of four response variables in this study the stepwise regression was conducted based on response variable 'TimelinessInfoUse'. The analysis was concluded in two iterations.

In the first iteration the regression of X-variable, RslvDataIntgIssue, on Y-variable, TimelinessInfoUse, provided the highest adjusted R^2 (0.1259 or 12%). In the second iteration we have included other X-variables with this variable ('RslvDataIntgIssue'). The second iteration X-variables, 'RslvDataIntgIssue' and 'UserFuncReq' (see Table 1), together provided the highest adjusted R^2 (0.2015 or 20%), which is much higher than that of first iteration adjusted R^2. The third iteration along with three X-variables, 'RslvDataIntgIssue', 'UserFuncReq', and 'ProjObj' (see Table 1), provided the highest adjusted R-squared (0.2210 or 22%). The fourth iteration did not provide any better adjusted R^2 compared to the third iteration.

The conclusion is that, with an adjusted R^2 of 22%, the predictive variables 'RslvDataIntgIssue' (We have a process for identifying & resolving data integration issues), 'UserFuncReq', and 'ProjObj' are the best predictors of the response variable 'TimelinessInfoUse' (The DW has improved the timeliness of information for use) with a p-value of 0.000,8742, which is significantly less than .05 (the 95% confidence interval). The significance of having a process in place to identify and resolve data integration issues is an important finding of this study and confirms the assertion made by Sen and Jacob (1998).

Collecting user functional requirements (the variable 'UserFuncReq') at the beginning of a project and providing a flawless solution based on those requirements are critical to satisfying the user community. Deciding on a clear set of project objectives (the variable 'ProjObj') before starting the DW project is important for work on the project to have a clear purpose and to achieve the desired goals.

6. Research limitations

The survey asked 13 questions and 12 of them were designed on a five-point scale. How much statistical error might be generated by such a scale remains an open question. In management information systems (MISs) and behavioral sciences, scale development and a framework for developing valid measures are challenging activities (Hevner et al., 2004; MacKenzie et al., 2011; March & Smith, 1995). If we had designed it on a one-to-ten scale it would have allowed respondents more granularity in choosing the points on the scale. That could have been helpful for statistical computation and allowed normal probability distributions to be used. In general, response scale formats of this type do not allow respondents to qualify or clarify answers. The research did not solicit any open-ended questions. Hence, it was not possible to collect any additional comments or thoughts about data warehouse effectiveness.

7. Findings and discussions

This study is based on a survey questionnaire consisting of eight predictive variables and four response variables. Using correlation and regression analysis methods we attempted to find the relationship of each predictive variable to each response variable. Our findings suggest that, out of the eight predictive variables, five of them (ProjChamp, ProjObj, CapSysDevDeliv, UserFuncReq, and RslvDataIntgIssue) have influences on four of theresponse variables. As expected, most of the predictive variables have an influence on each of the response variables. In the data warehousing industry, there is a widely-held belief that these factors are determinants of successful data warehouse implementation. This study found that variable 'ProjObj' (We follow a clear set of DW project objectives) has a strong positive influence on as many as three response variables (see Sections 5.1.2–5.1.4). This significant finding suggests that in order to achieve business value out of DW project implementation there needs to be a clear set of project objectives at the outset. This study also found that each of the four independent variables (ProjChamp, CapSysDevDeliv, UserFuncRq, and RslvDataIntgIssue) in Table 1 have a strong positive influence on all four response variables (see Sections 5.1.1–5.1.4).

When developing a data warehouse, the project team's ability to design and develop a system, their comprehension of users' functional requirements, and the identification of a process to resolve data integration issues are all instrumental in contributing to the success of the project and ultimately contribute to successful business performance. The findings of this study confirm the assertion of Mithas et al. (2011) that information technology capabilities, including customer management capability, process management capability, and performance management capability, contribute to a firm's performance (Chakravarty et al., 2013; Goncalves et al., 2015).

The study found that three variables, i.e. UserProjStaffRel (Excellent relationship between user group and DW project staff), IntegMetadata (We maintain and manage integrated metadata for the DW), and ProjMgmtExp (We have strong DW project management experience), had no influence on any of those four response variables. The users–project team relationship (during the project life cycle) is generally considered to be effective in implementing a project flawlessly (Keil & Carmel, 1995). However, this study found no strong evidence in support of this. DW metadata is generally thought of as ensuring data reliability and quality (Shankaranarayanan & Even, 2006), and project managers' experience is generally considered very important in completing data warehousing projects on time and within scope. However, this study did not find any direct relation between project managers' experience and data warehouse implementation effectiveness.

The findings of this study suggest that users' functional requirements need to be understood well. There is a strong correlation between a project team's understanding of users' functional requirements and the resulting improved quality of the data used for decision-making pulled from the data warehousing system. The previous study by DeLone and McLean (1992) found that user information satisfaction is strongly correlated with information and system quality.

As stated by Shmueli (2011), an empirical study should contribute to knowledge in many areas including discovering new relationships, measuring development, improving existing theoretical models, comparing existing theories, establishing the relevance of existing models, and assessing predictability. This study contributed to some of the above identified areas. For example, this study discovered a new relationship, i.e. that putting a standard process in place to identify and resolve data integration issues can help in making data available in a timely fashion. This helps in resolving the data latency issue, which is a data warehouse refresh bottleneck.

8. Concluding remarks and future research

In this article, we have reported the findings of an empirical study of enterprise data warehouse implementation effectiveness. We identified eight independent variables based on previous studies that had found them to be key influencers of successful data warehousing. We also identified four response variables based previous research that indicated them to be key factors in keeping data warehouse project stakeholders, including customers, satisfied. We used correlation and regression analysis methods and hypothesis testing to find relationships between each predictive variable and each response variable.

We found that successful data warehouse implementation is dependent on (1) a clear set of data warehouse project objectives; (2) data warehouse champions who can oversee data warehouse operations and take effective steps to keep the data warehouse up and running in a healthy state; (3) the capability of the data warehouse technical team, including architects and application developers, to deliver flawless applications that run efficiently without causing data integrity issue or performance bottleneck; (4) the project team's understanding of users' functional requirements; and (5) processes developed by data warehouse architects and developers to identify and resolve data integrity issues at any time. We found that these factors are key to providing data warehouse stakeholders, including report users, the BI community, and company executives, with (a) the availability of timely information; (b) support for business intelligence and reporting needs; (c) improved quality decision-making; and (d) improved timeliness of information for use. Thus, our findings have provided significant insight into building successful data warehousing.

From a broader organizational perspective, successful data warehouse implementation provides an organization with business value creation, cost avoidance, innovation, user satisfaction, internal operations efficiency, data warehouse performance, and stability (Akhter & Rahman, 2015; Chakravarty et al., 2013; Rahman, 2013). Given that the computing industry is fast-moving and business conditions also change fast (Rahman, 2013; Akhter et al., 2014), data warehouse implementation effectiveness needs to be evaluated from time to time. For example, recently a new phenomenon called 'Big Data' has come into the picture. As part of future work, we would like to explore how this new kind of data could bring new insights and business value to an organization, and how big data could be transformed and integrated with existing data sitting within a data warehouse to provide an organization with improved capability to make strategic and tactical decisions.

Acknowledgements

The author would like to thank two referees for their very useful comments and suggestions on earlier versions of the manuscript. Many thanks to Joan Schnitzer, Senior Systems Analyst at Intel, for her thoughtful comments and suggestions on improving this paper. The author also thanks Tracy Hornschuch, Senior Application Developer at Intel, for excellent editing.

Disclosure statement

No potential conflict of interest was reported by the author.

References

Akhter, S., & Rahman, N. (2015). Building a customer inquiry database system. *International of Journal of Technology Diffusion (IJTD), 6*, 59–76.

Akhter, S., Rahman, N., & Rahman, M. N. (2014). Competitive Strategies in the Computer Industry. *International Journal of Technology Diffusion (IJTD), 5*, 73–88.

AlMabhouh, A., & Ahmad, A. (2010). Identifying quality factors within data warehouse. *Proceedings of the Second International Conference on Computer Research and Development, IEEE,*. doi: 10.1109/ICCRD.2010.18, 65-72.

Ballou, D. P., & Tayi, G. K. (1999). Enhancing data quality in data warehouse environments. *Communications of the ACM, 42*, 1.

Brohman, M. K., & Parent, M. (2001). Gaining insight from the data warehouse: The competence maturity model. *Proceedings of the 34th Hawaii International Conference on System Sciences (HICSS)*, IEEE, 1–10.

Brohman, M. K., Parent, M., Pearce, M. R., & Wade, M. (2000). The business intelligence value chain: Data-driven decision support in a data warehouse environment: An exploratory study. *Proceedings of the 33rd Hawaii International Conference on System Sciences (HICSS)*, IEEE, 1–10.

Cataldo, M., & Herbsleb, J. D. (2013). Coordination breakdowns and their impact on development productivity and software failures. *IEEE Transactions on Software Engineering, 39*, 343–360.

Chakravarty, A., Grewal, R., & Sambamurthy, V. (2013). Information technology competencies, organizational agility, and firm performance: enabling and facilitating roles. *Information Systems Research (ISR), 24*, 976–997.

Cooper, B. L., Watson, H. J., Wixom, B. H., & Goodhue, D. L. (2000). Data warehousing supports corporate strategy at first American corporation. *MIS Quarterly, 24*, 547–567.

DeLone, W. H., & McLean, E. R. (1992). Information systems success: The quest for the dependent variable. *Information Systems Research (ISR), 3*, 60–95.

DeLone, W. J., & McLean, E. R. (2002). Information systems success revisited. *Proceedings of the 35th Hawaii International Conference on System Sciences (HICSS)*, IEEE Computer Society Press, 2002.

Field, A., Miles, J., & Field, Z. (2012). *Discovering Statistics Using R* (1st ed.). Thousand Oaks, CA: SAGE Publications Ltd.

Gefen, D., Wyss, S., & Lichtenstein, Y. (2008). Business familiarity as risk mitigation in software development outsourcing contracts. *MIS Quarterly, 32*, 531–551.

Golfarelli, M., & Rizzi, S. (2009). *Data warehouse design: Modern principles and methodologies*. New York: McGraw-Hill Osborne Media.

Goncalves, C. D. F., Dias, J. A. M., & Machado, V. A. C. (2015). Multi-criteria decision methodology for selecting maintenance key performance indicators. *International Journal of Management Science and Engineering Management (IJMSEM), 10,* 215–223.

Hevner, A. R., March, S. T., Park, J., & Ram, S. (2004). Design science in information systems research. *MIS Quarterly, 28,* 75–105.

Huber, G. P. (1990). A theory of the effects of advanced information technologies on organizational design, intelligence, and decision making. *Academy of Management Review, 15,* 47–71.

Idris, N., & Ahmad, K. (2011). Managing data source quality for data warehouse in manufacturing services. Proceedings of the International Conference on Electrical Engineering and Informatics, 17-19 July 2011, Bandung, Indonesia.

Isik, O., Jones, M. C., & Sidorova, A. (2013). Business intelligence success: The roles of BI capabilities and decision environments. *Information & Management, 50,* 13–23.

Keil, M., & Carmel, E. (1995). Customer-developer links in software development. *Communications of the ACM, 38,* 33–44.

Kharbanda, O. P., & Pinto, J. K. (1996). What made Gertie gallop? Learning from project failures. Van Nostrand Reinhold, International Thompson Publishing, Inc., 115 Fifth Avenue, New York, NY 10003, USA.

Leitheiser, R. L. (2001). Data quality in health care data warehouse environments. *Proceedings of the 34th Hawaii International Conference on System Sciences (HICSS),* IEEE, 1–10.

Lu, Y., & Ramamurthy, K. (2011). Understanding the link between information technology capability and organizational agility: An empirical examination. *MIS Quarterly, 35,* 931–954.

MacKenzie, S. B., Podsakoff, P. M., & Podsakoff, N. P. (2011). Construct measurement and validation procedures in MIS and behavioral research: Integrating new and existing techniques. *MIS Quarterly, 35,* 293–334.

Mannino, M. V., & Walter, Z. (2006). A framework for data warehouse refresh policies. *Decision Support Systems (DSS), 42,* 121–143.

March, S. T., & Hevner, A. R. (2007). Integrated decision support systems: A data warehousing perspective. *Decision Support Systems (DSS), 43,* 1031–1043.

March, S. T., & Smith, G. F. (1995). Design and natural science research on information technology. *Decision Support Systems (DSS), 15,* 251–266.

Mithas, S., Ramasubbu, N., & Sambamurthy, V. (2011). How information management capability influences firm performance. *MIS Quarterly, 35,* 237–256.

Miyamoto, M. (2015). Application of competitive forces in the business intelligence of Japanese SMEs. *International Journal of Management Science and Engineering Management (IJMSEM), 10,* 273–287.

O'Donnell, P., Sipsma, S., & Watt, C. (2012). The critical issues facing business intelligence practitioners. *Journal of Decision Systems (DSS), 21,* 203–216.

Parssian, A., Sarker, S., & Jacob, V. S. (2009). Impact of the union and difference operations on the quality of information products. *Information Systems Research (ISR), 20,* 99–120.

Rahman, N. (2013). Measuring performance for data warehouses - A balanced scorecard approach. *International Journal of Computer and Information Technology (IJCIT), 4,* 1–7.

Rahman, N. (2014). Temporal data update methodologies for data warehousing. *Journal of the Southern Association for Information Systems (JSAIS), 2,* 25–41. doi:10.3998/jsais.11880084.0002.103.

Rahman, N., Marz, J., & Akhter, S. (2012). An ETL metadata model for data warehousing. *Journal of Computing and Information Technology (CIT), 20,* 95–111.

Rahman, N., & Rutz, D. (2015). Building data warehouses using automation. *International Journal of Intelligent Information Technologies (IJIIT), 11,* 1–22.

Rahman, N., Rutz, D., & Akhter, S. (2011). Agile development in data warehousing. *International Journal of Business Intelligence Research (IJBIR), 2,* 64–77.

Rahman, N., Rutz, D., Akhter, S., & Aldhaban, F. (2014). Emerging technologies in business intelligence and advanced analytics. *ULAB Journal of Science and Engineering (JSE), 5,* 7–17.

Redman, T. C. (1998). The impact of poor data quality on the typical enterprise. *Communications of the ACM, 41,* 79–82.

Rundensteiner, E. A., Koeller, A., & Zhang, X. (2000). Maintaining data warehouses over changing information sources. *Communications of the ACM, 43,* 57–62.

Rutz, D., Nelakanti, T. K., & Rahman, N. (2012). Practical implications of real time business intelligence. *Journal of Computing and Information Technology (CIT), 20,* 257–264.

Schlegel, K., Sallam, R. L., Yuen, D., & Tapadinhas, J. (2013). Magic quadrant for business intelligence and analytics platforms, Gartner, Inc. *Research ID, G00239854,* 1–64.

Sen, A., & Jacob, V. S. (1998). Industrial-strength data warehousing. *Communications of the ACM, 41,* 29–31.

Shankaranarayanan, G., & Cai, Y. (2006). Supporting data quality management in decision-making. *Decision Support Systems (DSS), 42,* 302–317.

Shankaranarayanan, G., & Even, A. (2006). The metadata enigma. *Communications of the ACM, 49,* 88–94.

Shin, B. (2003). An exploratory investigation of system success factors in data warehousing. *Journal of the Association for Information Systems (JAIS), 4,* 141–170.

Shmueli, G. (2011). Predictive analytics in information systems research. *MIS Quarterly, 35,* 553–572.

Simitsis, A., Vassiliadis, P., & Sellis, T. (2005). Optimizing ETL processes in data warehouses. Proceedings of the 21st International Conference on Data Engineering (ICDE), Tokyo, Japan, April 5-8, 2005.

Weill, W., Subramani, M., & Broadbent, M. (2002). Building IT infrastructure for strategic agility. *MIT Sloan Management Review,* fall 2002.

Weli (2014). Manager satisfaction in using the enterprise resource planning (ERP) system and the managerial performance. *Australasian Journal of Information Systems (AJIS), 18,* 119–135.

Wixom, B. H., & Watson, H. J. (2001). An empirical investigation of the factors affecting data warehousing success. *MIS Quarterly, 25,* 17–41.

Developing a preliminary cost estimation model for tall buildings based on machine learning

Muizz O. Sanni-Anibire, Rosli Mohamad Zin and Sunday Olusanya Olatunji

ABSTRACT

The last half-century has witnessed an astronomical rise in the number of tall building projects in urban centers globally. These projects however frequently experience delays and total abandonment due to economic reasons. This study presents the application of Machine Learning techniques in the systematic development of a model to estimate the preliminary cost of tall building projects. The techniques considered include Multi-Linear Regression Analysis (MLRA), k-Nearest Neighbors (KNN), Artificial Neural Networks (ANN), Support Vector Machines (SVM), and Multi Classifier Systems. Twelve models were developed and compared using standard performance metrics. The results revealed that the best performing model was based on a Multi Classifier System using KNN as the combining classifier, with a Correlation Coefficient (R^2) of 0.81, Root Mean Squared Error (RMSE) of 6.09, and Mean Absolute Percentage Error (MAPE) of 80.95%. This research showed the potential of modern digital technologies such as machine learning to solve problems of the construction industry. The procedure described in this study is of significant value to research and practice in the development of preliminary cost estimation models. The developed model can function as a decision support tool in the preliminary cost estimation stage of tall building projects.

1. Introduction

The construction industry, despite its continuous boom, is still being plagued by traditional challenges such as high risks, poor quality, cost, and time overruns. Stakeholders in the industry unanimously agree that the success of a project is determined by the triple constraint of time, cost, and quality (Gunduz et al., 2015; Ghosh, Kabir, & Hasin, 2017). It is however widely acknowledged that the construction industry is lagging in terms of efficiency and productivity when compared to the service and manufacturing industries (Forbes et al., 2010). One such problem area is the variation that occurs between the estimated and actual cost of large construction projects. The unique nature of construction projects presents a problem of variability in the estimated and actual cost of the projects, and consequently, most construction projects routinely overrun their cost estimates (Ahiaga-Dagbui & Smith, 2014). Alzara, Kashiwagi, Kashiwagi, and Al-Tassan (2016) note that variations between actual and estimated values range from 50% to 150%.

Tall buildings especially have suffered delays and total abandonment due to the lack of financial resources (Sanni-Anibire, Zin, & Olatunji, 2020). Al-Kodmany (2018) noted that the financing of a tall building is a critical task, and many ambitious tall building projects end up unfinished due to financial hurdles. Notably, the Council of Tall Buildings and Urban Habitat (CTBUH) in a research report mapped out 50 projects of 150 m or taller that were never completed (CTBUH, 2014a). Despite the potential of tall buildings to be a viable solution to an impeding urban housing crisis

consequent of massive urbanization, such megastructures can only be considered sustainable if they fulfill the economic aspect of sustainability's triple bottom line: 'planet, people and profit'. Interestingly, CTBUH in its 'Roadmap on the Future Research Needs of Tall Buildings' suggested that research on the economic and cost aspects of tall buildings should seek to reduce construction costs of tall buildings (CTBUH, 2014b). Though the research domain, for many decades, has flourished with abundant literature on the factors influencing variations between actual and estimated construction costs (Doloi, 2012; Enshassi, Al-Najjar, & Kumaraswamy, 2009; Le-Hoai, Dai Lee, & Lee, 2008; Mansfield, Ugwu, & Doran, 1994; Rahman, Memon, & Karim, 2013) these studies are however inadequate in solving the inherent problem due to their exploratory nature. Hence, the underestimation of the cost of construction projects is still a prevalent problem in the industry (Ballesteros-Perez et al., 2020).

Furthermore, an accurate estimate of construction costs is crucial in the early stages of a project and carries far-reaching consequences in the later stages of the project. The early stages of a project require preliminary cost estimates to enable clients and owners to evaluate the feasibility of a project through cost-benefit analysis, life cycle costing, and similar studies. Therefore, an effective preliminary cost estimate is so vital it can seal a project's financial fate (Ahiaga-Dagbui & Smith, 2014). Moreover, real estate developers and investors consider tall building projects as costly and risky investments, and thus, require preliminary cost estimates for decision making. Preliminary estimates of construction costs also support architects and engineers in their design decisions related to the selection of architectural systems for the building project (Al-Kodmany, 2018). Despite, the recognized need for preliminary construction estimates, the early stages of a project is a period of high uncertainty (Ghosh et al., 2017). There is a huge number of unknowns and sparse information is available for an accurate estimation to be achieved. The evolution of construction automation and data analytics has however presented an opportunity for smarter approaches in construction through the study of historical data to make inferences about new cases in the form of forecasts and predictions.

The past few decades have witnessed the rise of smarter approaches to enhance optimization in engineering management due to the fourth industrial revolution (Buakum & Wisittipanich, 2020; Kamel, Aly, Mohib, & Afefy, 2020). In the construction industry, this rising phenomenon is termed 'Construction 4.0'. Notable amongst the technologies to facilitate 'Construction 4.0' is machine learning, a cogent part of Artificial Intelligence. Machine Learning (ML) algorithms, also referred to as black-box models are used to transform input from relevant databases into useable output. ML techniques such as Artificial Neural Network (ANN) and Support Vector Machines (SVM) are considered efficient in solving complex engineering problems (Ebtehaj & Bonakdari, 2016b; Sharafi, Ebtehaj, Bonakdari, & Zaji, 2016). Studies seeking ML application in the construction industry have intensified, including hydraulic engineering (Ebtehaj & Bonakdari, 2016a, 2016b; Sharafi et al., 2016) structural engineering and materials (Apostolopoulou et al., 2020; Lu, Koopialipoor, Asteris, Bahri, & Armaghani, 2020), geotechnical engineering (Bayat, Monjezi, Rezakhah, & Armaghani, 2020; Lim, Mohamad, Motahari, Armaghani, & Saad, 2020)

Though, the research landscape features studies in the application of machine learning in estimating the preliminary costs of construction projects (Ahiaga-Dagbui & Smith, 2014; An, Park, Kang, Cho, & Cho, 2007; Yeung & Skitmore, 2012); there is a dearth of literature in its application to tall building projects, despite the status of such projects in the urban center of the 21st century. The proliferation of tall building construction as a dominant building typology has made tall building construction technology an important area in construction management research (Chew, 2017). The complexity of tall building projects embodied in its number of floors, structural systems, large material quantities, and professionals required, are some of the factors that contribute to studying this specific building typology separate from other building types.

Therefore, this study aims to examine a selection of common machine learning techniques to develop models for the estimation of the preliminary cost of tall building projects. The significance of the study is characterized by its adoption of machine learning for the preliminary cost estimation of tall building projects. This comes at a time when the construction industry is seeking to be more efficient through digitalization. Additionally, the application of different machine learning methods is of considerable value to the research community. Specifically, the study considered Multi Linear Regression Analysis (MLRA), k-Nearest Neighbors (KNN), Support Vector Machines (SVM), and Artificial Neural Network (ANN), while finally exploring Multi Classifier Systems (ensemble techniques). The performance

of these models was compared using standard performance metrics such as the Correlation Coefficient (R^2), Root Mean Squared Error (RMSE), and Mean Absolute Percentage Error (MAPE). The final result of this study is the selection of a model considered to be the best performing model, which was based on a multi classifier system that combines the outputs of other models using KNN as the combining classifier.

2. Literature review

2.1. Overview of construction cost estimation

Construction costs are usually developed in a deterministic manner where a single value is computed as the most likely estimate (Nasir, McCabe, & Hartono, 2003). In developing estimates, documents of past projects, data available from trade associations and construction companies, building codes, and standards are consulted. However, these values usually exhibit huge variances with the actual cost values. The accuracy of the estimate is largely dependent on the quantity take-off as well as the unit costs and the production rates. Other factors include the estimator's background and experience, material, and labor price variations/fluctuations, and inflation (Mahamid, 2015). Modern research trends have been geared towards the application of digital technologies in solving problems related to the under-estimation of construction costs. The following sections describe some of the work that has been achieved thus far.

2.2. Construction cost estimation models

Abu Hammad, Ali, Sweis, and Bashir (2008) utilized data from 140 projects in Jordan to develop regression models and concluded that there is a probability of 95% that the proposed models could accurately predict project cost and duration with a precision of ±0.035% of the mean cost and time. Mahamid (2011) developed early cost estimating models for road construction projects based on 131 sets of data collected in the West Bank in Palestine. The study compared the performance of 11 regression models and concluded that the coefficient of determination of the developed models ranged from 0.92 to 0.98, while values of MAPE ranged from 13% to 31% in line with past research works, which have shown that the estimate accuracy in the early stages of a project is between ±25% and ±50%. Lekan (2011) developed a cost-predicting model for building projects in Nigeria based on ANN. The results showed that the model had a relative average efficiency of 0.763. Similarly, Arafa and Alqedra (2011) developed a model to estimate the cost of building construction projects at early stages using ANN with a database of 71 building projects in the Gaza Strip. The performance of the model was reported to be R^2 of 90%. The study also showed that the ground floor area, number of storeys, type of foundation, and number of elevators in the buildings are the most effective parameters influencing the early estimates of building cost. Peško et al. (2017) also compared ANN and SVM for the estimation of costs and duration in construction projects. A database of 198 projects in the Republic of Serbia was used. The study concluded that SVM displayed better performance in estimating cost with a MAPE of 7.06% compared to 25.38% in ANN.

3. Methods

3.1. Dataset establishment

The dataset was established from two sources including the Mega Project Case Study Center of China available at http://www.mpcsc.org/case_search.htm, and CTBUH's skyscraper center available at http://www.skyscrapercenter.com/country/china. A total number of 53 projects were identified in the database with completion dates ranging from 1993 and 2015. The retrieved data was further reviewed for relevant information so that a final set of 30 projects suitable for the study was derived. The dataset was split into a train-test ratio of 66% to 34%.

3.2. Data pre-processing

It is well acknowledged that raw data from the real world require pre-processing to become suitable for machine learning. In this study, the Waikato Environment for Knowledge Analysis (Weka 3.8.3) has been used. This is an open-source machine learning software written in Java and developed at the University of Waikato, New Zealand (Witten, Frank, Hall, & Pal, 2016). It is popular for being user-friendly and its capability to deploy a large number of common machine learning algorithms Larrañaga et al. (2018). Table 1 provides descriptive statistics of the numerical features of the dataset, while Table 2 describes the non-numerical features of the dataset and their conversion to dummy variables.

3.3. Views of the dataset

The views of the data set refer to copies of the dataset created based on some systems such as normalization and standardization. Comparing the performance of various views of the dataset provides an idea of the views that are better suitable for the machine-learning problem (Brownlee, 2019). Firstly, the use of raw cost values as the dependent variable has been critiqued by previous studies as not being suitable for modeling (Lowe, Emsley, & Harding, 2006). Thus, this study compared various forms of the dependent variable as presented in Table 3. Furthermore, Table 4 shows four various views of the independent variables that were examined to determine the most suitable view of the data for the machine-learning problem (Brownlee, 2018). To create the views of the dataset, three filtering methods were used including normalization, standardization, and replacing missing values. These are briefly described as follows:

- Normalized view entails rescaling values in the input dataset to a range of 0 and 1, such that the largest value for each feature is 1 and the lowest is 0. The formula for normalization is expressed as follows:

$$x_{new} = \frac{x - x_{min}}{x_{max} - x_{min}} \tag{1}$$

- The standardized view entails rescaling the input values such that the arithmetic mean is set at 0, and the standard deviation is 1. The process is executed according to the following formula (where μ represents the arithmetic mean and σ the standard deviation):

$$x_{new} = \frac{x - \mu}{\sigma} \tag{2}$$

- Replace missing values entails the imputation of missing values with the mean of the distribution for numerical features, and the mode for categorical features respectively.

To compare the performance of various views of the dataset, four ML algorithms have been considered including MLRA, ANN, KNN, and SVM. There are abundant sources that provide detailed theoretical and mathematical descriptions of these techniques.

3.4. Feature selection

Real-world data suffers from the 'curse of dimensionality', and thus, feature selection is required to determine the subset of independent features contributing to the predictive performance of a model. The 'CorrelationAttributeEval' technique in Weka's 'select attributes' module was used. It is based on the ranking of the correlation of various features in the dataset to the prediction output, and further selection based on the Recursive Feature Elimination (RFE) process (Akande, Owolabi, & Olatunji, 2015). In RFE, the entire feature set (V) ranked according to the correlation coefficient is split in half to derive the best V/2 features, and the worst V/2 features are eliminated. The splitting process continues recursively until only one best feature is left. Thereafter, the feature subset that achieved the best accuracy/or the best performance measure is finally chosen as the best subset to be used.

3.5. Hyperparameter optimization

The performance of ML algorithms is dependent on searching for the hyperparameters that result in the best performance. The ML algorithms used in this study are described in the Weka environment as follows: MLRA: 'LinearRegression', k-NN: 'IBk', ANN: 'Multilayer Perceptron', and SVM: 'SMOReg'. MLRA does not require the optimization process, on the other hand, the hyperparameter for KNN is the k value, as well as the search and distance function, while ANN depends on the learning rate and hidden layers (Brownlee, 2018). SVM optimization depends on the regularization factor C, the type of kernel

Table 1. Descriptive statistics of the dataset.

	Mean	Standard deviation	Maximum	Minimum	Missing values
GDP (bill USD)	309.29	113.64	446.31	80.77	0
# of elevators	51.81	31.18	130	6	4
Building area (m^2)	293, 0	621.53	146, 971.91	602, 401	91, 600
Floor area (m^2)	34, 5	185.39	47, 611.45	197, 000	4, 126
Height to tip (m^2)	385.76	111.58	632	237.5	0
# of floors above GF	76.8	23.00	128	37	0
Height of occupied floors (m)	337.12	110.48	584.1	213.9	0
# of total floors	80.57	23.35	133	39	0
# of basement floors	6.33	5.62	30	2	6
# of parking spaces	1, 6	133.5	623.32	2, 702	203
Cost (bill Yuan)	8.34	8.53	30	0.38	0

Table 2. Attribute conversion.

Attribute	Description	Conversion	Missing values
Facility type	O/Office, BOH/Business, office, hotel, ROH/Residential, office, hotel, BO/Business, office, BOR/Business, office, residential	O = 1; BOH = 2; ROH = 3; BO = 4; BOR = 5	0
Structural form	T-T/Tube in Tube, D/Diagrid, C-T/Core-Tube, T/Tubular	T-T = 1; D = 2; C-T = 3; T = 4	8
Structural material	RC/Reinforced concrete, RCS/Reinforced concrete and steel, S/Steel C/Composite	RC = 1; RCS = 2; S = 3; C = 4	0
Commencement period	Summer, autumn, winter and spring	Summer = 1; Autumn = 2; Winter = 3; Spring = 4	0

Table 3. Performance of various views of the dependent variable cost.

ML Algorithm	Performance measure	Raw cost	LOG (raw cost)	Cost/m^2	LOG (cost/m^2)
MLRA (*LinearRegression*)	R^2	0.67	**0.86**	−0.261	0.57
	RMSE	8.19	**6.36**	14.08	8.03
	MAPE (%)	325.66	**146.36**	252.78	179.19

Table 4. Performance of ML algorithms for various views of the dataset.

ML Algorithm	Performance measure	Raw data	Replace missing values	Normalized view	Standardized view
MLRA (*LinearRegression*)	R^2	0.86	0.74	0.86	**0.86**
	RMSE	6.36	11.54	6.36	**6.36**
	MAPE (%)	146.36	157.74	146.36	**146.36**
ANN (*Multilayer Perceptron*)	R^2	0.65	**0.59**	−0.26	−0.15
	RMSE	11.11	**10.74**	70.84	49.47
	MAPE (%)	113.54	**99.09**	828.26	734.53
KNN (*IBk*)	R^2	0.23	**0.28**	0.23	0.23
	RMSE	10.77	**11.01**	10.77	10.77
	MAPE (%)	638.6	**81.19**	638.6	638.6
SVM (*SMOReg*)	R^2	0	0	0.24	**0.28**
	RMSE	11.37	11.37	11.47	**10.75**
	MAPE (%)	164.61	164.61	126.16	**105.33**

function, as well as ε-insensitive loss function (Larrañaga et al., 2018). In determining the hyperparameters that yield optimal model performance, a modified systematic search was executed i.e. a range of randomly spaced values are searched first, and then the range that performs best is zoomed in for further investigation. The optimal hyperparameter for KNN is the k value (search range 1–30), as well as the search and distance function, while ANN depends on the learning rate (search range 0.1–0.3) and network typology. SVM optimization depends on the regularization factor C (search range 1–1000), the type of kernel function, as well as *epsilon parameter* (search range 0.1–0.00001).

3.6. Performance measurement

The Correlation Coefficient (R^2), Root Mean Squared Error (RMSE), and Mean Absolute Percentage Error (MAPE) are the performance metrics used in this study. They are described mathematically as follows:

$$R^2 = \frac{\sum \left(y_a - y'_a\right)\left(y_p - y'_p\right)}{\sqrt{\sum \left(y_a - y'_a\right)^2 \sum \left(y_p - y'_p\right)^2}} \quad (3)$$

Where y_a and y_p are the actual and predicted values while y'_a and y'_p are the mean of the actual and predicted values.

$$RMSE = \sqrt{\frac{\left(y_a - y_p\right)^2 + \left(y_a - y_p\right)^2 + \ldots + \left(y_a - y_p\right)^2}{n}} \quad (4)$$

Where $(y_a - y_p)$ is the difference between the actual and predicted values and n is the size of the dataset used.

$$MAPE = \frac{1}{n} \sum_{t=1}^{n} \left| \frac{y_a - y_p}{y_p} \right| \quad (5)$$

Where y_a is the actual value and y_p is the predicted value, and n is the size of the dataset used.

3.7. Combining classifiers

Multi-classifier systems also known as ensemble methods combine the prediction outcomes of a set of models with the same or different sets of features. They help to improve the predictive performance of machine learning models compared to the outcomes of a single model. This can be achieved through averaging (fixed rules) and stacking (trained rules) (Xia, Zong, & Li, 2011; Kuncheva, 2014), as illustrated in Figure 1. Averaging is a simple aggregation of the predictions of other models based on a fixed rule such as the mean, maximum and minimum values. Stacking is an extension of averaging which allows another algorithm to learn how best to combine the predictions of other models (Brownlee, 2018).

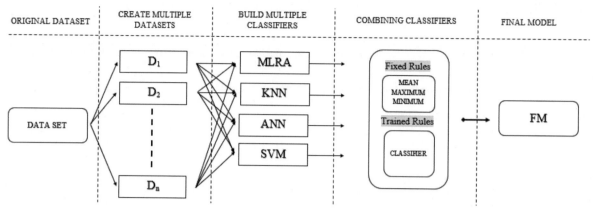

Figure 1. Architecture of the proposed multi-classifier system.

4. Results and findings

4.1. Comparison of various views of the dataset

Firstly, the suitability of the raw cost as the dependent variable was examined. This was demonstrated by comparing the results of linear regression analysis with three other forms as suggested by Lowe et al. (2006). These include the cost/m², the log of cost, and the log of cost/m². The results as presented in Table 3 show that the best performance was achieved with the log of raw cost as the dependent variable in agreement with Lowe et al. (2006)'s study where the same conclusion was reached. There was a 55.06% reduction in the MAPE values when the log of raw cost is compared to the raw cost. Furthermore, the performance of four various views of the independent variables was compared. As shown in Table 4, this included the raw data, 'replace missing values', normalized and standardized views deployed through Weka's filter. The performance of the four selected ML algorithms (MLRA, ANN, KNN & SVM) are presented in Table 4, and the results showed that ANN and KNN performed best with the 'replace missing values' view. SVM performed better with the standardized view with a 36.01% reduction in the MAPE values. MLRA performed equally for

three views, except the 'replace missing values' view which had the poorest performance, and thus the standardized view was adopted for MLRA and SVM.

4.2. Performance of machine learning algorithms

In this study, the 'CorrelationAttributeEval' and RFE techniques discussed previously were used to determine the combination of features that yields the optimum performance of a machine learning algorithm. Thus, four additional feature sets were developed and presented in Table 5. It can be observed from the table, that the floor area was determined to be the highest correlating feature to the cost. In addition to the floor area, the table also shows that the structural material, height of occupied floors, and height to tip were the most important features influencing the cost of tall building projects. This also confirms the results of previous studies that suggest that the cost of tall buildings is mainly influenced by the floor area and height (Arafa & Alqedra, 2011).

The performance of the four algorithms on the various feature sets is shown in Table 6. MLRA and SVM exhibited the best performance with the best four features i.e. 'floor area, structural material, the height of occupied floors, and

Table 5. Description of feature sets based on *CorrelationAttributeEval*.

Recursive Elimination process	Feature	No. of features	Description
Best V/2 features		8	Floor area; structural material; height of occupied floors; height to tip; # of parking spaces; building area; # of total floors; # of floors above ground floors
Best V/4 features		4	Floor area; structural material; height of occupied floors; height to tip
Best V/8 features		2	Floor area; structural material
Best feature		1	Floor area

Table 6. Performance of ML algorithms for various feature sets.

ML Algorithm	Performance measure	All features	Best V/2	Best V/4	Best V/8	Best feature
MLRA (*LinearRegression*)	R^2	0.86	0.86	**0.76**	0.68	0.66
	RMSE	6.36	6.36	**7.15**	8.48	8.94
	MAPE (%)	146.36	146.36	**109.3**	174.42	141.11
ANN (*Multilayer Perceptron*)	R^2	**0.59**	−0.65	0	0	0
	RMSE	**10.74**	10.37	10.34	10.34	10.94
	MAPE (%)	**99.09**	241.85	241.79	241.79	194.29
KNN (*IBk*)	R^2	0.28	−0.39	0.54	0.72	**0.73**
	RMSE	11.01	15.34	9.75	8.08	**8.01**
	MAPE (%)	81.19	640.74	86.11	107.29	**106.12**
SVM (*SMOReg*)	R^2	0.28	**0.36**	**0.71**	0.67	0.65
	RMSE	10.75	**10.67**	**9.25**	10.47	10.88
	MAPE (%)	105.33	**96.68**	**98.43**	150.27	139.64

height to tip'. ANN performed best when all features are used. KNN performed best with the best feature. The results presented in Table 6 formed the basis for the development of the initial models for further investigation through hyperparameter tuning and optimization. Therefore, five initial models labeled MOD1, MOD2, MOD3, MOD4, and MOD5 have been selected. The highlighted figures in Table 6 indicate the selected feature sets to form these models. Further improvement in the performance of ML algorithms requires searching for their optimization hyperparameters. Hence, Table 7 presents the developed models showing the combination of ML algorithms, feature sets, and hyperparameters. The RMSE, MAPE, and R^2 values of these models are presented in Table 8. It can be observed that MOD1, MOD4, and MOD5 performed best when the RMSE, MAPE, and R^2 results are compared. Though MOD2 had a lower MAPE value (i.e. lower MAPE means better performance), it had a poorer performance in terms of its RMSE and R^2 values.

Table 10. Performance of ML models based on MCS.

Performance measure	MOD6	MOD7	MOD8	MOD9	MOD10	MOD11	MOD12
RMSE	6.86	6.68	6.11	5.99	6.11	6.09	5.89
R^2	0.78	0.82	0.79	0.79	0.81	0.81	0.8
MAPE	79.3	118.96	94.66	123.99	153.62	80.95	113.87

4.3. Performance of multi-classifier systems

A multi classifier system as described previously is a system to combine the predictions of selected algorithms in a specified format. In this study, three best performing models (MOD1, MOD4 & MOD5) were selected to be combined using fixed and trained rules also referred to as averaging and stacking respectively. Thus, seven more models were created for further investigation as shown in Table 9.

Table 7. ML models (combinations of classifiers, optimized parameters and selected feature sets).

Model	ML Algorithm	Selected features	Optimization hyperparameters
MOD1	MLRA (*LinearRegression*)	Floor area; structural material; height of occupied floors; height to tip	Not Applicable
MOD2	ANN (*Multilayer Perceptron*)	All features described in Tables 1 and 2	0.3 learning rate; one hidden layer with four nodes
MOD3	KNN (*IBk*)	Floor area	Nearest Neighbor: LinearNN Distance function: Euclidean Distance K: 1
MOD4	SVM (*SMOReg*)	Floor area; structural material; height of occupied floors; height to tip; # of parking spaces; building area; # of total floors; # of floors above ground floors	Kernel: Polykernel Cost function, C: 106 Epsilon: 1E −12 Epsilon parameter: 0.12
MOD5	SVM (*SMOReg*)	Floor area; structural material; height of occupied floors; height to tip	Kernel: RBFkernel Cost function, C: 3 Epsilon: 0.1 Epsilon parameter: 0.001

Table 8. Performance of initial ML models.

Performance measure	MOD1	MOD2	MOD3	MOD4	MOD5
RMSE	7.15	10.74	8.01	5.96	6.66
R^2	0.76	0.59	0.73	0.79	0.77
MAPE (%)	109.3	99.09	106.12	114.81	77.53

4.3.1. Averaging (fixed rules)

The predictive outcomes of the selected models (MOD1, MOD4 & MOD5) were combined through a fixed rule system, including the mean, maximum and minimum values. These were described as MOD6, MOD7 & MOD8, and are presented in Table 9. The performance in terms of the RMSE, MAPE, and R^2 are presented in Table 10.

Table 9. ML models based on Multi Classifier Systems (MCS).

Model	Multi Classifier system	Selected input models	Combiner system
MOD6	Averaging	MOD1; MOD4; MOD5	Minimum
MOD7			Maximum
MOD8			Mean
MOD9	Stacking		MLRA
MOD10			ANN (1) learning rate; one hidden layer with 4 nodes
MOD11			KNN Nearest Neighbor: LineraNN Distance function: Euclidean Distance K: 1
MOD12			SVM Kernel: PolyKernel Cost function, C: 1 Epsilon: 1E −12 Epsilon parameter: 0.11

4.3.2. Stacking (trained rules)

The three best-performing models (MOD1, MOD4 & MOD5) were also combined using the trained rules, where another algorithm is selected to learn how best to combine these models for improved performance. The combiner systems as well as their hyperparameters are described in Table 9. These combinations have been labeled as MOD9, MOD10, MOD11 & MOD12. As shown in Table 9, the best performing model was considered to be MOD11 based on the relatively low values of RMSE and MAPE. It can be observed that the RMSE values and correlation coefficient (R^2) of the models were very close, and in some cases, approximately equal. Consequently, the performance was decided based on the reduced error observed in the MAPE values. Figure 2 shows a cross-plots of the actual cost values versus the

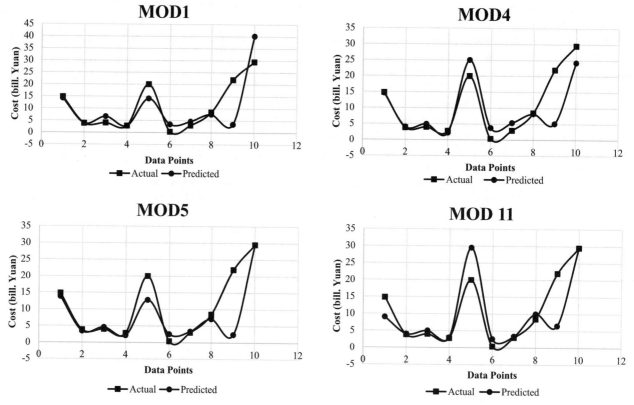

Figure 2. Cross-plots of the actual vs. predicted cost values of selected models.

predicted values, where the data points were closely matching in most instances.

5. Discussion

The rapid growth of tall building projects is viewed as a sustainable solution to challenges related to urbanization. However, these projects are subject to construction delays and total abandonment due to inadequate financial resources (Al-Kodmany, 2018). Insufficient financial risk assessment due to gross underestimation of the project's financial requirements is a significant risk trigger. Moreover, the construction industry, in general, is still plagued with the problem of construction cost underestimation (Ballesteros-Perez et al., 2020). Thus, previous studies have sought to develop nonparametric cost estimation models for construction projects, notably through the application of linear regression and neural networks. The studies that dominate the research arena are limited in the techniques employed, especially in the case of tall building projects. Therefore, this study developed a machine learning model based on a systematic examination and further combination of common machine learning algorithms. Firstly, a dataset was established from online databases on tall buildings, notably the Mega Project Case Study Center of China, and CTBUH's skyscraper center. Industrial data is usually not suitable for machine learning applications in their raw format, thus pre-processing of the dataset becomes necessary. This study adopted the hypothesis by Lowe et al. (2006) that the raw cost as a dependent variable is not suitable for modeling purposes, and thus, the log of

cost, cost/m^2, and log of cost/m^2 were also examined alongside the raw cost. The results showed that the best performing view of the dependent variable was the log of raw cost, and thus it was subsequently adopted for the study. Likewise, various views of the independent variables were examined for the four algorithms considered in this study, and the most appropriate view suitable for the machine learning algorithm was adopted. The study also compared various feature sets to control a popular phenomenon in machine learning known as the 'curse of dimensionality' characteristic of real data. In this study, the most relevant features in determining the cost of tall buildings are the floor area, structural material, height of occupied floors, and height to tip.

Furthermore, the evaluation of the various algorithms (MLRA, ANN, KNN & SVM) was executed. A systematic search for the hyperparameters of the selected algorithms was performed, and therefore five initial models were formed as previously described (MOD1, MOD2, MOD3, MOD4 & MOD5). Three best performing models (MOD1, MOD4 & MOD5) were further combined through multi classifier systems/ensemble techniques i.e. fixed and trained rules (see Figure 1). Thus, the combination yielded seven more models, while the best performing model (MOD11) was based on the combination of three models (MOD1, MOD4 & MOD5) using KNN as the combining classifier. The best performing model in this study described as MOD11 had an R^2 of 0.81, MAPE of 80.95%, and RMSE of 6.09. The model's performance falls within acceptable ranges in terms of the correlation coefficient (i.e. > 70%) as reported by previous studies (Lekan, 2011; Lowe et al., 2006). However, Mahamid (2011) suggests that previous researchers have shown that the estimate accuracy in the early stages of a project should be between ±25% and ±50%. Despite the model's performance in terms of its correlation coefficient, it fell out of range in terms of the MAPE. It can be concluded that further improvement in the predictive performance of the models requires some other strategies such as the establishment of a larger dataset which is currently unavailable. Interestingly, Ray (2019) notes that potential barriers hindering the deployment of machine learning and artificial intelligence in the construction industry could be attributed to the huge amounts of data required. The construction industry is generally deficient in recording and publishing data suitable for ML applications. Thus, this study is limited in the source and size of the dataset used. Although, this limitation in the dataset being sourced from China can be ignored due to China being the major driver of tall building construction globally (CTBUH, 2018).

5.1. Research contributions

The contribution of the current study is the development of a model for the preliminary cost estimation of tall building projects. The relevance of the research findings comes at a time where the construction industry is seeking for improved productivity through digitization. Moreover, the abandonment of tall buildings has become a menace due to the high financial risk involved. Though, studies exist to explore the causes behind cost overruns in capital projects, such exploratory studies do not offer practical solutions. This study thus proposed as a solution predictive models of the preliminary cost of tall buildings based on insights derived from historical data with the aid of machine learning. Furthermore, the study showed the advantage of combining various ML algorithms through multi classifier systems over individual methods such as MLRA and ANN, which are popular in previous studies. Although the performance of the various machine learning techniques depends on the dataset used. This study showed that the use of a multi classifier system improves the predictive performance of the cost estimation models. Another contribution of this study is the confirmation of the log of raw cost as the most suitable view of the dependent variable in developing cost estimation models as was previously noted by Lowe et al. (2006). This study also revealed that the most significant factors that influence the cost of tall buildings include the floor area, structural material, height of occupied floors, and height to tip. Ultimately, this research proposed a solution to the problem of cost underestimation at the preliminary stages of tall building projects based on the application of machine learning.

6. Conclusion

Tall buildings are considered to be high-risk investments and are subject to abandonment as a result of financial hurdles. Early estimation of the cost of tall buildings is crucial to the sustainability of such investments. This study demonstrated the significance of adopting modern digital tools such as machine learning for the preliminary cost estimation of tall building projects. The outcome of this study was the proposal of a model which uses KNN in multi classifier system. The model proposed in this study is limited in its level of

generalization, as is the case with data-driven models. This emphasizes the need to establish other datasets for similar machine learning applications in the construction industry. The study has significant implications for research and engineering practice. Further research could seek to adopt the systematic procedure described herein to other datasets, as well as incorporate such models into computing tools for automating construction cost estimation. Similarly, managerial frameworks and digital tools incorporating the cost estimation model will be of significant value to decision-makers including consultants, contractors, engineering managers, and real estate investors in establishing initial cost estimates for budgeting, bidding purposes, and financial risk assessments.

Data Availability Statement

Some or all data, models, or code that support the findings of this study are available from the corresponding author upon reasonable request.

Disclosure statement

No potential conflict of interest was reported by the authors.

References

Abu Hammad, A. A. A., Ali, S. M. A., Sweis, G. J., & Bashir, A. (2008). Prediction model for construction cost and duration in Jordan. *Jordan Journal of Civil Engineering, 2*(3), 250–266.

Ahiaga-Dagbui, D. D., & Smith, S. D. (2014). Dealing with construction cost overruns using data mining. *Construction Management and Economics, 32*(7–8), 682–694.

Akande, K. O., Owolabi, T. O., & Olatunji, S. O. (2015). Investigating the effect of correlation-based feature selection on the performance of support vector machines in reservoir characterization. *Journal of Natural Gas Science and Engineering, 22*, 515–522.

Al-Kodmany, K. (2018). The sustainability of tall building development: A conceptual framework. *Buildings, 8*(1), 7.

Alzara, M., Kashiwagi, J., Kashiwagi, D., & Al-Tassan, A. (2016). Using PIPS to minimize causes of delay in Saudi Arabian construction projects: University case study. *Procedia Engineering, 145*, 932–939.

An, S. H., Park, U. Y., Kang, K. I., Cho, M. Y., & Cho, H. H. (2007). Application of support vector machines in assessing conceptual cost estimates. *Journal of Computing in Civil Engineering, 21*(4), 259–264.

Apostolopoulou, M., Asteris, P. G., Armaghani, D. J., Douvika, M. G., Lourenço, P. B., Cavaleri, L., ... Moropoulou, A. (2020). Mapping and holistic design of natural hydraulic lime mortars. *Cement and Concrete Research, 136*, 106167.

Arafa, M., & Alqedra, M. (2011). Early stage cost estimation of buildings construction projects using artificial neural networks. *Journal of Artificial Intelligence, 4*(1), 63–75.

Ballesteros-Perez, P., Sanz-Ablanedo, E., Soetanto, R., Gonzalez-Cruz, M. C., Larsen, G. D., & Cerezo-Narvaez, A. (2020). On the duration and cost variability of construction activities: An empirical study. *Journal of Construction Engineering and Management, 146*(1), 04019093.

Bayat, P., Monjezi, M., Rezakhah, M., & Armaghani, D. J. (2020). Artificial neural network and firefly algorithm for estimation and minimization of ground vibration induced by blasting in a mine. *Natural Resources Research, 29*(6), 4121–4132.

Brownlee, J. (2019). Machine learning mastery with Weka. Ebook. Edition: v. 1.4

Buakum, D., & Wisittipanich, W. (2020). Stochastic internal task scheduling in cross docking using chance-constrained programming. *International Journal of Management Science and Engineering Management, 15*(4), 258–264.

Chew, M. Y. L. (2017). *Construction technology for tall buildings* (5th ed.). USA: World scientific Publishing.

Council of Tall Buildings and Urban Habitat (CTBUH). (2014b). Roadmap on the Future Research Needs of Tall Buildings.

Council of Tall Buildings and Urban Habitat CTBUH. (2014a). Dreams deferred: Unfinished tall buildings. *CTBUH Journal*, (4).

CTBUH (2018). Tall Buildings in Numbers: 2018 Year in Review. Available at: https://www.skyscrapercenter.com/year-in-review/2018Accessed 25/3/2021

Doloi, H. (2012). Cost overruns and failure in project management: Understanding the roles of key stakeholders in construction projects. *Journal of Construction Engineering and Management*, *139*(3), 267–279.

Ebtehaj, I., & Bonakdari, H. (2016a). Bed load sediment transport estimation in a clean pipe using multilayer perceptron with different training algorithms. *KSCE Journal of Civil Engineering*, *20*(2), 581–589.

Ebtehaj, I., & Bonakdari, H. (2016b). A support vector regression-firefly algorithm-based model for limiting velocity prediction in sewer pipes. *Water Science and Technology*, *73*(9), 2244–2250.

Enshassi, A., Al-Najjar, J., & Kumaraswamy, M. (2009). Delays and cost overruns in the construction projects in the Gaza Strip. *Journal of Financial Management of Property and Construction*, *14*(2), 126–151.

Forbes, L. H., & Ahmed, S. M. (2010). Modern construction: lean project delivery and integrated practices. CRC press

Forbes, L. H., & Ahmed, S. M. (2010). Modern construction: lean project delivery and integrated practices. CRC press

Ghosh, M., Kabir, G., & Hasin, M. A. A. (2017). Project time–cost trade-off: A Bayesian approach to update project time and cost estimates. *International Journal of Management Science and Engineering Management*, *12*(3), 206–215.

Gunduz, M., Nielsen, Y., & Ozdemir, M. (2015). Fuzzy assessment model to estimate the probability of delay in Turkish construction projects. Journal of Management in Engineering, 31(4), 04014055

Kamel, G., Aly, M. F., Mohib, A., & Afefy, I. H. (2020). Optimization of a multilevel integrated preventive maintenance scheduling mathematical model using genetic algorithm. *International Journal of Management Science and Engineering Management*, *15*(4), 247–257.

Kuncheva, L. I., & Rodríguez, J. J. (2014). A weighted voting framework for classifiers ensembles. Knowledge and Information Systems, 38 (2), 259–275

Larrañaga, P., Atienza, D., Diaz-Rozo, J., Ogbechie, A., Puerto-Santana, C. E., & Bielza, C. (2018). *Industrial applications of machine learning.* CRC Press, Taylor & Francis Group, United Kingdom.

Le-Hoai, L., Dai Lee, Y., & Lee, J. Y. (2008). Delay and cost overruns in Vietnam large construction projects: A comparison with other selected countries. *KSCE Journal of Civil Engineering*, *12*(6), 367–377.

Lekan, A. (2011). *Neural network-based cost predictive model for building works* [Thesis (PhD)]. Covenant University.

Lim, C. S., Mohamad, E. T., Motahari, M. R., Armaghani, D. J., & Saad, R. (2020). Machine learning classifiers for modeling soil

characteristics by geophysics investigations: A comparative study. *Applied Sciences*, *10*(17), 5734.

Lowe, D. J., Emsley, M. W., & Harding, A. (2006). Predicting construction cost using multiple regression techniques. *Journal of Construction Engineering and Management*, *132*(7), 750–758.

Lu, S., Koopialipoor, M., Asteris, P. G., Bahri, M., & Armaghani, D. J. (2020). A novel feature selection approach based on tree models for evaluating the punching shear capacity of steel fiber-reinforced concrete flat slabs. *Materials*, *13*(17), 3902.

Mahamid, I. (2011). Early cost estimating for road construction projects using multiple regression techniques. *Construction Economics and Building*, *11*(4), 87–101.

Mahamid, I. (2015). Factors affecting cost estimate accuracy: Evidence from Palestinian construction projects. *International Journal of Management Science and Engineering Management*, *10*(2), 117–125.

Mansfield, N. R., Ugwu, O. O., & Doran, T. (1994). Causes of delay and cost overruns in Nigerian construction projects. *International Journal of Project Management*, *12*(4), 254–260.

Nasir, D., McCabe, B., & Hartono, L. (2003). Evaluating Risk in Construction–Schedule Model (ERIC–S): Construction schedule risk model. *Journal of Construction Engineering and Management*, *129*(5), 518–527.

Peško, I., I, V. M., Šešlija, M., T, N. R., Vujkov, A., T, D. B., & Krklješ, M. (2017). Estimation of costs and durations of construction of urban roads using ANN and SVM. *Hindawi Complexity*, 2017, Article ID 2450370, 13.

Rahman, I. A., Memon, A. H., & Karim, A. T. A. (2013). Significant factors causing cost overruns in large construction projects in Malaysia. *Journal of Applied Sciences*, *13*(2), 286–293.

Ray, D. (2019). Breakthrough: how AI and machine learning could transform construction. Available online:. https://www.building.co.uk/focus/break-through-how-ai-and-machine-learning-could-transform-construction/5097559.article Accessed 25/3/2021

Sanni-Anibire, M. O., Zin, R. M., & Olatunji, S. O. (2020). Machine learning model for delay risk assessment in tall building projects. *International Journal of Construction Management*, 1–10.

Sharafi, H., Ebtehaj, I., Bonakdari, H., & Zaji, A. H. (2016). Design of a support vector machine with different kernel functions to predict scour depth around bridge piers. *Natural Hazards*, *84*(3), 2145–2162.

Witten, I. H., Frank, E., Hall, M. A., & Pal, C. J. (2016). *Data mining: Practical machine learning tools and techniques.* Massachusetts, United States of America.

Xia, R., Zong, C., & Li, S. (2011). Ensemble of feature sets and classification algorithms for sentiment classification. *Information Sciences*, *181*(6), 1138–1152.

Yeung, D., & Skitmore, M. (2012). A method for systematically pooling data in very early stage construction price forecasting. *Construction Management and Economics*, *30*(11), 929–939.

A framework for managing uncertainty in information system project selection: an intelligent fuzzy approach

Dipika Pramanik, Samar Chandra Mondal and Anupam Haldar

ABSTRACT

Information System Project (ISP) Selection is the most significant strategic consideration to each management of organizations, in terms of business intelligence (BI) as critical factors must be considered from large volume of information, known as Big Data (BD). In today's competitive environment, the main objective is selecting suitable and effective ISP to reduce the risk of investment, maximize overall performance of management of organization by mitigating uncertainty. As these types of decisions generally involve several criteria and it is often necessary to compromise among possibly conflicting factors, the multiple criteria decision making (MCDM) becomes a useful approach to solve this kind of problem. This paper establishes a novel intelligent model by integrating fuzzy Shannon entropy and Fuzzy Technique for Order Preference by Similarity to Ideal Solution Method (FTOPSIS) techniques as a decision tool for solving MCDM problem using linguistic values, which smoothly aids decision makers dealing with uncertain or incomplete information without losing existing quantitative information. The novelty of this paper is to propose a framework of BI in management of an organization to determine suitable ISP where all the meaningful information, relevant knowledge and visualization retrieved by analyzing BD based on decision making to enhance any organizational performance worldwide.

1. Introduction

Now-a-days it is very common for management of an organization to deal with development of an ISP selection which needs to be planned, organized, conducted, monitored and controlled as organizations have to face an enormous business competition presently to facilitate rapid decisions, allocations of optimum resource and an unambiguous focus definition. Several types of ISP are projected with diverse objectives wherein need strategic management consistent with organizational aspirations. ISPs are fundamental for any organizations' achievement over and above behavior which directs them to novel products, services and business enhancement. Successful projects direct to sales increase, reduction of costs, improvement of quality and quantity, end-users satisfaction, work surroundings, and additional benefits. Consequently, a lot of business organizations use ISP selection as a most important strategy to maintain competition in terms of BI. At the process of ISP selection many quantitative and qualitative critical factors must be considered from a large volume of information known as BD which is a relatively new term (Manyika et al., 2011). BD (popularly characterized by 5Vs) is used to characterize data sets that are large in size (volume), miscellaneous (variety i.e. different types of data or data with different structure) but we have to extract valuable information from data (value) related to proper data governance and privacy concern (veracity), and rapidly changing (Velocity i.e. speed of data transfer), as seen by ever increasing numbers of organizations (Arora & Goyal, 2018; Blazquez & Domenech, 2018; Feng & Shanthikumar, 2018). The decision-making problem to select ISP of management

of an organization may be expressed as complex multi-objective job which are derived from uncertain data. According to Jauch and Kraft (1986), technically uncertainty is 'the state of knowledge in which each alternative leads to a set of results but the probability of occurrence of each outcome is unknown to the decision maker'.

According to Gandomi and Haider (2015) BD tools can make available more information to business organization than ever before, but it does not guarantee quality data. The information can be vague, imprecise, and a source of uncertainty. On the other hand, organizations have also faced troubles to treat and transform the data into meaningful information to improve their BI strategy. Many business organizations fail to overcome the challenges presented by BD. The wide range of uncertainties affects the design and operation of complex systems and creates risks and opportunities of a business organization. The system architects develop strategies that can be used to mitigate uncertainties or take advantage of them and thus resulting in improved system attributes. McAfee and Brynjolfsson (2012) conclude that BD has the prospective to modernize the management of an organization and because of BD managers can know radically more about their businesses by measuring how decisions are made and who makes these decisions. Apparently, very less number of organization consider their investment in BD analytics and successfully improving the performance of the organizations (Ghasemaghaei, Ebrahimi, & Hassanein, 2018; KošCielniak & Puto, 2015). Since, information system hardly considers the impact of uncertainties on the project, the threats caused by uncertainty in a business organization must be identified and minimized for the smooth running of the organization. Hence the problem may be defined as a MCDM problem under uncertain condition and there is a need for reliable, flexible solution methods that will help to achieve the success of organizations. Organizations provide ideas for improving BI strategy by integrating all risk factors collected from BD in a logical and consistent as well as coherent manner to make different contributions of ISP performance containing different levels of inherent uncertainty for better understanding of various uncertainties.

In addition the introductory section, this article is prearranged as follows: Section 2 gives the summary about the literature review on information system project selection and the uncertainty related to it and different types of methodologies applied by various authors to manage it; Section 3 presents the basic definition and notations which are used in the proposed methodology; Section 4 represents the proposed methodology with an example which is a guide for uncertainty management in information system project selection; Section 5 discuss and analyzes the result; and last Section 6 concludes the article.

2. Literature review

A large number of business organization use ISP management as a crucial strategy to maintain today's business competition and add value to their BI strategy. ISPs are fundamental for success of any organization as well as activities which conduct them to produce new products, services and business development. According to Chen, Chiang, and Storey (2010) and Williams (2011) BI is the 'technologies, systems, practices, methodologies, and applications' employed to analyze large amounts of various business data, known as BD, to help organizations to convert into meaningful information to support efficiently and effectively decision-making. By means of the development of information systems, the key issue for making decisions on ISP selection and applications must be on their own (Shemshadi, Soroor, & Tarokh, 2008; Soroor, Tarokh, & Shemshadi, 2009). A well planed decision-making process must be organized by sufficiently improved software architecture. According to LaValle, Lesser, Shockley, Hopkins, and Kruschwitz (2011), a business organization that recognizes BD and analytics as a differentiation strategy are likely to be a top performer in their business fragment. The decision problem of selecting ISP can be expressed as a complex, multi-objective task, as well as a MCDM problem based on uncertain data and its solution requires reliable methods that can integrate all risk factors in a methodical approach under uncertain environment. Looking into critical skills necessary to create business value, He (2014) provides an overview of the current status of BD business analytics and discusses the probable applications in various organizations. Klievink, Romijn, Cunningham, and de Bruijn (2016) introduced a framework which provides a methodology for public organizations to reflect on the uncertainties that may hamper their decision-making on big data projects. Sun et al. (2018) proposed ontology of BD analytics, and discuss the association between BD analytics and BI by introducing a BD analytics service-oriented architecture (BASOA) and discuss how to use BASOA to improve BI. Popović, Hackney, Tassabehji, and Castelli (2018) investigated the impact of BDA on operations management in the manufacturing sector

by highlighting the real-business value and thus encouraging beneficial economic societal changes. Pham (2018) discussed maturity model concept, which offers a systematic approach for an organization to measure and improve its maturity level by successful implementation of BD cyber security analytics within organizations. By integrating machine learning algorithms and expert judgments De Mauro, Greco, Grimaldi, and Ritala (2018) proposed a novel analytical methodology which can support business leaders and HR managers semi-automatically in establishing clear strategies semi-automatically for the achievement and the development of the right skills needed to control BD at best.

The basic cause of uncertainty is the lack of available information, unquantifiable information, incomplete information and partial ignorance (Yeh & Deng, 1997), available knowledge or competence (Christensen & Kreiner, 1991). In a project context, uncertainty management has traditionally been synonymous with risk management and for large and complex projects such predictability is not the reality Hillson and Simon (2012), Rolstadås, Hetland, Jergeas, and Westney (2011). Olsson (2007) established that major uncertainties play a large role in important areas and especially under such conditions, it will not be a good strategy to struggle for maximum predictability, but rather to choose a strategy of flexibility in the project, in order to be able to face changes. Rolstadås et al. (2011), Artto, Martinsuo, and Kujala (2011), and Alessandri, Ford, Lander, Leggio, and Taylor (2004) described that it is a dilemma for decision makers that they have to make decisions based on very little information that is available in the early stage of the project. Rodríguez, Ortega, and Concepción (2015) proposed a new integrated risk assessment method based on fuzzy MCDM approaches for the evaluation of risk in IT projects by considering the different levels of uncertainty. Vafaei, Ribeiro, and Camarinha-Matos (2018) determines that as it is required of performing data reduction and synthesis to facilitate intelligible information and computational efficiency for supporting decision makers, choosing an appropriate normalization technique is a big challenge as BD is collected from many different sources.

An ISP selection problem can be designed as a MCDM problem in which alternatives of the ISP or software packages to be selected and criteria are those attributes under consideration. MCDM methodologies has been extensively used to work out different types of problems such as election forecasting (Roycs & Bastos, 2001), selecting robots for manufacturing companies (Chu & Lin, 2003), assessment of military threat (Changwen & You, 1998), financial decision making (Zopounidis & Doumpos, 2002), facility location selection (Chu, 2002a, 2002b), evaluation of initial training aircraft (Wang & Chang, 2007), human resource management, supply chain management (Zhou, Xu, & Deng, 2008), sensor network (Sridhar, Madni, & Jamshidi, 2008), and so on. Under various situations where performance rating and weights cannot be specified accurately, the fuzzy set theory is introduced by Zadeh (1965) to model the uncertainty of human judgments. Fuzzy set theory first introduced by Bellman and Zadeh (1970) introduced fuzzy set into MCDM as an approach to successfully dealing with the inherent imprecision, vagueness and ambiguity of the human decision-making process and also developed a more realistic approach for the ratings and weights of the criteria in a problem by means of linguistic variables instead of numerical values. An integrated fuzzy TOPSIS (FTOPSIS) method was developed by Ding (2011) to improve the quality of decision-making for ranking the alternatives. Chen and Chao (2012) proposed that the linguistic ratings may be expressed as trapezoidal or triangular fuzzy numbers integrated with TOPSIS to rank suppliers. Arikan (2013) established a fuzzy mathematical model and a novel solution approach to satisfy the decision maker's aspirations for fuzzy goals. Pramanik et al. (2015) proposed a framework on resilient supplier selection under a fuzzy environment and also a supplier selection index is calculated which produces less imprecise and more realistic by resolving the problem of loss of information.

A new selection approach was established by Chang, Yeh, and Chang (2013) to concentrate on the ranking inconsistency problem in fuzzy group MCDM. Wang et al. (2007; Wang & Lee 2009) and many researchers categorize weighting methods into two categories: subjective methods as well as objective methods to obtain a better weighting system. Preference or judgments of decision makers are considered in the calculation of subjective methods. Objective methods utilize mathematical computations which reduce the subjectiveness and vagueness caused by human preference. Deng et al., (2000) described that, the approach with objective weighting is particularly applicable for situations where reliable subjective weights cannot be obtained. The entropy concept proposed by Shannon and Weaver (1947),is a measure of uncertainty in information formulated in terms of probability theory is well suited for measuring the relative contrast intensities of attributes.(Cui, Yoo, Choi, & Youn, 2011). Zou, Sun, and Ren (2005) proposed that entropy method is highly reliable and can be easily adopted in information measurement. A scheme for multi-criteria group decision making using fuzzy TOPSIS and entropy-based method to decide the weighting of the criteria presented by Cui et al. (2011) and the proposed scheme employed linguistic variables instead of numerical values to assess the alternatives with respect to the criteria. A new fuzzy TOPSIS approach with entropy measure by integrating subjective and objective weights established by Wang et al. (2007) to rank solutions from available alternatives under uncertainty, prompting the need for the method to handle imprecise judgments from decision makers. A framework developed by Tavana and Hatami-Marbini (2011) to integrate subjective judgments derived from the Analytic Hierarchy Process (AHP) with entropy information and TOPSIS into a series of preference models for the human exploration of Mars. A supplier selection process using the Shannon Entropy method has been developed by Haldar, Ray, Banerjee, and Ghosh (2012) and also by Shemshadi et al. (2011) where author introduced a fuzzy VIKOR method with entropy measure for objective weighting. Kacprzak (2017) proposed concept of Shannon entropy by extending using Ordered Fuzzy Numbers (OFNs) which allows obtaining the weights of criteria in the form of OFNs for the multi-criteria problem of selecting a provider of medical equipment to a medical centre. Mousavi, Vahdani, and Behzadi (2016) developed a VIKOR method based on intuitionistic fuzzy sets with multi-judges and multi-attributes in real-life situations. Zavadskas, Turskis, Vilutien Úe, and Lepkova (2017) proposed real-case study which is versatile and can be adapted for any management problems to facilities management strategy

selection using an integrated MCDM approach. Yazdani, Zarate, Coulibaly, and Zavadskas (2017) established an efficient decision support system (DSS) by integrating MCDM methods which analyze the strategic decisions of decision makers under fuzzy environment for managing uncertain situations of an agricultural Supply chain management to enhance quality and reliability of that particular supply chain management. Markou, Koulinas, and Vavatsikos (2017) established an intelligent and efficient approach combining standard optimization techniques and Multi-Attribute decision models for Project Resources Scheduling in Project Management. Babbar and Amin (2018) developed a Fuzzy Quality Function Deployment (QFD) for supplier selection as well as a stochastic multi-objective programming model for order allocation in green supply chain management to manage the vagueness in human judgments and to handle the uncertainty respectively where qualitative and quantitative both criteria has been considered.

On conclusion, the above literature survey illustrates that an appropriate ISP selection can be the most crucial BI strategy for the management of an organization to mitigate unexpected risks as well as uncertainty accumulated from BD and to the best of the authors' knowledge, no better study has developed Fuzzy MCDM with Fuzzy Entropy using linguistic variables in the meadow of the improvement of the performance of a business organization for the improvement of BI strategy. In this paper, a novel integrated as well as intelligent fuzzy multi-criteria group decision-making approach based on TOPSIS and Entropy using linguistic values for ISP Selection under uncertain data which constructed from BD is developed for the improvement of BI strategy of an organizational management. The proposed approach calculates both the weights of ISP Selection criteria and the ratings of the ISP by using fuzzy MCDM and entropy method, which produces less imprecise and more realistic overall desirability levels.

3. Shannon's entropy in calculating objective weight

Shannon and Weaver (1947) established the famous entropy concept, in measuring uncertainty within information invented in terms of probability theory and be able to obtain the objective weights known as entropy weights. Zeleny (1996) established that the entropy concept is appropriate in measuring the relative contrast intensities of criteria in representing the regular essential information transmitted to the decision maker. Shi-Fei and Zhong-Zhi (2005) proposed that entropy is also explained as the average amount of information in information theory.

Following are the steps for developing the concept of entropy to determine the objective weights:

Step 1: Entropy measure in determining the objective weights:

Calculation of the projection value of each element,

$$pv_{ij} = \frac{X_{ij}}{\sum_{i=1}^{g} X_{ij}} \tag{1}$$

X_{ij} is the element of decision matrix, which means the value of jth risk parameters under the ith failure modes.

Step 2: The entropy,

$$E_j = -k \sum_{i=1}^{g} pv_{ij} * In(pv_{ij}) \qquad (2)$$

where, g = the number of failure modes and k is a constant and calculated as:

$$k = \frac{1}{In(g)} \qquad (3)$$

Step 3: The degree of divergence ddv_j of the inherent information of each jth parameter is calculated as follows:

$$ddv_j = (1 - E_j) \qquad (4)$$

The value ddv_j represents the intrinsic contrast intensity of jth parameter. Larger value of ddv_j, represents more important j^{th} parameter for the problem. The objective weight for each jth parameter can be obtained by the following equation as:

$$EW_j = ddv_j / \sum_{j=1}^{h} ddv_j \qquad (5)$$

where, h = the number of risk element.

4. The proposed methodology

Based on the FTOPSIS method (Haldar, Ray, Banerjee, & Ghosh, 2014), a new multi-criteria group decision-making approach is proposed under fuzzy environment to successfully dealing with the inherent imprecision, vagueness and ambiguity of the human decision-making process. Depending upon the nature of the problem and available information decision makers prefer to describe their feeling in the fuzzy term of 'very bad', 'bad', 'medium', 'very good', etc as the decision-making problem is made under uncertainties, vagueness, fuzziness due to some incomplete information and it is difficult for decision makers to give an exact value to express their opinion on an organization's capability. A fuzzy set is characterized by a membership function, which assigns to each component a grade of membership within the range [0, 1], to a certain extent than absolute membership (Pramanik et al., 2014) representing to what degree that element is a member of the set (Bevilacqua et al., 2006). The Fuzzy membership function of a triangular fuzzy number is represented in Figure 1. According to decision makers, an appropriate linguistic variables and corresponding membership functions which

can be obtained from their assessment and past data, and can be modified to incorporate individual situations to give right judgments on decisions are expressed in Table 1, using triangular fuzzy numbers to estimate the importance weights of each criterion as well as alternatives. We used the triangular fuzzy number for its simplicity and are used most frequently for expressing linguistic terms in research (Chen, 2000; Yong, 2006).

4.1. Description of the problem

An ISP normally deals with different types of decisions with various types of uncertainty in an organization to fulfill the desire requirement. Selecting the best feasible ISP which are suitable and robust within the management information system of an organization is a challenge and also is an opportunity to that particular organization for successful business implementation as the selection process of ISP is a qualitative measurement process which needs or deals with the real-life information those are often vague in nature and cannot estimate with an exact numerical value. As shown in Figure 3, a business organization desires to select an appropriate ISP in order to improve work productivity. After preliminary screening, five alternatives ISP1, ISP2, ISP3, ISP4, and ISP5 have remained in the candidate list and a committee of decision makers is formed by four experts, including project manager (*DM1*), IT security manager (*DM2*), quality testing manager (*DM3*), purchasing manager (*DM4*), who considered following four criteria for this selection process:

    C1: Organizational Behavior,
    C2: Quality of the project,
    C3: Applied Technologies and Innovations,
    C4: Cost of Hardware/Software Investment.

Here, all the criteria are matched to the alternatives as the alternative's performance in terms of the criteria scores are modeled and on the basis of which the alternatives would be evaluated and selected.The schematic representation of proposed methodology is shown in Figure 2.

The proposed new integrated approach by employing Fuzzy entropy and Fuzzy TOPSIS [FTOPSIS] technique is summarized step by step as follows:

Step 1: The linguistic rating variables made by decision makers are listed in Table 1 to assess the rating of five possible alternatives (ISP1 to ISP5) with respect to each criterion.

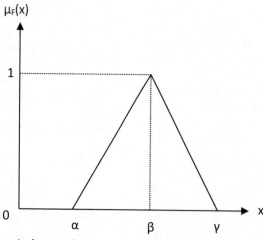

Figure 1. Fuzzy membership function of a triangular fuzzy number.

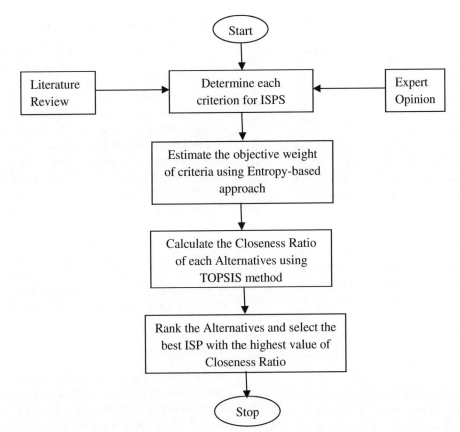

Figure 2. Schematic representation of proposed methodology.

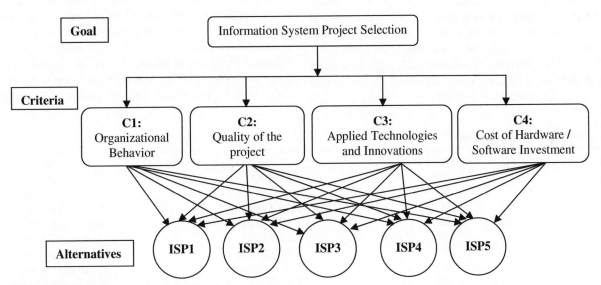

Figure 3. Hierarchical diagram of proposed methodology.

Table 1. Fuzzy linguistic variables and respective fuzzy number in the interval [0, 1].

IMPORTANCE	ABBREVIATION	FUZZY NUMBER
VERY BAD	VB	(0,0,0.05,0.1)
BAD	B	(0.05,0.15,0.3)
MEDIUM BAD	MB	(0.15,0.3,0.5)
MEDIUM	M	(0.3,0.5,0.7)
MEDIUM GOOD	MG	(0.5,0.7,0.9)
GOOD	G	(0.7,0.9,1)
VERY GOOD	VG	(0.9,0.95,1)

Step 2: According to Wang et al. (2007), with the purpose of making criterion value comparable and Vafaei, Ribeiro, and Camarinha-Matos (2015) ensures the obtained different dimensional units collected from heterogeneous data measurements have to aggregate for rating and ranking decision alternatives, normalization is very essential for all kind of decision making. In Table 2, linguistic values are converted into triangular fuzzy numbers to establish the aggregated fuzzy weight (AFW) (Haldar et al., 2014) and normalized aggregated fuzzy weight (NAFW) to create the normalized decision matrix as the following Table 3.

Table 2. The ratings of alternatives with respect to the criteria.

CRITERIA	ALTERNATIVES	DM1	DM2	DM3	DM4
C1	ISP1	B	VG	G	MB
	ISP2	M	G	VG	B
	ISP3	G	M	VG	G
	ISP4	G	VG	VB	MB
	ISP5	VG	B	MB	VG
C2	ISP1	M	MB	G	G
	ISP2	G	M	VG	B
	ISP3	VG	B	G	M
	ISP4	VG	G	VG	MB
	ISP5	B	VG	VB	M
C3	ISP1	M	G	MB	VG
	ISP2	G	VG	B	MB
	ISP3	VG	M	MG	VB
	ISP4	B	M	VG	G
	ISP5	MB	G	M	MB
C4	ISP1	MB	VG	G	G
	ISP2	G	B	VG	MB
	ISP3	G	VG	MB	VG
	ISP4	B	G	B	VG
	ISP5	VG	M	G	B

Step 3: Based on linguistic variables listed in Table 1, the objective weight of each criteria is calculated using the Shannon's entropy (Equations 1–5). The result is shown in the following Table 4:

Step 4: Weighted normalized decision matrix is developed and fuzzy positive ideal and negative ideal solution (Dalah et. al., 2011, and Bojadziev et al., 1995) for each decision maker is determined and tabulated in Table 5.

Step 5: The Closeness Coefficient (CC_i^*) of alternatives are calculated and by comparing CC_i^* values, the ranking of alternatives are determined in Table 6:

5. Discussion & result analysis

From Table 6, the priority of each alternative was done by considering criteria. Based on the Closeness Coefficients of individual ISP, the alternative ISP5 is the highest and as the higher the better is most suitable, so ISP5 is chosen.

The graph in Figure 4 illustrates the Closeness Coefficients of each alternative. According to the calculation results, it is revealed from Table 6 that the priority order of the information system projects can be represented as ISP5> ISP2> ISP4> ISP1> ISP3. It means that the best information system project is ISP5 and the worst information system project is ISP3. From Figure 4, the alternative ISP5 also has the highest alternative weight. It reveals that the alternative ISP5 is the most preferable alternative over the others. Therefore for selecting information system projects from many experts and a variety of projects for improvement of BI strategy of the management of an organization with multiple criteria collected from BD, the ISP5 is the best one.

6. Conclusion

In the present highly competitive business environment, the management of any business organization has to work firmly to highlight their own reward by collecting the valuable information which is constructed from BD for improvement of BI strategy for the enhancement of the performance against their challengers. They demand a clear focus as many types of project are proposed with different objectives which need strategic management according to organizational goals. The purpose of uncertainty management within ISP selection can be an influential factor in the success of business organization. This study used fuzzy TOPSIS method to determine the priority ranks of the performance for ISP projects. By using the

Table 3. The normalized decision matrix.

CRITERIA	ALTERNATIVES	AFW	NAFW
C1	ISP1	(0.45,0.575,0.7)	(0.486486,0.621622,0.756757)
	ISP2	(0.4875,0.625,0.75)	(0.527027,0.675676,0.810811)
	ISP3	(0.65,0.8125,0.925)	(0.702703,0.878378,1)
	ISP4	(0.4375,0.55,0.65)	(0.472973,0.594595,0.702703)
	ISP5	(0.5,0.5875,0.7)	(0.540541,0.635135,0.756757)
C2	ISP1	(0.4625,0.65,0.8)	(0.528571,0.742857,0.914286)
	ISP2	(0.4875,0.625,0.75)	(0.557143,0.714286,0.857143)
	ISP3	(0.4875,0.625,0.75)	(0.557143,0.714286,0.857143)
	ISP4	(0.6625,0.775,0.875)	(0.757143,0.885714,1)
	ISP5	(0.3125,0.4125,0.525)	(0.357143,0.471429,0.6)
C3	ISP1	(0.5125,0.6625,0.8)	(0.640625,0.828125,1)
	ISP2	(0.45,0.575,0.7)	(0.5625,0.71875,0.875)
	ISP3	(0.425,0.55,0.675)	(0.53125,0.6875,0.84375)
	ISP4	(0.4875,0.625,0.75)	(0.609375,0.78125,0.9375)
	ISP5	(0.325,0.5,0.675)	(0.40625,0.625,0.84375)
C4	ISP1	(0.6125,0.7625,0.875)	(0.7,0.871429,1)
	ISP2	(0.45,0.575,0.7)	(0.514286,0.657143,0.8)
	ISP3	(0.6625,0.775,0.875)	(0.757143,0.885714,1)
	ISP4	(0.425,0.5375,0.65)	(0.485714,0.614286,0.742857)
	ISP5	(0.4875,0.625,0.75)	(0.557143,0.714286,0.857143)

Table 4. Obtain entropy value, degree of divergence, and the objective weights of criteria.

	C1	C2	C3	C4
DM1	M	MG	G	B
DM2	MG	VG	MB	MG
DM3	G	B	M	VG
DM4	VG	M	MG	G
E_j	(0.83142,0.897751,0.94356)	(0.895214,0.950504,0.978446)	(0.834285,0.897563,0.941832)	(0.947787,0.979373,0.993027)
dv_j	(0.16858,0.102249,0.05644)	(0.104786,0.049496,0.021554)	(0.165715,0.102437,0.058168)	(0.052213,0.020627,0.006973)
EW_j	(0.343134,0.372072,0.394312)	(0.213286,0.18011,0.150584)	(0.337303,0.372757,0.406386)	(0.106277,0.075061,0.048717)

Table 5. Calculation of weighted normalize matrix and fuzzy positive ideal and negative ideal solution.

CRITERIA	ALTERNATIVES	WEIGHTED NAFW	PIS^+	NIS^-
C1	ISP1	(0.12346,0.171401,0.196084)	(0.178331,0.242197,0.259111)	(0.12003,0.163948,0.182078)
	ISP2	(0.133748,0.186305,0.21009)		
	ISP3	(0.178331,0.242197,0.259111)		
	ISP4	(0.12003,0.163948,0.182078)		
	ISP5	(0.137177,0.175127,0.196084)		
C2	ISP1	(0.127508,0.188206,0.224099)	(0.182647,0.224399,0.245108)	(0.086154,0.119438,0.147065)
	ISP2	(0.134401,0.180967,0.210093)		
	ISP3	(0.134401,0.180967,0.210093)		
	ISP4	(0.182647,0.224399,0.245108)		
	ISP5	(0.086154,0.119438,0.147065)		
C3	ISP1	(0.162368,0.207687,0.246688)	(0.162368,0.207687,0.246688)	(0.102965,0.156745,0.208143)
	ISP2	(0.142567,0.180256,0.215852)		
	ISP3	(0.134647,0.172419,0.208143)		
	ISP4	(0.154448,0.195931,0.23127)		
	ISP5	(0.102965,0.156745,0.208143)		
C4	ISP1	(0.176073,0.191819,0.249091)	(0.190447,0.194964,0.249091)	(0.122173,0.135217,0.185039)
	ISP2	(0.12936,0.14465,0.199272)		
	ISP3	(0.190447,0.194964,0.249091)		
	ISP4	(0.122173,0.135217,0.185039)		
	ISP5	(0.14014,0.157229,0.213506)		

Table 6. Obtain the closeness coefficient and rank of alternatives.

ALTERNATIVES	CC_i^*	RANK
ISP1	0.529679	4
ISP2	0.533775	2
ISP3	0.52869	5
ISP4	0.532419	3
ISP5	0.538728	1

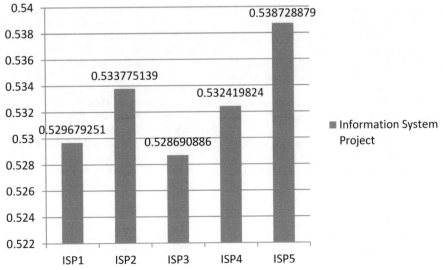

Figure 4. Graphical representation of CC_i^* of each alternative ISP's.

suggested approach, the ambiguities involved in the assessment of ISP projects could be effectively represented and processed to assure a more effective evaluation process. Based on the result, this study can provide management implication for the business organizations who wish to take counter measures. The primary reason of this article is to develop a fuzzy TOPSIS method by integrating subjective and objective weights, where subjective weights are obtained directly from the decision makers and objective weights are determined using Shannon entropy to rank the performance of compared alternatives. The described problem is a new fuzzy modification of the TOPSIS method considering subjective weights and objective weights under uncertainty. Closeness Co-efficient (CC_i^*) of each alternative ISP's are plotted in Figure 4 which shows, ISP5 as the best one for improvement of BI strategy of the management of an organization. Although this study try to represent a full analysis on ISP selection under various types of uncertainty, but still there are some improvements can be made in the future by developing a more refined approach to further enhance the performance of the proposed scheme to calculate overall rating scores of the alternatives.

Disclosure statement

No potential conflict of interest was reported by the authors.

References

Akyene, T. (2012). Cell phone evaluation base on entropy and TOPSIS. *Interdisciplinary Journal of Research in Business*, 1(12), 9–15.

Alessandri, T. M., Ford, D. N., Lander, D. M., Leggio, K. B., & Taylor, M. (2004). Managing risk and uncertainty in complex capital projects. *The Quarterly Review of Economics and Finance*, 44(5), 751–767.

Arikan, F. (2013). A fuzzy solution approach for multi objective supplier selection. *Expert Systems with Applications*, 40(3), 947–952.

Arora, Y., & Goyal, D. (2018). Review of data analysis framework for variety of big data. In *Emerging Trends in Expert Applications and Security: Proceedings of ICETEAS [Springer]* held at Jaipur Engineering College and Research Centre, on February 17–18 (Vols. 55–62). Jaipur, India. Online ISBN978-981-13-2285-3; https://doi.org/10.1007/978-981-13-2285-3

Artto, K., Martinsuo, M., & Kujala, J. (2011). *Project business*. Helsinki, Finland. Retrieved from http://pbgroup.tkk.fi/en/. (ISBN 978-952-92-8535-8)

Babbar, C., & Amin, S. H. (2018). A multi-objective mathematical model integrating environmental concerns for supplier selection and order allocation based on Fuzzy QFD in beverages industry. *Expert Systems With Applications*. doi:10.1016/j.eswa.2017.09.041

Bellman, R. E., & Zadeh, L. A. (1970). Decision-making in a fuzzy environment. *Management Science*, 17, 141–164.

Bevilacqua, M., Ciarapica, F., & Giacchetta, G. (2006). A fuzzy-QFD approach to supplier selection. *Journal of Purchasing and Supply Management*, 12, 14–27.

Blazquez, D., & Domenech, J. (2018). Big data sources and methods for social and economic analyses. *Technological Forecasting & Social Change*, 130, 99–113.

Bojadziev, G., & Bojadziev, M. (1995). *Fuzzy sets, fuzzy logic, applications, advances in fuzzy systems – applications and theory* (Vol. 5, pp. 113–140). World Scientific Publishing Co Pte Ltd, Singapore.

Chang, Y. H., Yeh, C. H., & Chang, Y. W. (2013). A new method selection approach for fuzzy group multi-criteria decision making. *Applied Soft Computing*, 13, 2179–2187.

Changwen, Q., & You, H. (1998). A method of heat assessment using multiple attribute decision making. In *Frontiers in education conferences* (Vol. 3, pp. 992–997). Tempe, AZ.

Chen, C. T. (2000). Extensions of the TOPSIS for group decision-making under fuzzy environment. *Fuzzy Sets and Systems*, 114(1), 1–9.

Chen, H., Chiang, R. H. L., & Storey, V. C. (2010). Business intelligence research. *MIS Quarterly*, 34(1), 201–203.

Chen, M. F., Tzeng, G. H., & Ding, C. G. (2003). Fuzzy MCDM approach to select service provider. In Proc. of the *12th IEEE international conference on fuzzy systems* (Vol. 1, pp. 25–28). St. Louis, MO.

Chen, Y. H., & Chao, R. J. (2012). Supplier selection using consistent fuzzy preference relations. *Expert Systems with Applications*, 39, 3233–3240.

Christensen, S., & Kreiner, K. (1991). *Prosjektledelse under usikkerhet* [Project management under uncertainty]. Oslo: Universitetsforlaget.

Chu, T. C. (2002a). Facility location selection using fuzzy TOPSIS under group decisions. *International Journal of Uncertainty, Fuzziness and Knowledge-Based Systems*, 10, 687–701.

Chu, T. C. (2002b). Selecting plant location via a fuzzy TOPSIS approach. *The International Journal of Advanced Manufacturing Technology*, 20, 859–864.

Chu, T. C., & Lin, Y. C. (2003). A fuzzy TOPSIS method for robot selection. *The International Journal of Advanced Manufacturing Technology*, 21, 284–290.

Cui, Z. X., Yoo, H. K., Choi, J. Y., & Youn, H. Y. (2011). Multi-criteria group decision making with fuzzy logic and entropy based weighting. In *ICUIMC'11*, Seoul, Korea.

Dalalah, D., Hayajneh, M., & Batieha, F. (2011). A fuzzy multi-criteria decision making model for supplier selection. *Expert Systems with Applications*, 38, 8384–8391.

De Mauro, A., Greco, M., Grimaldi, M., & Ritala, P. (2018). Human resources for big data professions: A systematic classification of job roles and required skill sets. *Information Processing & Management*, 54(5), 807–817.

Deng, H., Yeh, C. H., & Willis, R. J. (2000). Inter-company comparison using modified TOPSIS with objective weights. *Computers & Operations Research*, 27, 963–973.

Ding, J. (2011). An integrated fuzzy TOPSIS method for ranking alternatives and its application. *Journal of Marine Science and Technology*, 19(4), 341–352.

Feng, O., & Shanthikumar, J. G. (2018). How research in production and operations management may evolve in the era of big data. *Production and Operations Management*, 27(9), 1670–1684.

Gandomi, A., & Haider, M. (2015). Beyond the hype: Big data concepts, methods, and analytics. *International Journal of Information Management*, 35(2), 137–144.

Ghasemaghaei, M., Ebrahimi, S., & Hassanein, K. (2018). Data analytics competency for improving firm decision making performance. *The Journal of Strategic Information Systems*, 27(1), 101–113.

Haldar, A., Ray, A., Banerjee, D., & Ghosh, S. (2012, December 14–16). Supplier selection in the intuitionistic environment under requirement perspective. In *Proceedings of the 4th international and 25th AIMTDR conference (2012)* (Vol. 2, pp. 1287–1292). Jadavpur University, Kolkata, India.

Haldar, A., Ray, A., Banerjee, D., & Ghosh, S. (2014). Resilient supplier selection under a fuzzy environment. *International Journal of Management Science and Engineering Management*, 9(2), 147–156.

He, X. J. (2014).Business intelligence and big data analytics: An overview. *Communications of the IIMA*, 14, Article 1.

Hillson, D., & Simon, P. (2012). *Practical project risk management – The ATOM methodology* (2nd ed.), Vienna: Berrett-Koehler.

Hwang, C. L., & Yoon, K. S. (1981). *Multiple attribute decision making: Methods and applications*. Berlin, Germany: Springer-Verlag.

Jauch, L., & Kraft, K. (1986). Strategic management of uncertainty. *Academy of Management Review*, 11, 777–790.

Kacprzak, D. (2017). Objective weights based on ordered fuzzy numbers for fuzzy multiple criteria decision-making methods. *Entropy*, 19, 373.

Klievink, B., Romijn, B.-J., Cunningham, S., & de Bruijn, H. (2016). Big data in the public sector: Uncertainties and readiness. *Information Systems Frontiers*, 19(2), 267–283.

KošCielniak, H., & Puto, A. (2015). BIG DATA in decision making processes of enterprises. *Procedia Computer Science*, 65, 1052–1058.

LaValle, S., Lesser, E., Shockley, R., Hopkins, M., & Kruschwitz, N. (2011). Big data, analytics and the path from insights to value. *MITSloan Management Review*, 52(2), 21–32.

Manyika, J., Chui, M., Brown, B., Bughin, J., Dobbs, R., Roxburgh, C., & Byers, A. H. (2011). *Big data: The next frontier for innovation, competition, and productivity.* San Francisco, CA: McKinsey Global Institute.

Marinho, M. L. M., Sampaio, S. C. D. B., Lima, T. L. D. A., & Moura, H. P. D. (2015). Uncertainty management in software projects. *Journal of Software, 10*(3).

Markou, C., Koulinas, G. K., & Vavatsikos, A. P. (2017). Project resources scheduling and leveling using multi-attribute decision models: Models implementation and case study. *Expert Systems With Applications, 77,* 160–169.

McAfee, A., & Brynjolfsson, E. (2012). Big data: The management revolution. *Harvard Business Review, 90,* 60–68.

Mousavi, S. M., Vahdani, B., & Behzadi, S. S. (2016). Designing a model of intutionistic fuzzy VIKOR in multi-attribute group decision-making problems. *Iranian Journal of Fuzzy Systems, 13*(1), 45–65.

Olsson, R. (2007). In search of opportunity management: Is the risk management process enough? *International Journal of Project Management, 25*(8), 745–752.

Pham, C. M. 2018. Building a maturity framework for big data cyber security analytics. In *Applying business intelligence initiatives in healthcare and organizational settings* (Vols. 164–183). doi: 10.4018/978-1-5225-5718-0.ch009

Popovič, A., Hackney, R., Tassabehji, R., & Castelli, M. (2018). The impact of big data analytics on firms' high value business performance. *Information Systems Frontiers", 20*(2), 209–222.

Pramanik, D., & Haldar, A. (2014). Design of fuzzy decision support system (FDSS) in technical employee recruitment. *International Journal of Emerging Technology and Advanced Engineering, 4*(2), 5–15.

Pramanik, D., Haldar, A., Mondal, S. C., Naskar, S. K., & Ray, A. (2015). Resilient supplier selection using AHP-TOPSIS-QFD under a fuzzy environment. *International Journal of Management Science and Engineering Management, 12,* 45–54.

Rodríguez, A., Ortega, F., & Concepción, R. (2015). A method for the evaluation of risk in IT projects. *Expert Systems With Applications.* doi:10.1016/j.eswa.2015.09.056

Rolstadås, A., Hetland, P. W., Jergeas, G. F., & Westney, R. E. (2011). *Risk navigation strategies for major capital projects: Beyond the myth of predictability.* London: Springer-Verlag London Limited.

Roycs, G. F., & Bastos, R. C. (2001). Fuzzy MCDM in election prediction. In *IEEE international conference on systems, Mon. and cybernetics,* October 7–10, (Vol. 5, pp. 3258–3263). Tucson, AZ. doi:10.1109/ICSMC.2001.972021

Shannon, C. E., & Weaver, W. (1947). *The mathematical theory of communication.* Urbana: The University of Illinois Press.

Shemshadi, A., Shirazi, H., Toreihi, M., & Tarokh, M. J. (2011). A fuzzy VIKOR method for supplier selection based on entropy measure for objective weighting. *Expert Systems with Applications, 38,* 12160–12167.

Shemshadi, A., Soroor, J., & Tarokh, M. J. (2008). Implementing a multi-agent system for the real-time coordination of a typical supply chain based on the JADE Technology, In *3rd IEEE SMC international conference on system of systems engineering* (pp. 1–6). Singapore.

Shi-Fei, D., & Zhong-Zhi, S. (2005). Studies on incidence pattern recognition based on information entropy. *Journal of Information Science, 31*(6), 497–502.

Soroor, J., Tarokh, M. J., & Shemshadi, A. (2009). Initiating a state of the art system for real-time supply chain coordination. *European Journal of Operational Research, 196*(2), 635–650.

Sridhar, P., Madni, A. M., & Jamshidi, M. (2008). Multicriteria decision making in sensor networks. *IEEE Instrumentation & Measurement Magazine, 11,* 24–29.

Sun, Z., Sun, L., & Strang, K. (2018). Big data analytics services for enhancing business intelligence. *Journal of Computer Information Systems (JCIS), 58*(2), 162–169. doi:10.1080/08874417.2016.1220239

Tavana, M., & Hatami-Marbini, A. (2011). A group AHPTOPSIS framework for human space flight mission planning at NASA. *Expert Systems with Applications, 387,* 13588–13603.

Vafaei, N., Ribeiro, R. A., & Camarinha-Matos, L. M. (2015, May 27–29). Importance of data normalization in decision making: Case study with TOPSIS method. In *ICDSST 2015 Proceedings – The 1st International Conference on Decision Support Systems Technologies, An EWG-DSS Conference. Theme: Big Data Analytics for Decision-Making,* May 27–29, Belgrade, Serbia.

Vafaei, N., Ribeiro, R. A., & Camarinha-Matos, L. M. (2018). Data normalisation techniques in decision making: Case study with TOPSIS method. *International Journal of Information and Decision Sciences, 10*(1), 19–38.

Wang, T. C., & Chang, T. H. (2007). Application of TOPSIS in evaluating initial training aircraft under a fuzzy environment. *Expert Systems with Applications: an International Journal, 33,* 870–880.

Wang, T. C., & Lee, H. D. (2009). Developing a fuzzy TOPSIS approach based on subjective weights and objective weights. *Expert Systems with Applications, 36,* 8980–8985.

Wang, T. C., Lee, H. D., & Chang, M. C. S. (2007). *A fuzzy TOPSIS approach with entropy measure for decision-making problem.* IEEE, IEEE International Conference on Industrial Engineering and Engineering Management, December 2–4. doi: 10.1109/IEEM.2007.4419164.

Williams, S. (2011). 5 barriers to BI success and how to overcome them. *Strategic Finance, 93*(1), 27–33.

Yazdani, M., Zarate, P., Coulibaly, A., & Zavadskas, E. K. (2017). A group decision making support system in logistics and supply chain management. *Expert Systems with Applications, 88,* 376–392.

Yeh, C. H., & Deng, H. (1997). An algorithm for fuzzy multi- criteria decision making. In *IEEE international conference on intelligent processing systems* (pp. 1564–1568), Beijing, China.

Yong, D. (2006). Plant location selection based on fuzzy TOPSIS. *The International Journal of Advanced Manufacturing Technology, 28* (7–8), 839–844.

Zadeh, L. A. (1965). Fuzzy sets. *Information Control, 8,* 338–353.

Zavadskas, E. K., Turskis, Z., Vilutien Úe, T., & Lepkova, N. (2017). Integrated group fuzzy multi-criteria model: Case of facilities management strategy selection. *Expert Systems with Applications, 82,* 317–331.

Zeleny, M. (1996). *Multiple criteria decision making.* New York: Springer.

Zhou, L., Xu, X., & Deng, S. (2008). An ANP model for service policy decision in SCM. In *4th International Conference on Wireless Communication, Networking and Mobile Computing,* October 12–17 (pp. 1–5). Dalian, China.

Zopounidis, C., & Doumpos, M. (2002). Multi-criteria decision aid in financial decision making: Methodologies and literature review. *Journal of Multi-Criteria Decision Analysis, 11,* 167–186.

Zou, Z., Sun, J., & Ren, G. (2005). Study and application on the entropy method for determination of weight of evaluating indicators in fuzzy synthetic evaluation for water quality assessment. *ACTA Scientiae Circumstantiae, 25*(4), 552–556.

Index

For Product Safety Concerns and Information please contact our
EU representative GPSR@taylorandfrancis.com Taylor & Francis
Verlag GmbH, Kaufingerstraße 24, 80331 München, Germany